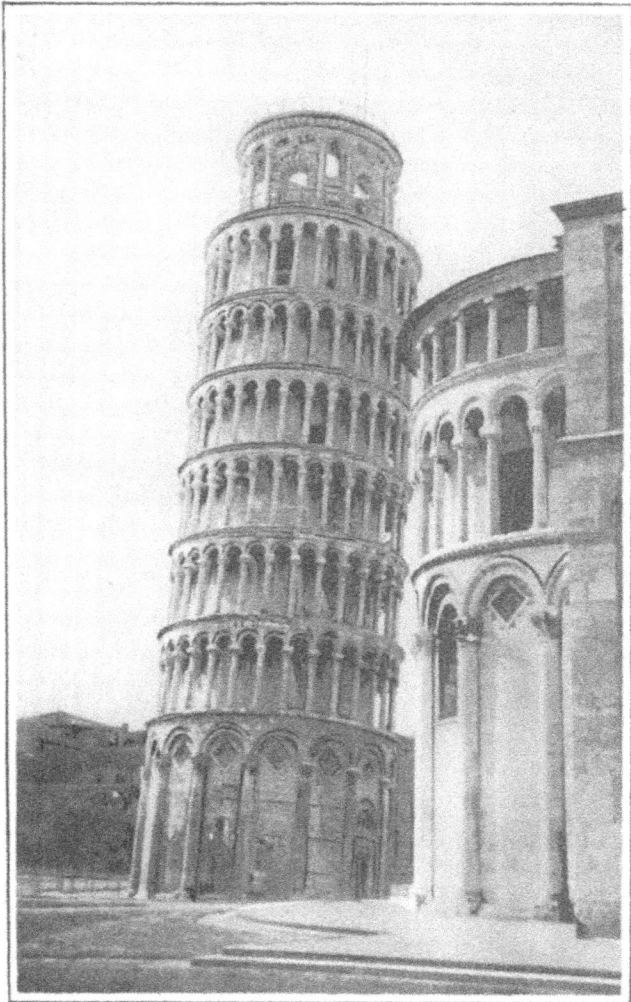

THE LEANING TOWER OF PISA

PRACTICAL
ITALIAN GRAMMAR

BY

JOSEPH LOUIS RUSSO Ph.D.
UNIVERSITY OF WISCONSIN

WILDSIDE PRESS

PREFACE

As ITS title implies, the present work aims to present in the simplest form the elements of the Italian language. In preparing it, the author has made no attempt at completeness; on the contrary, his efforts have tended to omit whatever seemed to him non-essential and apt to cause confusion in the beginner's mind. The needs of our High School and College classes have guided him throughout his task and, believing that extensive drill should be emphasized in the study of any modern language, he has consistently followed the system of giving *few rules and many exercises* in each lesson.

The grammar is taught inductively. Experience has shown that by placing the rules after the examples, the principles of language are more likely to leave a lasting impression upon the student: they appear to him more concrete, more real.

In the following particulars this work will perhaps prove of special interest to teachers:

1. A thorough treatment of Italian pronunciation, followed by graded exercises in which the difficulties are overcome one by one, and in which, among other things, the student is made familiar with the names of the most important Italian cities and of the men most prominent in Italian civilization.

2. Short lesson assignments, containing few basic principles of grammar clearly stated.

3. Practical and, on the average, short vocabularies.

grouped by topics, dealing with subjects that will interest young women as well as young men.

4. Substitution and completion exercises, generally based on the vocabularies of the preceding lessons, thus serving as a kind of review while drilling the student on the grammar rules just studied.

5. Reading matter composed of connected Italian passages based on everyday experience, in the first thirty-three lessons, and of a series of brief articles relating the story of Italy from the beginning of last century up to and including the Great War, in the remaining seventeen lessons.

6. Two sets of sentences with each lesson for translation from English into Italian, to be used at the option of the teacher and according to the needs of his class. These sentences form a connected story in which one main subject is treated coherently, thus giving an adequate opportunity for the correct use of the tenses.

7. Ample oral drill based on the material presented in each lesson.

8. A brief account of Italian geography, accompanied by a map of Italy and conveniently placed right before the story of Italy is told.

9. Drill in idiomatic expressions.

10. Direct-Method exercises made possible by the inclusion of fourteen appropriate drawings. These drawings, all of which are correlated with *Heath's Modern Language Wall Charts*, cover a wide range of subjects considered sufficient for an elementary conversation course and vocabulary drill. They are printed at convenient places in the book, in connection with lessons containing identical or related topics. The Special Vocabularies accompanying these charts are listed toward the end of the book.

11. Five intensive review lessons.

12. A collection of fifteen short poems at the end of the

volume, forming in their variety excellent material for memory exercises, apt to awaken among the students an interest for Italian literature.

An effort has been made in the preparation of this work to follow the latest pedagogical principles, with the aim of rendering easy and attractive the study of Italian for which such increasing interest is being shown at present in our schools.

SUGGESTIONS TO TEACHERS

The fifty lessons contained in this volume are intended to cover the work of two years in High School. It is suggested that the first year program should include the first thirty-three lessons.

In the first year each lesson may be divided into two parts: Grammar rules and exercises A and B, for the first day; exercises C and E, for the second. Exercise D may be reserved as an alternative assignment to exercise C, or used for review work.

In the second year of High School work the last seventeen lessons may be used, each divided into three parts: Grammar rules and exercise A, for the first day; exercises B and C, for the second; exercises D and E, for the third. The increased difficulty of the material presented in the grammar part and in the topics which the exercises cover, justifies this more intensive study.

For College classes each lesson can be covered in one day, omitting either exercise C or D, which may be used in alternate years or in different sections.

The success of this work depends in great part on the way in which the oral drill (exercise E) will be conducted. It is suggested that the instructor read each question, aloud and clearly, naming the student who is to answer it only after the question has been asked. Thus the attention of the whole class will be maintained.

The author desires to express his thanks to his students in the University of Wisconsin with whom this work has been tried in several classes; to his assistants, Miss Augusta C. Boschini and Miss Doris L. Bennett, who have given him valuable assistance both in class work and in the reading of the proofs. He is also under great obligation to Professors Herbert H. Vaughan of the University of California, Kenneth McKenzie of Princeton University, and James E. Shaw of the University of Toronto, to whom he is indebted for useful suggestions. Finally he wishes to express his deep sense of appreciation to Professor E. C. Hills of the University of California and to Dr. Alexander Green of D. C. Heath and Company, both of whom went over this work in its manuscript form and offered a great deal of constructive criticism and advice.

J. L. R.

UNIVERSITY OF WISCONSIN
February, 1927

To his many friends and well-wishers throughout the country, in both High Schools and Colleges, who have used this book with their classes and have favored the author with constructive suggestions here utilized in a new edition, he desires to express his deep appreciation.

J. L. R.

April, 1929

CONTENTS

vii

CONTENTS

ILLUSTRATIONS

ITALIAN GRAMMAR

INTRODUCTION

THE ALPHABET

1. The Italian alphabet consists of the following twenty-one letters:

LETTER	NAME	LETTER	NAME	LETTER	NAME
a	a	h	acca	q	cu
b	bi	i	i	r	ɛrre
c	ci	l	ɛlle	s	ɛsse
d	di	m	ɛmme	t	ti
e	ɛ	n	ɛnne	u	u
f	ɛffe	o	ɔ	v	vu
g	gi	p	pi	z	zɛta

The letter **j** (*i lungo*) is rarely used in modern Italian, i having taken its place; **x** (*iccase*) is found only in such expressions as **ex deputato, ex ministro,** etc.; the letters **k** (*cappa*), **w** (*doppio vu*) and **y** (*ipsilon*) are used exclusively for the spelling of foreign words.

PRONUNCIATION

2. Stress Marks. When a word has two or more vowels, one vowel is stressed more than the other or others. Usually only a word stressed on the last vowel is marked in Italian with an accent; no sign marks the stress when it is on any other vowel. For the convenience of the student, however, certain symbols have been adopted in this book to mark the

1

stress: printing in italic type; in the special type ɛ (called
" open *e* "); and in the special type ɔ (called " open *o* ").

c*a*mera　　　　　　　m*ɛ*dico　　　　　　　m*ɔ*bile

If none of the vowels is specially printed, the stress is on
the next-to-the-last vowel.

veranda　　　　　　**cantare**　　　　　　locomotiva

While these symbols will be used in all Italian words occurring in
the grammar rules, in the special vocabularies and in the complete
vocabulary at the end of the volume, they will be omitted in the exercises so as to accustom the student to read Italian without this guide.

3. Vowels. 1. The five vowel signs represent seven
different sounds, and are pronounced as follows: [1]

a	as *a* in *father*	carta	sala	stalla
e (*clóse*)	as *a* in *late*	mele	vedere	temere
e (*open*)	as *e* in *let*	sɛlla	tɛma	tɛnda
i	as *i* in *machine*	siti	vini	finiti
o (*clóse*)	as *o* in *rope*	sole	coda	colore
o (*open*)	as *o* in *soft*	pɔrta	tɔro	vɔlta
u	as *oo* in *moon*	fumo	luna	tutto

Close and *open* vowels are not differentiated in spelling, but their
pronunciation follows somewhat definite rules (*see* § 9).

2. In pronouncing Italian vowels an effort should be made
to avoid nasal resonance entirely, and to carry the voice
well forward in the mouth. The mouth should be well
opened in pronouncing **a**, **e** *open* and **o** *open*, and almost
closed with the lips drawn back when making the sound **i**.
The student should note also that, while in English long

---

[1] For practical purpose, the pronunciation will be explained by comparison with English sounds. It must never be forgotten, however, that the
sounds of any two languages seldom correspond exactly. As for the vowels,
note that those which occur in unstressed position at the end of a word are
uttered slightly more rapidly than the others.

vowels tend to become diphthongal (like *a* in *late* and *o* in *rope*), this tendency does not appear in Italian: Italian vowels are uniform throughout their utterance.

3. A marked difference in pronunciation between Italian and English is that in Italian the unstressed vowels keep their pure sound, while in English unstressed vowels are often slurred. This is due to the fact that Italian is not, like English, an explosive language, but rather a singing (chromatic) language. Accents are not strong stresses which mutilate preceding and following vowels, but rather soft stresses that are shown in the lengthening of the vowel sounds.

4. It may be useful to call the beginner's attention to the following cases in which Italian vowels are frequently mispronounced by English-speaking students:

(*a*) Initial or final unstressed a, which should not be slurred: **amica, aroma, arɛna.**

(*b*) The vowels e, i, u, when followed by r should not be incorrectly pronounced like the *i* in *girl:* **Verdi, Curci, permesso, firma.**

(*c*) Initial, unstressed o should not be mispronounced like the *o* in *office:* **occupare, ostacolare, osservare.**

(*d*) The vowel u, followed by l or n, should not be pronounced like the *u* in *full:* **ultimo, punto.**

The beginner should strive to overcome such tendencies from the start, bearing in mind that the sound of the Italian vowels should be kept pure and distinct without regard to their position.

4. **Semivowels.** Unstressed i and u, placed before another vowel, are pronounced respectively like *y* in *yet* and *w* in *well*. They are often called semivowels.[1]

ieri   aiuto   uomo   nuovo

5. **Diphthongs.** A combination of two vowels, uttered as one syllable, constitutes a diphthong. The vowels a, e and

[1] Semivowel i is written j by a few writers (ex. **ajuto**), but this usage is rapidly growing obsolete.

o may combine with **i** or **u**, in which case the stress falls on the **a**, **e** or **o**; or the diphthong may be **iu** or **ui**, in which case it is the second vowel which is stressed.

piɛno   biada   mai   rɑuco   pɔi   guida   suɔno

6. Consonants. The following consonants are pronounced approximately as in English: **b, d, f, l, m, n, p, q, t** and **v**. In pronouncing **d, l, n** and **t**, however, the tip of the tongue should touch the upper teeth, and **p** should be made with an effort to avoid the explosive aspiration which accompanies the same sound in English. It should also be noted that the letter **n**, when standing before a **c** which has the sound of *c* in *cap*, a **g** which has the sound of *g* in *go*, or a **q**, has the sound of *ng* in *bang*.

bianco   lungo   dovunque

c and **g** have either a *palatal* sound, or a *guttural* sound. Before **e** or **i**, they take the palatal sound, that is, they are pronounced toward the front of the mouth: **c** like *ch* in *chill*, and **g** like *g* in *general*.[1] In all other cases the guttural sound occurs, that is they are pronounced to the rear of the mouth, and **c** corresponds to the English *k*, **g** to the *g* in *go*.

PALATAL: **aceto   vicino   gentile   regina**
GUTTURAL: **sicuro   credo   gallo   grande**

h   is always silent. It appears in a few short words.

      ha   hai   ahi   hɔ

r   is trilled, that is, pronounced with a vibration of the tongue against the upper teeth.

      caro   sera   mare   marito

s   has two different sounds: unvoiced **s**, like *s* in *sand*, and voiced **s**, like *s* in *rose*.

UNVOICED: **spillo   sabbia   destino   frusta**
VOICED: **sleale   smemorato   prɔsa   esame**

---

[1] In Tuscany and in some other parts of Italy, **c** and **g** between two vowels, the second of which is **e** or **i**, are pronounced respectively like the *sh* in *ship* and the *s* in *pleasure*.

z   also is pronounced in two different ways: like a vigorous *ts* (unvoiced z), or like a prolonged *dz* (voiced z).

UNVOICED:	marzɔ	azione	zio	terzo
VOICED:	romanzo	bronzo	zɛro	manzo

Each Italian consonant, except those forming digraphs (*see* § 8), has a distinct and separate sound value, and should be clearly pronounced.

The letters **l, m, n** and **r,** when preceded by a stressed vowel and followed by another consonant, are uttered longer than usually.

    palma   **ambo**   **banca**   **parte**

7. Double Consonants. Note carefully that in Italian the double consonant is always more prolonged and emphatic than the single, except in the case of **zz,** which is pronounced almost like **z.** A similar doubling occurs in English only when two words, the first of which ends and the second of which begins with the same consonant sound, are pronounced without a pause between, as *good day, penknife,* etc.

In Italian, double consonants always represent a single, energetic and prolonged sound. This is true also of double **c** and double **g,** which are never pronounced separately, as two distinct sounds, as in the English words *accept, suggest,* etc., but together, with more intensity and length than if they were single. Their palatal or guttural nature is determined by their being followed or not by **e** or **i.**

    atto   **vacca**   **accento**   **aggettivo**   **palla**

8. Combined Letters. The following combinations, or digraphs, which really represent single sounds, are to be noted:

ch and **gh** (used only before **e** or **i**), the first representing the sound of a *k,* the second that of *g* in *go.*

    chiave   **laghi**   **schiavo**

ci and gi, pronounced respectively like *ch* in *chill* and *g* in *general*, when followed by **a, o, u.** In the resulting groups (**cia, cio, ciu; gia, gio, giu**) the i, unless stressed, merely indicates that the **c** or **g** has the palatal sound before **a, o,** or **u.**

provincia	ciottolo	fanciullo
giallo	ragione	giusto

gli   which is pronounced somewhat like *lli* in *billiards* and *million*, but with the tip of the tongue against the lower teeth. When no vowel follows gli, the i is pronounced.

figlio	figli	egli	paglia	gigli

In the following words, however, gl sounds as in the English word *angle:* **Anglia,** poetic name of England; **anglicano,** *Anglican;* **anglicismo,** *Anglicism;* **glicerina,** *glycerine;* **geroglifico,** *hieroglyphic;* **negligere,** *to neglect;* the derivatives of **negligere,** and a few other uncommon words.

gn   which has a sound similar to that of *ni* in *onion*, but with the tip of the tongue against the lower teeth.

bagno	ogni	guadagno	ognuno

qu   pronounced always like *kw.*

quattro	quanto	questo

sc   pronounced like *sh* before e or i, like *sk* in any other case.

bolscevichi	fascismo	oscuro	escluso

In the groups **scia, scio, sciu,** the vowel **i,** unless it is stressed, is not sounded, serving only to indicate that **sc** must be pronounced *sh.*

sciabola	lascio	sciupare

9. The Vowels *e* and *o*.   The vowels e and o are always *close* in unstressed syllables.

fame	delirio	domandare

In *stressed syllables*, e and o are *open* in the following cases:

e: (a) In the ending –ero of words of more than two syllables.

impɛro ministɛro sevɛro

(b) In the diphthong iɛ, or when e stands for ie.

piɛno liɛto altiɛro or altɛro

(c) When followed by another vowel.

idɛa rɛo nɛo dɛa

(d) In many words in which e is followed by two or more consonants.[1]

tɛrra vɛspa fɛbbre pɛtto

(e) When e appears in the third-from-the-last syllable and is stressed.[2]

sɛcolo mɛdico pɛttine ventɛsimo

o: (a) In the diphthong uo, or when o stands for uo.

uɔmo buɔno uɔvo or ɔvo

(b) When followed by another vowel.[3]

pɔi nɔia giɔia stɔia

(c) If followed by double consonants.

fɔssa gɔbbo dɔnna lɔtta

(d) When o appears in the third-from-the-last syllable and is stressed.

mɔnaco pɔvero ɔttimo ɔttico

(e) If at the end of a monosyllable or of a word stressed on the last syllable.

fɔ dɔmɔ sɔ parlɔ

[1] But in the endings –egno, –emmo, –enna, –esco, –etto, –ezza, –mente, e is *close*.

[2] Except in the ending –evole, in which e is *close*.

[3] But the o of noi and voi is *close*.

(*f*) When one or more consonants and a diphthong follow the **o**.

gloria	proprio	odio	fandonia

10. The Consonants *s* and *z*. 1. The letter **s** is pronounced as a voiceless sibilant, like *s* in *sand:*

(*a*) When initial before a vowel.

sabato	seta	silɛnzio	santo

(*b*) When double (but it is here prolonged).

tassa	basso	assai	lusso

(*c*) If followed by the voiceless consonants **c, f, p, q,** or **t.**

scudo	sforzo	astio	aspettare

2. In the following cases **s** is pronounced as a voiced sibilant, like *s* in *rose:*

(*a*) When followed by the voiced consonants **b, d, g, l, m, n, r,** or **v.**

sbadato	slitta	smalto	snɛllo

(*b*) Between vowels.

vaso	tesoro	esame	uso

This latter rule has, however, some important exceptions. Though between vowels, **s** has the unvoiced sound:

(*a*) After a prefix, provided that the **s** is the first letter of the original word.

presentimento	risalutare	but **disonore**

(*b*) In the adjective endings −ese,[1] −oso, and in words derived from such adjectives.

inglese	curioso	curiosità

(*c*) In the past absolute and past participle of certain irregular verbs and their derivatives.

difesi	raso	rasoio

---

[1] But **cortese,** *courteous,* **francese,** *French,* and **palese,** *evident,* are pronounced with a voiced **s.**

(*d*) In the following words and their derivatives:

annusare to smell	**fuso** spindle	**posa** pose
asino donkey	**mese** month	**raso** satin
casa house	**naso** nose	**riposo** rest
cosa thing	**peso** weight	**riso** rice, laughter
così thus	**Pisa** (Ital. city)	**susina** plum
desiderio desire	**pisello** pea	**susurro** whisper

3. The letter **z** has the unvoiced sound (*ts*):

  (*a*) When followed by **ia, ie,** or **io.**

  amicizia   **grazie**   **vizio**

  (*b*) In all cases not mentioned in the following paragraph.

4. The letter **z** has the voiced sound (*dz*):

  (*a*) In all verbs ending in –**izzare** which have more than four syllables in the infinitive.

  analizzare   **scandalizzare**   **fertilizzare**

  (*b*) In words derived from Greek, Hebrew, or Arabic.

  protozoi   **azzurro**   **zenit**

  (*c*) When initial, except in the following words, their derivatives, and others of minor importance:

zampa paw	**zitella** spinster
zampillo spurt	**zitto** hush
zampogna bagpipe	**zoccolo** wooden shoe
zanna tusk	**zolfo** sulphur
zappa hoe	**zoppo** lame
zattera raft	**zucca** pumpkin
zecca mint	**zucchero** sugar
zeppa wedge	**zuffa** fray
zingaro gipsy	**zuppa** soup
zio uncle	

  (*d*) In **mezzo**, *half*, and its compounds.

11. Special Doubling of Consonant Sounds. When, in a natural word group, a monosyllable ending with a vowel, or a word stressed on the final vowel, precedes a word beginning

with a consonant, this consonant is generally pronounced as
if it were double. There is no such doubling after **di**, *of*.

a Roma (*arroma*)	**chi sa** (*chissà*)
lunedì sera (*lunedissera*)	**più caro** (*piuccaro*)

STRESS AND ACCENT

12. In an Italian word the stress falls nearly always on the
same syllable on which it falls in the corresponding Latin
word. We may find it on one of the following syllables:

on the last	**fabbricò**
on the next-to-the-last	**fabbricare**
on the third-from-the-last	**fabbrico**
on the fourth-from-the-last	**fabbricano**

Words having the stress on the final vowel are marked
with a grave accent (`` ` ``). No written accent is used on other
words, except occasionally in order to avoid ambiguity, but
it may be a help for the student to remember: (*a*) that most
Italian words are stressed on the next-to-the-last syllable,
fewer on the third-from-the-last, and only a very limited
number on the fourth-from-the-last; (*b*) that *e open* (ɛ) and
o open (ɔ) are always stressed.

13. Besides being used on words stressed on the last
syllable, as stated above, the grave accent is used also on the
words **già, giù, più, può,** and on the following monosyllables
which otherwise might be confused with others of the same
spelling but of different meaning:

chè because	**che** that
dà gives	**da** by, from
dì day	**di** of
è is	**e** and
là, lì there	**la, li** *articles*
nè nor	**ne** of it, of them
sè himself	**se** if
sì yes	**si** himself
tè tea	**te** thee

SYLLABICATION

14. Italian words are divided into syllables according to these rules:

1. A single consonant between vowels belongs to the syllable which follows.

ma-ri-to ru-mo-re re-gi-na

2. Double consonants are separated.

sab-bia at-to vac-ca

3. Two consonants, the first of which is l, m, n or r, are also separated.

al-to an-ti-co cor-dia-le

4. Two consonants in any other combination belong to the syllable which follows.

giu-sto fi-glio u-scio

5. Of three consonants, the first one belongs to the preceding syllable, provided it is not an s.

com-pro al-tro com-plɛ-to
but a-stro ma-sche-ra co-stru-zio-ne

6. Vowels forming a diphthong are never separated.

glɔ-ria uɔ-mo piɛ-no

ELISION AND APOCOPATION

15. Elision is the dropping of the final vowel of a word, before another word beginning with a vowel. It is indicated by the apostrophe.

l'amico (= lo amico)
un'ɔpera d'arte (= una ɔpera di arte)
un onɛst'uɔmo (= un onɛsto uɔmo)
dovrɛbb'ɛssere (= dovrɛbbe ɛssere)

While optional otherwise, the elision is generally required in the following cases: (*a*) articles; (*b*) conjunctive personal pronouns; (*c*) demonstrative adjectives; (*d*) the adjectives bɛllo, buɔno, grande and santo: (*e*) the preposition di.

16. Apocopation (called in Italian troncamento) is the dropping of the final vowel or of the entire final syllable of a word, before another word, no matter how it begins. No apostrophe is required when the apocopation affects only the last vowel; when the entire final syllable is dropped, the apostrophe is used in certain instances, while in others it is omitted.

The apocopation is in most cases a matter of choice, being based on euphony and current usage. As a rule, it takes place with words of more than one syllable, ending with an e or an o, preceded by l, m, n or r.

fatal(e) **destino**	fatal destiny	**son**(o) **andati**	they have gone
siam(o) **perduti**	we are lost	**lasciar**(e) **tutto**	to leave all

CAPITALS

17. Capital letters are used in Italian as they are in English, except that small letters are used:

(a) With proper adjectives, unless used as nouns.

    una grammatica italiana   an Italian grammar
    But **gl'Italiani**   the Italians

(b) With names of months and days.

    ogni giovedì di marzo   every Thursday in March

(c) With titles, when followed by a proper name.

    il principe Colonna   Prince Colonna
    il signor Guidi   Mr. Guidi

(d) In contemporary poetry, with the first word of each line, unless a capital letter should be required by the rules of prose.

(e) With the pronoun io, *I*.

    s'io fossi in Italia   if I were in Italy

On the other hand, the personal pronouns **Ella, Lei, Loro**, *you* (singular and plural), used in formal address, are generally capitalized.

    verrò con Lei   I shall come with you

PUNCTUATION

18. The same punctuation marks exist in Italian, as in English. Their Italian names are:

. punto	— lineetta
, virgola	. . . punti sospensivi
; punto e virgola	« » virgolette
: due punti	( ) parentesi
? punto interrogativo	[ ] parentesi quadra
! punto esclamativo	⌒ grappa
- stanghetta	* asterisco

They are used as in English, except that the **punti sospensivi** are often employed in place of the English dash, while the latter (**lineetta**) commonly serves to denote a change of speaker in a conversation.

EXERCISES IN PRONUNCIATION

NOTE. — *The following exercises should be carefully read under the supervision of the instructor, and used as material for dictation and drill in syllabication.*

I

1. **Consonants and the Vowels** *a, i, u.* Luna pila gala vanga diga durata vita unità tutta culla palla urna finiti cara partita gita laguna fucili lacci baci ha hai tara pura piccina animali dalia labbri caduta impavida annata italiana anima frutta guida vini vicini cappa minuti carri libri caricatura naviganti cicala diritti mai fanali fanti buca unica lampi lima marina mulatta margarina mutilati natura ninfa nuca nulla minima nutriti banditi punta radunati riadattati ricci fulmini prima rifugi ripuliti pallida tardi vivai muri crudi lividi mulini gai litiganti birilli.

2. **Close** *e.* Cena vela veduta pena fedele cera catena temere vegetale pere vendetta ferire decadere bere rete penetrare mene pregare tenere tela generare mela rene regina gretti refe emendare cenni ceppi prevedere te candele capelli maledetti stretti.

3. **Open** *e.* Imperi erba ferri genti affetti concetti ieri bella cieli fiera greci terra guerra grevi pecca merci dieci cappelli parenti

lena lenti tenda perla pelli letti dialetti attenta venti verbi centri medici treni anelli lei sella tendini pessima meriti.

4. Close o. Moneta rotto rovo voce calore timore noce foce dottore bocca croce atroce tromba trionfo tondo ora onda pompa pronto rumori amore bolla borgo colore colpa dove ardore bottega colmo conto forma orlo pollo proporre.

5. Open o. Forte cuore morte rocca olio ho lotta otto prova boia porta oggi volta cattolico colla uovo donna galoppo troppo nuova cotta ottimo dotta roba fuoco tono torto notte do dogma ricotta solito moda mole monaca nodo noia docile flora gotico portico.

6. Unvoiced s and z. Rosso solo zio zanna ozioso peso casa pezzo razzolare spero stanza semenza pazzo zitto sazio vista morso naso azione corso vizio zappa vezzo nozze danza professore massaia sudore grazioso prezioso puzza nazione.

7. Voiced s and z. Tesi tesoro uso viso zero mezzano positivo vaso zaffiro garza improvvisare grezzo caso smorto esatto visitare utilizzare fertilizzare mezzo dose entusiasmo donzella gazzetta miseria svernare sguardo manzo pranzo sbucare smania.

II

8. Italia Roma Napoli Milano Torino Palermo Genova Firenze Venezia Trieste Dante Petrarca Boiardo Lorenzo de' Medici Poliziano Sannazaro Ariosto Vittoria Colonna Berni Caro Guarini Tasso Testi Redi Filicaia Frugoni Metastasio Goldoni Parini Gozzi Alfieri Monti Foscolo Rossetti Manzoni Leopardi Tommaseo Aleardi Carducci Rapisardi Pascoli Fogazzaro D'Annunzio Benelli Pirandello Zuccoli Papini Perugino Raffaello Donatello Leonardo da Vinci Buonarroti Cellini Tiziano Tintoretto Salvator Rosa Canova Monteverde Morelli Galilei Torricelli Galvani Volta Marconi Marco Polo Cristoforo Colombo Caboto Amerigo Vespucci Napoleone Bonaparte Garibaldi Diaz Mazzini Vittorio Emanuele Crispi Mussolini

III

9. Combined letters. Giugno luglio chimera ghermire maglia scusa sciupare discesa camicia meglio fascisti pigliare ogni figlio

unghia negligente poichè quaglia scontro sciorinare sciame liscio
lagnarsi stagno sciocco fichi facchino freschi foglia amichevole
strigliare lasciare magnolia ognuno scivolare vecchia ghianda scemo
aglio trascinare guadagno boschi.

10. Bologna Brescia Reggio Perugia Chieti Cagliari Aiaccio
Alighieri Boccaccio Machiavelli Guicciardini Chiabrera D'Azeglio
Giusti Stecchetti Michelangelo Correggio Ghirlandaio Ponchielli
Mascagni Giordano

11. Non si move foglia che Dio non voglia. Chi dorme non
piglia pesci. La superbia è figlia dell'ignoranza. Amore e signoria
non voglion compagnia. Scherzo di mano, scherzo di villano.
D'un cattivo legno non può venire una buona scheggia. Ogni
diritto ha il suo rovescio. I ragli dei ciuchi non arrivano al cielo.
Qual vuol la figlia, tal moglie piglia. Le chiacchiere non fan farina.
Dimmi chi pratichi e ti dirò chi sei. Chi vuol la noce schiacci il
guscio. Chi taglia taglia, e chi cuce ragguaglia. Chi sbaglia nelle
diecine, sbaglia nelle migliaia. Chi ride in gioventù, piange in
vecchiaia. Non bisogna fasciarsi il capo prima di romperselo.
Dall'unghia si conosce il leone.

IV

12. Amate l'Umanità. Ad ogni opera vostra nel cerchio della
Patria o della Famiglia, chiedete a voi stessi: « se questo ch'io
fo fosse fatto da tutti e per tutti, gioverebbe o nocerebbe all'Umanità? » e se la coscienza vi risponde: « nocerebbe, » desistete quand'
anche vi sembri che dall'azione vostra escirebbe un vantaggio immediato per la Patria o per la Famiglia. Siate apostoli di questa
fede, apostoli della fratellanza delle Nazioni e dell'unità, oggi
ammessa in principio, ma nel fatto negata, del genere umano.
Siatelo dove potete e come potete. Nè Dio, nè gli uomini possono
esigere più da voi. Ma io dico che facendovi tali — facendovi tali
dov'altro non possiate, in voi stessi — voi gioverete all'Umanità.
Dio misura i gradi d'educazione ch'Ei fa salire al genere umano sul
numero e sulla purità dei credenti. Quando sarete puri e numerosi,
Dio, che vi conta, v'aprirà il varco all'azione.

— *Giuseppe Mazzini* (1805–1872)

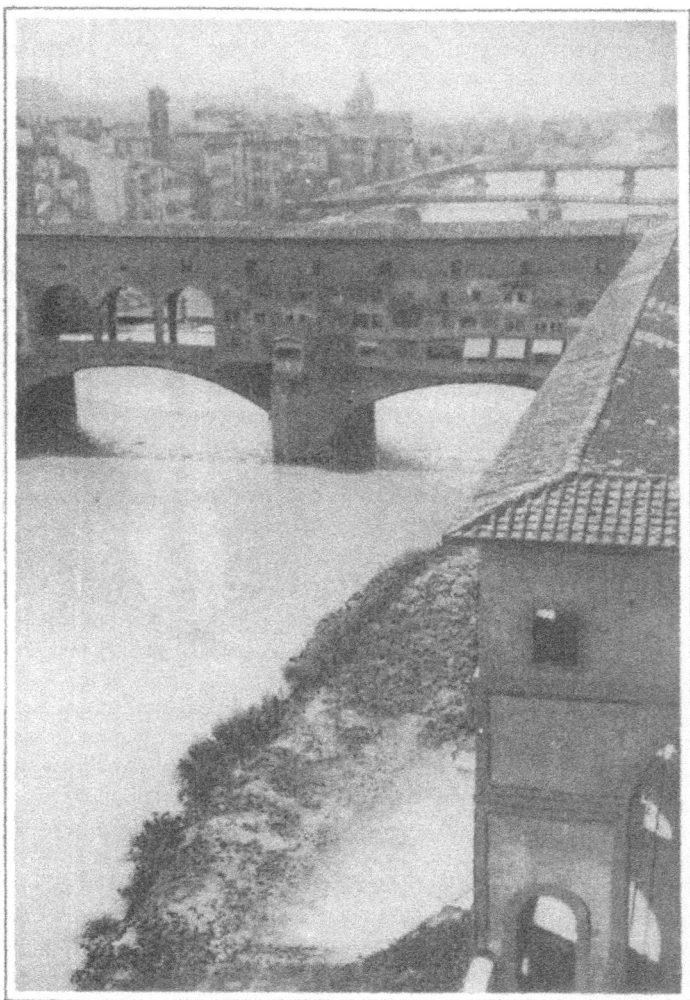

PONTE VECCHIO, FLORENCE

LESSON I

19. Indefinite Article

Masculine		Feminine	
un		una (un') } *a* or *an*	
uno			
un fratello	a brother	una sorella	a sister
un alunno	a pupil (*m.*)	un'alunna	a pupil (*f.*)
uno sbaglio	a mistake	una lavagna	a blackboard
uno zero	a zero	una matita	a pencil

1. Before a masculine word the usual form of the indefinite article is **un.** Uno is used only before a masculine word beginning with s impure (that is s followed by another consonant) or with z.

2. **Una** is the feminine form of the indefinite article; it becomes **un'** before a feminine word beginning with a vowel.

3.   **un fratello e una sorella,** a brother and sister

The indefinite article must be repeated before each noun to which it refers.

20. Gender. As seen in the examples above, there are only two genders in Italian, the masculine and the feminine. There are no neuter nouns in Italian.

21. Noun Ending. Italian nouns, unless shortened by apocopation (*see* § 16), end with a vowel.[1] Those ending in –o are all masculine, except **mano,** *hand,* **radio,** *radio,* **dinamo** *dynamo* ; those ending in –a are usually feminine.

[1] There are a few nouns which end with a consonant, but they are of foreign origin, as **alcool, gas, revolver, sport,** etc.

17

C

EXERCISE I

Élena Helen	dà gives
Carlo Charles	è is
Giovanni John	ha has
Maria Mary	mi mostri! show me!
	siamo we are *or* are we?
finestra window	
libro book	a to, at
muro wall	che? *or* che cosa? what?
porta door	chi? who? whom?
quaderno exercise book	dove? where? (dov'è?
sedia chair	where is?)
scuola school	e *or* ed and [1]
specchio mirror	in in

buon giorno! good day! good morning!
ecco here is, here are, there is, there are

A. (1) *Insert the indefinite article in each of the following sentences:* 1. Giovanni ha —— sorella. 2. Mi mostri —— finestra! 3. Elena ha —— fratello. 4. Carlo dà —— libro a —— alunna. 5. Mi mostri —— sbaglio! 6. Dov'è —— muro? 7. Ecco —— porta. 8. Maria ha —— quaderno. 9. Ecco —— zero. 10. Giovanni è —— alunno. 11. Siamo in —— scuola. 12. Elena è —— alunna. 13. Dov'è —— lavagna? 14. Giovanni dà —— matita a Carlo. 15. Maria ha —— specchio.

(2) *Divide and pronounce by syllables all proper names and nouns given in the vocabulary of this exercise.*

(3) *Read aloud Exercise I in Pronunciation (see §§ 1–7).*

B. **Buon giorno!**

1. Buon giorno, Elena! 2. — Buon giorno, Carlo! 3. Dov'è un quaderno? 4. — Ecco un quaderno ed ecco un libro. 5. Chi ha una matita? 6. — Carlo ha una

---
[1] Use ed before words beginning with e.

matita. 7. Dove siamo, Maria? 8. — Siamo in una scuola.
9. Chi ha uno specchio? 10. — Elena ha uno specchio.
11. Mi mostri una sedia. 12. — Ecco una sedia. 13. Carlo
dà una sedia a Elena. 14. Chi ha una sorella? 15. — Giovanni ha una sorella. 16. Che cosa ha Elena? 17. — Elena
ha un quaderno e una matita. 18. Chi è Carlo? 19. — Carlo
è un alunno. 20. Dov'è un muro, Giovanni? 21. — Ecco
un muro. 22. Carlo, mi mostri uno sbaglio. 23. — Ecco
uno sbaglio. 24. Ha un fratello Elena? 25. — Elena ha un
fratello e una sorella. 26. Dov'è una lavagna? 27. — Ecco
una lavagna. 28. Mi mostri una porta. 29. — Ecco una
porta, ed ecco una finestra. 30. Maria dà una matita a
Elena.

C. 1. Good morning, Charles! 2. Where is Mary? 3. — Here
is Mary, and here is Helen. 4. Has Helen a book? 5. — Helen
has a book and an exercise book. 6. Show me a door, John.
7. — Here is a door. 8. Where is a window? 9. — Here is a
window. 10. What has Mary? 11. — Mary has a mirror.
12. Who is Mary? 13. — Mary is a pupil. 14. Helen gives an
exercise book to Charles. 15. Where are we, Charles? 16. — We
are in a school. 17. Show me a mistake, Helen. 18. — Here is
a mistake.

D. 1. Where is a pupil? 2. — Here is Charles; Charles is a
pupil. 3. John gives a pencil to Mary. 4. Who has a pencil?
5. — Mary has a pencil. 6. What is a chair, Mary? 7. — Here
is a chair. 8. Where is a chair, Helen? 9. — Here is a chair,
and here is a blackboard. 10. What has John? 11. — John has
a book and a pencil. 12. Show me a door and a window, Charles.
13. — Here is a door, and here is a window. 14. Show me a wall.
15. — Here is a wall. 16. Who has a sister? 17. — John has a
sister. 18. Who has a brother? 19. — Mary has a brother.
20. John and Mary, a brother and sister.

LESSON II

22.   Conjugations

I		II		III	
comprare	to buy	vendere	to sell	finire	to finish, end
cancellare	to erase	ripetere	to repeat	capire	to understand
mostrare	to show	scrivere	to write	partire	to depart, leave

1. Italian verbs are divided, according to their infinitive endings, –are, –ere, –ire, into three conjugations.

2. The stem of any regular verb (found by dropping the infinitive ending) remains unchanged throughout the conjugation. To it are added the endings which indicate mood, tense, person and number.

23.   Present Indicative of *comprare* and *vendere*

Singular	compr o	I buy	vendo	I sell
	compr i	you buy	vend i	you sell
	compr a	he, she, it buys	vend e	he, she, it sells
Plural	compr **iamo**	we buy	vend **iamo**	we sell
	compr **ate**	you buy	vend **ete**	you sell
	compr **ano**	they buy	vend **ono**	they sell

1. The Italian present indicative renders not only the English simple present, but also the emphatic and, very often, the progressive present tenses: **compro** = *I buy, I do buy, I am buying.*

An Italian progressive present exists, however, and will be studied in a later lesson.

2. As the endings of the tenses ordinarily indicate person and number, the subject pronouns are seldom necessary for clearness and, unless emphasis is desired, may be omitted.

24. **Interrogative Sentences**

Carlo scrive con una penna? ⎫
Scrive Carlo con una penna? ⎬ Does Charles write with a pen?
Scrive con una penna Carlo? ⎭

1. A sentence can be made interrogative merely by the inflection of the voice and the use of the interrogation point.

2. The subject may follow the verb (yet less frequently than in English) or be placed at the very end of the sentence.

3. The verb *to do*, used as an auxiliary, is not translated in Italian.

25. **Possession**

Il libro d'Εlena — Helen's book
I libri d'Εlena e di Maria — Helen's and Mary's books

Possession is denoted by the preposition di which becomes d' before a vowel. This preposition must be repeated before each noun that it modifies.

EXERCISE II

carta paper	**ricevere** to receive
foglio sheet of paper	**usare** to use
gεsso chalk	**abbiamo** we have
inchiostro ink	**sono** they are
parola word	
penna pen	**anche** also
pεzzo piece	**con** with
ragazza girl	**mentre** while
ragazzo boy	**poi** then, afterward
sala hall, room	**prima** first, before

A. (1) *Continue the following throughout the singular and plural:* 1. Compro un quaderno, compri un quaderno, etc. 2. Vendo un libro, vendi un libro, etc. 3. Mostro una matita, mostri una matita, etc. 4. Ripeto uno sbaglio, ripeti uno sbaglio, etc.

La Classe

(*See page* 283)

(2) *Supply the correct form of the present indicative of the verb given in the infinitive:* 1. (*usare*) Maria —— una penna. 2. (*ricevere*) Carlo —— uno zero. 3. (*comprare*) Carlo e Giovanni —— un libro. 4. (*ripetere*) Elena e Maria —— una parola. 5. (*scrivere*) Elena —— con un pezzo di gesso. 6. (*cancellare*) Giovanni —— uno sbaglio.

(3) *Translate into Italian:* I receive, we show, they erase, you buy (*two ways*), he repeats, they write, I use, you show (*two ways*), we receive, she erases, it shows, we are, they use, we have, you sell (*two ways*), we write, they are, they repeat, she shows, you erase (*two ways*), we sell.

(4) *Divide and pronounce by syllables all nouns and verbs given in the vocabulary of this exercise.*

(5) *Read aloud Exercise II in Pronunciation (see § 8).*

B.   **A scuola**

1. Siamo in una sala. 2. Scriviamo. 3. Un alunno scrive con un pezzo di gesso. 4. Prima scrive e poi cancella. 5. Con che cosa scrivono Elena e Maria? 6. — Elena e Maria scrivono con penna e inchiostro. 7. Anche [1]Carlo scrive con penna e inchiostro. 8. Chi riceve uno zero? 9. — Un alunno riceve uno zero. 10. Carlo ha un foglio e una penna. 11. Mentre Carlo scrive, Giovanni mostra uno sbaglio a un ragazzo. 12. Elena ha un pezzo di carta. 13. Ha anche una matita. 14. Carlo usa una matita di Giovanni. 15. Chi è Maria? 16. — Maria è una ragazza. 17. Che cosa mostra Maria? 18. — Maria mostra uno specchio a Elena. 19. Che cosa vendi, ragazzo? 20. — Vendo un libro. 21. Vendiamo un libro e compriamo un quaderno. 22. Elena e Maria con chi sono? 23. — Sono con Carlo. 24. Con chi è Giovanni? 25. — Giovanni è con una ragazza. 26. Che cosa mostro?

---

[1] **Anche** generally precedes the noun or pronoun it modifies.

C. 1. Where are Charles and Helen? 2. — They are in a room.
3. They are writing. 4. With what does Charles write?
5. — Charles writes with pen and ink. 6. Helen is writing with a
pencil. 7. John, with what are you writing? 8. — I am writing
with a piece of chalk. 9. Where is Mary? 10. — Mary is with a
girl. 11. She is buying a book. 12. We write, and while we write
we use a pen and a sheet of paper. 13. First we write, then we
erase. 14. I am erasing a word. 15. Does John erase a zero?
16. — John erases a zero. 17. Who has a pen? 18. — A boy has
a pen.

D. 1. Good morning, John! 2. Where is Mary? 3. — Mary
is with Helen. 4. While Mary is with Helen, I use Mary's book.
5. What are you writing, Charles? 6. — I am writing a word.
7. A girl also is writing. 8. She is writing with a piece of chalk.
9. First she writes, and then she erases. 10. Does a pupil (*fem.*)
receive a zero? 11. Who is she? 12. — She is a sister of Helen?
13. Has John a piece of paper? 14. — John has a piece of paper
and also a pencil. 15. We have pen and ink, and we write. 16. Who
has a sheet of paper? 17. — A boy has a sheet of paper. 18. Here
is also an exercise book.

LESSON III

26. **Subject Pronouns**

As has been stated, clearness or emphasis may require the
use of the subject pronouns. Their more common forms are:

	SINGULAR		PLURAL	
1*st person*	io	I	noi	we
2*d person*	tu	thou, you	voi	you
3*d person*	egli	he		
	ella	she		
	esso	he, it	essi	they (*m.*)
	essa	she, it	esse	they (*f.*)
	Ella *or* Lei	you	Loro	you

1. Note that **egli** and **ella** refer to persons only, while **esso** and **essa, essi** and **esse**, may refer to persons, animals or things.

2. **Anch'io imparo.**   I also am learning.
   Egli detta e io scrivo.   He dictates and I write.

A subject pronoun is required: (*a*) when it is modified by an adverb; (*b*) when it is in contrast with a noun or another pronoun.

3. **Ella ascolta.**   }
   Lei ascolta.   }   You listen (*addressing one person*).
   Loro ascoltano.   You listen (*addressing more persons*).

Ella or, more familiarly, **Lei** with the verb in the 3d person singular, and **Loro** with the verb in the 3d person plural, are the normal forms of direct address in modern Italian. **Tu** and **voi** are used only in addressing very intimate persons, children, and dependents.

EXERCISE III

poesia poetry, poem	**guardare** to look, look at
racconto story	**imparare** to learn
regola rule	**insegnare** to teach
scrivania desk	**leggere** to read
verbo verb	**parlare** to speak
zio uncle	**perdere** to lose, miss
	recitare to recite
ascoltare to listen, listen to	
dettare to dictate	**oggi** today

A. (1) *Continue the following throughout the singular and plural:* 1. Io imparo una regola, tu impari una regola, etc. 2. Io leggo una poesia, tu leggi una poesia, etc. 3. Io perdo una matita, tu perdi una matita, etc. 4. Io parlo con un ragazzo, tu parli con un ragazzo, etc.

(2) *Insert the proper subject pronoun:* 1. —— scrivono. 2. —— insegniamo. 3. —— guardi. 4. —— mostra. 5. ——

dettate. 6. —— riceve. 7. —— scrivo. 8. —— cancellate.
9. —— perdi. 10. —— usano. 11. —— impariamo. 12. ——
ripetono. 13. —— cancella. 14. —— compri. 15. —— a-
scoltate. 16. —— guardiamo.

(3) *Supply the correct form of the present indicative of the
verb given in the infinitive:* 1. (*imparare*) Tu —— un verbo.
2. (*perdere*) Noi —— una penna. 3. (*recitare*) Esse —— una
poesia. 4. (*guardare*) Io —— un ragazzo. 5. (*ascoltare*) Voi
—— una ragazza. 6. (*dettare*) Lei —— un racconto. 7. (*leggere*) Egli —— una regola. 8. (*recitare*) Noi —— una poesia.
9. (*scrivere*) Loro —— con penna e inchiostro. 10. (*ripetere*)
Ella —— una parola. 11. (*cancellare*) Voi —— uno sbaglio.
12. (*mostrare*) Tu —— un muro. 13. (*ricevere*) Io —— uno
zero. 14. (*usare*) Egli —— un pezzo di gesso. 15. (*scrivere*)
Noi —— una parola. 16. (*insegnare*) Tu —— una regola.
17. (*mostrare*) Essi —— una scuola. 18. (*perdere*) Voi ——
un foglio.

(4) *Read aloud Exercise III in Pronunciation (see §§ 9–11).*

B. Impariamo

1. Che cosa recitiamo oggi? 2. — Oggi recitiamo una
poesia. 3. Che cosa impara Carlo? 4. — Carlo impara un
verbo. 5. Anche Giovanni impara un verbo. 6. Elena dà
un libro a una ragazza. 7. Io leggo e Maria ascolta.
8. Leggo un racconto. 9. Che cosa leggete voi? 10. — Noi
leggiamo una poesia. 11. Carlo detta e un alunno scrive.
12. Che cosa scrive? 13. — Essa scrive una regola.
14. Elena e Maria parlano con una ragazza. 15. Chi è
ella? 16. — È una sorella di Giovanni. 17. Noi guardiamo un libro. 18. Chi parla con Giovanni? 19. — Uno
zio di Carlo parla con Giovanni. 20. Mentre essi parlano,
noi mostriamo una scrivania a Elena. 21. Io insegno, e voi
imparate. 22. Chi perde un quaderno? 23. — Un alunno
perde un quaderno. 24. Egli perde un quaderno, e tu perdi
una matita.

C. 1. A pupil learns a poem. 2. Mary learns a verb. 3. What are you (tu) learning? 4. — I am learning a rule. 5. With whom is Helen speaking? 6. — She is speaking with an uncle of John. 7. While she speaks, we listen. 8. What do we read today? 9. — Today we read a story. 10. A boy dictates, and a girl writes. 11. Are you (voi) listening, Charles? 12. — I am listening. 13. They also are listening. 14. A pupil (fem.) is reciting. 15. Mary, show me a desk. 16. — Here is a desk, and here is also a chair. 17. Who teaches? 18. — You teach, and I learn.

D. 1. We show a desk, a chair and a blackboard to Helen. 2. We speak, and Helen listens. 3. Are you listening, Helen? 4. — I am listening. 5. I teach, and you learn. 6. What are you teaching? 7. — I am teaching a rule. 8. Does Mary look at a blackboard? 9. — She looks at a blackboard while John writes. 10. He is writing with a piece of chalk. 11. I dictate a poem. 12. Is Helen writing? 13. Has she paper and pencil? 14. — She has a sheet of paper, and she is writing with pen and ink. 15. Who recites today? 16. — Mary and Helen recite. 17. We also recite. 18. They (fem.) recite a verb, and you recite a poem.

LESSON IV

27.   Definite Article

	MASCULINE		FEMININE	
Singular	il	lo (l')	la (l')	= the
Plural	i	gli (gl')	le (l')	

1. il ragazzo, i ragazzi   the boy, the boys
   il muro, i muri   the wall, the walls
   lo scritto, gli scritti   the writing the writings
   lo zio, gli zii   the uncle, the uncles
   l'altro libro, gli altri libri the other book, the other books
   l'Italiano, gl'Italiani   the Italian, the Italians

Il and its plural, i are the usual masculine forms of the definite article. Lo and gli are used before masculine words beginning with a vowel, s impure or z. Before a vowel, however, lo becomes l', while gli becomes gl' only before i.

2. la sedia, le sedie, the chair, the chairs
l'altra sedia, le altre sedie the other chair, the other chairs
l'entrata, l'entrate the entrance, the entrances

La and its plural, **le,** are the feminine forms of the definite article. **La** becomes **l'** before any of the vowels, **le** becomes **l'** only before **e.**

3. la penna e l'inchiostro, the pen and ink

The definite article must be repeated before each noun to which it refers.

28. Plural of Nouns. From the examples given above it can be seen that nouns ending in **–o** form their plural by changing that **o** to **i** and that feminine nouns ending in **–a** form their plural by changing that **a** to **e.**

29. Adjectives in –o. The examples above (**altro, altri** — **altra, altre**) show also that:

1. Italian adjectives vary in gender and number, in agreement with their nouns.

2. Adjectives ending in **–o** have four forms:

	MASCULINE	FEMININE
Singular	–o	–a
Plural	–i	–e

EXERCISE IV

cosa thing
lettura reading
libro di lettura reader
maestro, –a teacher

americano American
attivo active
molto much (*pl.* many)
nuovo new
piccolo little, small
povero poor

questo this
stesso same
studioso studious

chiudere to close
cominciare to begin, start
imparare a memoria memorize
prendere to take
hanno they have

molto *adv.* very

A. (1) *Insert the definite article in each of the following sentences:* 1. Dov'è —— maestro? 2. Ecco —— maestro e —— maestra. 3. Mi mostri —— specchio. 4. Parlo con —— alunna. 5. Impariamo —— poesia. 6. Essi leggono —— racconti. 7. Noi ascoltiamo —— alunne. 8. Maria cancella —— zero. 9. Mi mostri —— entrata. 10. Chi prende —— matita? 11. —— ragazze scrivono. 12. Egli guarda —— zio. 13. —— maestro mostra —— sbaglio a Giovanni. 14. —— Americani [1] e —— Italiani sono molto attivi. 15. Voi cominciate —— lettura. 16. Ella mostra —— entrate. 17. Cancelliamo —— zeri. 18. Dove sono —— fratelli d'Elena? 19. —— alunni imparano. 20. Tu chiudi —— porta. 21. Ecco —— zii. 22. Compro —— inchiostro. 23. Impariamo —— verbi. 24. Mi mostri —— inchiostri. 25. —— specchi sono nuovi.

(2) *Supply the proper form of a suitable adjective in each case:* [2] 1. Un —— ragazzo. 2. Una —— sedia. 3. I —— libri. 4. Le —— entrate. 5. I —— pezzi di carta. 6. Le —— ragazze. 7. I —— alunni. 8. Impariamo —— cose. 9. Questi ragazzi sono ——. 10. Queste maestre sono ——.

(3) *Insert a suitable noun in each of the following sentences:* 1. Questa —— è nuova. 2. Dove sono gli altri ——? 3. Maria è una piccola ——. 4. La —— è americana. 5. I —— sono nuovi. 6. Compriamo molte ——. 7. Gli —— sono attivi. 8. Le —— sono studiose. 9. Questo è lo stesso ——. 10. Questa è la stessa ——. 11. Egli ha un altro ——. 12. Parlano a un povero ——.

(4) *Read aloud Exercise IV in Pronunciation (see § 12).*

B. **Parliamo italiano**

1. Il maestro parla, e noi ascoltiamo. 2. Egli parla italiano. 3. Anche noi cominciamo a parlare italiano.

---

[1] See §17 a.

[2] Do not use, in the first eight phrases, the adjectives **americano, attivo, italiano** and **studioso.**

4. Di che cosa parla il maestro? 5. — Egli parla di molte
cose. 6. Parliamo e leggiamo; poi scriviamo mentre egli
detta. 7. Oggi leggiamo in un nuovo libro di lettura.
8. Che legge Lei? 9. — Leggo un racconto. 10. È il racconto d'un povero ragazzo. 11. Chi legge poi? 12. — Poi
un altro alunno legge, e i ragazzi e le ragazze ascoltano.
13. Il maestro prende un pezzo di gesso e scrive una parola.
14. Gli alunni guardano la lavagna e scrivono la stessa
parola. 15. Scrivono con la penna. 16. Carlo scrive con la
matita. 17. Questi ragazzi sono molto studiosi e imparano.
18. È italiano il maestro? 19. — Il maestro è americano.
20. Ecco il fratello di Maria. 21. È un piccolo ragazzo.
22. Ha altri fratelli Maria? 23. — Maria ha molti fratelli.
24. Anche i fratelli di Maria sono in questa scuola.

C. 1. First we recite, then we speak Italian. 2. Today we recite a new poem. 3. Who memorizes the poem? 4. — The
pupils memorize the poem. 5. Have these boys the reader?
6. — They have the reader, and the reading begins. 7. We read
a new story today. 8. [It] [1] is the story of a poor girl. 9. Is this
girl American? 10. — This girl is Italian. 11. She is a little girl.
12. The pupils close the books and listen to the teacher. 13. He
takes a pencil. 14. He shows the pencil to a pupil (*fem.*). 15. What
is this, Helen? 16. Helen speaks Italian.

D. 1. Who are these boys? 2. — These are the same boys,
Charles and John. 3. They are very active and very studious.
4. They listen to the teacher and learn many things. 5. Helen
also is studious. 6. While the teacher speaks, she writes the new
words in an exercise book. 7. Then I read. 8. Are you listening,
Mary? 9. Mary is listening, and the other pupils also are listening. 10. I am reading a little story. 11. The story speaks of a
poor boy. 12. It begins with a little poem. 13. Afterward the
teacher dictates, and we write. 14. With what are the pupils
writing? 15. — They are writing with pen and ink. 16. Here is
a mistake, John. 17. The teacher shows the mistake to John.

---

[1] Omit words in brackets.

LESSON V

30.   Present Indicative of *finire* and *partire*

fin isc o	I finish	part o	I depart
fin isc i	you finish	part i	you depart
fin isc e	he, she, it finishes	part e	he, she, it departs
fin iamo	we finish	part iamo	we depart
fin ite	you finish	part ite	you depart
fin *isc* ono	they finish	part ono	they depart

The larger part of the verbs of the third conjugation, like **finire**, add –isc to their stem in all the persons of the singular and in the third person plural of the present indicative (present subjunctive and imperative). In all other tenses, all verbs of the third conjugation are inflected alike.

31.   Nouns and Adjectives in *–e*

1. **il padre, i padri**   the father, the fathers
   la madre, le madri   the mother, the mothers
   la lezione, le lezioni the lesson, the lessons

Italian nouns may end in –e in which case the ending gives no clue as to gender. Nouns in –e, whether masculine or feminine, form their plural in –i.

2. **Il libro è verde.**   The book is green.
   I libri sono verdi.   The books are green.
   La matita è verde.   The pencil is green.
   Le matite sono verdi.   The pencils are green.

Adjectives ending in –e have the same form for both masculine and feminine; their plural is in –i.

32.   *Lo* and *la* as Object Pronouns

Lo capisco.   I understand him (it).
La preferisco.   I prefer her (it).
Ecco la lezione: l'insegno. This is the lesson; I teach it.

The forms lo and la are also used as object pronouns. **Lo** means *him* or *it;* **la** means *her* or *it,* and both normally precede the verb. Like the definite article (*see* § 27) lo and la become l' before a following vowel.

EXERCISE V

Alberto Albert	**suonare** to sound, play, ring
Arturo Arthur	*Conjugated like* **finire:**
	capire to understand
campanello bell	**preferire** to prefer
eccezione *f.* exception	**pulire** to clean
lingua tongue, language	*Conjugated like* **partire:**
professore *m.* professor	**aprire** to open
violino violin	**seguire** to follow
diligente diligent	**ad** to, at [1]
inglese English	**da** by, from
tedesco German	**per** for, through, in order to

A. (1) *Continue the following throughout the singular and plural:* 1. Io finisco la lezione, tu finisci la lezione, etc. 2. Io capisco le parole di Carlo, etc. 3. Io parto da Roma, etc. 4. Io preferisco questo ragazzo, etc. 5. Io apro il libro, etc. 6. Io seguo il maestro, etc.

(2) *Supply the correct form of the present indicative of the verb given in the infinitive:* 1. (*finire*) Tu —— il racconto. 2. (*capire*) Noi —— queste parole. 3. (*cancellare*) Voi —— lo sbaglio. 4. (*preferire*) Voi —— Elena. 5. (*suonare*) Essi —— il campanello. 6. (*pulire*) Lei —— la lavagna. 7. (*seguire*) Esse —— Arturo. 8. (*finire*) Essi —— la poesia. 9. (*preferire*) Io —— questa scuola. 10. (*aprire*) Io —— il quaderno. 11. (*pulire*) Tu —— la scrivania. 12. (*comprare*) Voi —— le matite. 13. (*seguire*) Noi —— il professore. 14. (*capire*) Egli —— lo zio. 15. (*aprire*) Tu —— la

---

[1] Use the preposition **ad** before words beginning with **a;** in all other cases **a** is used.

finestra. 16. (*pulire*) Io —— le sedie. 17. (*aprire*) Loro —— le porte. 18. (*ricevere*) Voi —— un alunno. 19. (*preferire*) Tu —— un ragazzo diligente. 20. (*capire*) Voi —— le parole d'Alberto.

(3) *Give the plural of:* questa lezione, lo stesso padre, la stessa eccezione, la povera madre, il nuovo professore, l'alunno è diligente, la matita è verde, il professore è americano, la ragazza è inglese, l'inchiostro è verde.

B.   Recitiamo

1. Il maestro apre la finestra. 2. La lezione comincia. 3. È una lezione d'italiano. 4. Arturo recita, poi altri ragazzi recitano. 5. Alberto pulisce la lavagna e scrive. 6. Che cosa scrivi, Alberto? 7. — Scrivo le nuove parole di questa lezione. 8. Ecco uno sbaglio. 9. Capisci la regola? 10. — Non la capisco. 11. La capisco; questa è un'eccezione. 12. Molte regole hanno eccezioni. 13. Mentre Alberto scrive, noi apriamo i libri di lettura e leggiamo. 14. Molti alunni leggono. 15. Leggiamo in italiano e capiamo. 16. Gli alunni ascoltano; essi sono diligenti. 17. Poi il maestro parla ad Arturo. 18. Il maestro parla molte lingue. 19. Parla inglese, tedesco e italiano. 20. Preferisce parlare italiano in questa scuola. 21. Gli alunni capiscono e imparano. 22. Un campanello suona. 23. Chi suona il campanello? 24. I ragazzi chiudono i libri, e la lezione finisce.

C. 1. Who are these boys? 2. — They are Charles' brothers, Albert and Arthur. 3. They are studious and diligent. 4. Albert plays the violin. 5. He plays it. 6. These boys' father understands and speaks many languages. 7. Do you understand German?[1] 8. — I understand and speak German and Italian.

---

[1] The adjectives **inglese, italiano, tedesco**, etc. take the definite article whenever they stand for *the English language, the Italian language*, etc., except after the verb **parlare** or immediately after di or in.

D

9. What language do we speak? 10. — We speak English.
11. Today I prefer to speak Italian in order to learn this language.
12. I begin to (a) understand. 13. Many pupils (*fem.*) understand.
14. John, are these pencils green? 15. — The pencils are green,
and the book also is green.

D. 1. The professor begins the lesson. 2. He opens the book
and reads. 3. Then the pupils read. 4. John, what are you
listening to? 5. — I am listening to the reading of a story.
6. Mary and Helen, are you also listening? 7. They listen and
understand. 8. Charles finishes the story. 9. He finishes it.
10. Arthur cleans the blackboard. 11. The professor gives (to)
Arthur a piece of chalk, and Arthur writes. 12. He writes today's
lesson. 13. Mary, do you understand this rule? 14. We understand the rule and learn the exceptions. 15. The professor shows
the mistake to Arthur. 16. Albert and the other pupils look at
the blackboard in order to learn. 17. They are very diligent.
18. Mary gives the exercise book to John. 19. John receives the
exercise book from Mary. 20. The bell rings, and the lesson ends.

LESSON VI

33.   **Negative Sentences**

Egli non capisce.	He does not understand.
Non ha libri.	He hasn't any books.
Non ha nessun libro.	He hasn't any book.
Non parlo con nessuno.	I speak with nobody.
Non scriviamo niente.	We do not write anything.
Egli non ascolta mai.	He never listens.

1. A verb is made negative by placing **non** before it.

2. The English *any*, when followed by a plural word in a
negative sentence, is not translated; when followed by a
singular word, that may take a numerical modifier, it is usually rendered by **nessuno**, which takes the same endings as
the indefinite article (**nessun, nessuno, nessuna, nessun'**). As

nessuno really means *not one*, or *not any*, or *nobody*, the student will see that the *double negative* occurs rather frequently in Italian, conveying, however, only a single negative idea.

3. Other negative expressions used in connection with negative verbs are: mai *never*, niente or nulla *nothing*, nè ... nè *neither ... nor*, etc.

4. Also in negative sentences [1] the verb *to do*, used as an auxiliary, is not translated in Italian.

5. **Nessuno parte.**	Nobody leaves.
Nulla è impossìbile.	Nothing is impossible.
Egli mai capisce.	He never understands.
Nè Carlo nè Arturo impara.	Neither Charles nor Arthur learns.

When **nessuno**, or any of the other negative expressions mentioned in paragraph 3 of this section, precedes the verb, **non** is omitted.

34.   Some Interrogative Adjectives

Quale studio preferisce Lei?	Which study do you prefer?
Quali finestre sono aperte?	Which windows are open?
Quanta carta ha Lei?	How much paper have you?
Quanti racconti leggiamo?	How many stories do we read?

The most frequently used interrogative adjectives are **quale**, *which*, and **quanto**, *how much, how many*. Both are inflected, and agree with their nouns in gender and number.

35.   Some Cardinal Numerals

1	uno, –a	5	cinque	9	nove
2	due	6	sei	10	dieci
3	tre	7	sette	11	undici
4	quattro	8	otto	12	dodici

Uno has a feminine, **una** and when used adjectively has the forms of the indefinite article (*see* § 19). All other numbers are invariable.

[1] We have seen that the same occurs with interrogative sentences (*see* § 24, 3.)

EXERCISE VI

bidello school-janitor	**pigro** lazy
classe *f.* class	
studente *m.* student	**c'è** there is
traduzione *f.* translation	**ci sono** there are
verso line of poetry	
	no no
aperto open, opened	**ora** now
chiuso closed	**perchè?** why?
difficile difficult	**perchè** because, for
facile easy	**quando** when
grande large, big, great	**se** if
intelligente intelligent	**sì** yes

A. (1) *Continue the following throughout the singular and plural:* 1. Non preferisco io nulla? Non preferisci tu nulla? etc. 2. Io non apro nessuna finestra, etc. 3. Io non pulisco mai la lavagna, etc. 4. Seguo la regola io? etc. 5. Non prendo io niente? etc. 6. Io non ascolto nè Alberto nè Arturo, etc.

(2) *Translate into Italian:* 1. I don't open any door. 2. They have neither books nor exercise books. 3. She never understands. 4. We don't prefer anything. 5. He has no brothers. 6. She hasn't any uncle. 7. These lessons are never difficult. 8. Why does she never close the windows? 9. Mary has neither father nor mother. 10. Nobody learns. 11. They don't look at anything. 12. You (**voi**) speak neither Italian nor German.

(3) *Make the nouns in the following sentences singular or plural:* 1. Non abbiamo matite. 2. Non leggo nessun libro. 3. Non imparo nessuna poesia. 4. Non recitiamo verbi. 5. Voi non usate pezzi di gesso. 6. Non compriamo quaderni. 7. Non ascolto nessun racconto. 8. Essi non usano nessuna penna.

(4) *Count from 1 to 12. Count from 12 to 1.*

B.   **Rispondiamo**

1. Parlano italiano questi studenti? 2. È Arturo studioso e diligente? 3. La traduzione è facile? 4. Recita
Elena una poesia? 5. Apre il bidello una porta? 6. Chiudono i libri questi ragazzi? —— 7. No, Carlo non chiude
nessuna finestra. 8. Questa sala non è grande. 9. No,
questi ragazzi non sono nè attivi nè diligenti. 10. Sì, il
fratello d'Elena è pigro. 11. Sì, il bidello pulisce la sala.
12. Questa poesia ha dodici versi. —— 13. Quanti ragazzi
ci sono in questa classe? 14. — Ci sono undici ragazzi in
questa classe. 15. E quante ragazze ci sono? 16. — Ci
sono otto ragazze. 17. I quaderni sono aperti; perchè gli
studenti non scrivono? 18. — Non scrivono perchè non
hanno nè penne nè inchiostro. 19. Perchè non scrive Lei?
20. — Non scrivo perchè non capisco la nuova regola. 21. Lei
non è diligente. 22. Ora chiudiamo i libri e parliamo italiano. 23. I libri sono chiusi, un alunno parla, e gli altri
ascoltano. 24. Quando ascoltiamo e capiamo, impariamo.
25. Se non ascoltiamo, non impariamo nulla.

C. 1. If you don't listen to the professor, you don't learn anything. 2. Are these lessons difficult, John? 3. — No, they are
easy. 4. When I understand the rules, these lessons are never
difficult. 5. We learn rules and recite little poems. 6. Don't we
memorize anything today? 7. — Yes, we memorize ten lines.
8. How many new words [1] are there in this little poem? 9. — There
are nine new words. 10. Charles, where are you looking? 11. You
are looking neither at the blackboard nor at the professor; you are
not diligent. 12. Now we begin the reading of a new story. 13. We
read it.

D. 1. The door is open: why does Albert never close the door?
2. — He never closes the door because he is lazy. 3. Mary closes
it; now the door is closed. 4. Don't we learn any new verb today?

---

[1] For greater emphasis, place the adjective *new* after the noun *words*.

5. — No, we don't learn any verb today because no new verb is in this lesson. 6. We write a translation and memorize six lines of poetry. 7. Where is Helen's translation? 8. — She has neither the translation nor the exercise book. 9. Isn't there any new student in this class? 10. — Yes, there is a new student, and he is very intelligent and studious. 11. How many students are there in this class now? 12. — There are in this class eleven girls and seven boys. 13. I prefer a small class to a large [one].[1] 14. If the class is small, we learn better (**meglio**). 15. Now the janitor rings the bell, and the professor ends the lesson.

E. *Oral. The first six questions in B will be read aloud in class. The student should prepare himself to understand them without looking at the book, and to give to each of them first an affirmative, then a negative answer.*

Sentences 7 to 12 in B will likewise be read aloud. The student will be asked to form for each of them an appropriate interrogative sentence.

LESSON VII

36. Present Indicative of the Auxiliary Verbs

essere to be		*avere* to have	
sono	I am	hɔ	I have
sɛi	you are	hai	you have
ɛ̀	he, she, it is	ha	he, she, it has
siamo	we are	abbiamo	we have
siɛte	you are	avete	you have
sono	they are	hanno	they have

37. Definite Article before Titles

Il signor Fantoni ɛ̀ a casa.	Mr. Fantoni is at home.
Preferisco la contessa Bindi.	I prefer Countess Bindi.
Buɔn giorno, signor professore.	Good morning, professor.

---

[1] Omit.

A title followed by a proper name takes the definite article in Italian. The article is, however, omitted when the title is used in direct address.

38. Apocopation of Titles Ending in *–ore.* Titles ending in –ore (they are all of masculine gender), such as **signore, professore, senatore,** etc. drop the final e whenever followed by a proper name or another title, as seen in the examples in the preceding section.

EXERCISE VII

frase *f.* sentence
grammatica grammar
penna stilografica fountain pen
signore *m.* gentleman, sir, Mr.
signorina miss, young lady

ogni (*invariable*) every
qualche cosa something

aver [1] **bisogno di** to need
chiamare to call, call on
spiegare to explain
studiare to study

al pian terreno on the ground floor
al piano superiore on the upper floor

A. (1) *Continue the following throughout the singular and plural:* 1. Io sono in una scuola, etc. 2. Io non ho niente, etc. 3. Non sono io mai diligente? etc. 4. Ho io penna e inchiostro? etc. 5. Io non ho nessun fratello, etc. 6. Io sono americano, etc.

(2) *Place the correct form of the present indicative, first of* **essere** *and then of* **avere,** *after each of the following pronouns:* essi ——, tu ——, egli ——, esse ——, io ——, essa ——, voi ——, Lei ——, Loro ——.

(3) *Translate into Italian:* 1. They have eight books. 2. We are in a room. 3. Is he a teacher? 4. I am very active. 5. Have you a pencil? 6. She is not in this school. 7. You don't have any exercise books. 8. You are (**tu** *form*) Italian. 9. I am American. 10. She is a teacher.

[1] See § 16.

11. You have (**voi** *form*) a fountain pen. 12. They haven't any grammar. 13. They are with Miss Boni. 14. Is Mr. Tozzi at home?

B.   In classe

1. I ragazzi e le ragazze di questa classe studiano la lingua italiana. 2. Essi hanno una grammatica e un libro di lettura. 3. Hanno anche un quaderno e una penna stilografica. 4. Se non hanno la penna stilografica, hanno una matita. 5. Il professor Anselmi insegna e noi impariamo. 6. Impariamo se siamo diligenti. 7. Che cosa scrive Lei ora, signor Bruni? 8. — Scrivo una nuova parola. 9. Ogni alunno scrive quando il maestro detta. 10. Abbiamo un nuovo bidello in questa scuola. 11. Se abbiamo bisogno di qualche cosa, lo chiamiamo. 12. Egli è ora al pian terreno. 13. Noi siamo al piano superiore. 14. Questa sala è grande. 15. Non ogni sala di questa scuola è grande. 16. Molte sale sono piccole. 17. Ha Lei una matita, signorina Landini? 18. La signorina Landini ha una matita e ora scrive. 19. Voi anche scrivete perchè siete diligenti.

C. 1. We are in a large room on the ground floor. 2. They study the Italian[1] language in this class. 3. Professor Anselmi dictates and we write. 4. I write with a fountain pen. 5. Miss Landini writes with a pencil. 6. Mr. Bruni also writes with a pencil. 7. Now Professor Anselmi explains a new rule. 8. Every student understands it because he listens to the professor. 9. The lesson is not difficult. 10. I study and memorize every new word. 11. Which language do you prefer, Mr. Tozzi? 12. — I prefer the Italian language, sir.

D. 1. Today we are in a room on the upper floor. 2. This room has two windows and a door. 3. It has also a large blackboard. 4. Miss Alessandri is writing now. 5. I am looking at her; she is writing with a piece of chalk. 6. What are you writing, Miss Ales-

---

[1] Place the adjective *Italian* after the noun.

sandri? 7. — I am writing an Italian sentence. 8. Do you need
a grammar? 9. — No, sir: the lesson is easy today. 10. While
this girl writes, we read something. 11. Professor Anselmi calls on
Mr. Smith. 12. Mr. Smith opens his (= the) reader and reads.

E. *Oral.* 1. Dove siamo? 2. È questa sala al pian
terreno? 3. Che cosa studia Lei in questa classe, signor
——? 4. Chi è il professore d'italiano in questa scuola?
5. Chi è quest'alunno? 6. Chi è quest'alunna? 7. Con
che cosa scrive Lei, signorina ——? 8. Scriviamo ora, signor
——? 9. Che lingua parliamo? 10. Dov'è una grammatica? 11. Dov'è un altro libro? 12. Anche quest'altro libro è una grammatica? 13. Di che cosa abbiamo bisogno
per scrivere? 14. Chi spiega le lezioni?

LESSON VIII

39. Prepositions and Article. When the definite article
is preceded by one of the prepositions **a, con, da, di, in, per,
su,** the article and preposition are usually combined in one
word, as shown in the following table:

	il	i	lo	gli	la	le	l'
a to, at	al	ai *or* a'	allo	agli	alla	alle	all'
con with	col	coi *or* co'	(collo)	(cogli)	(colla)	(colle)	(coll')
da by, from	dal	dai *or* da'	dallo	dagli	dalla	dalle	dall'
di of	del	dei *or* de'	dello	degli	della	delle	dell'
in in, into	nel	nei *or* ne'	nello	negli	nella	nelle	nell'
per for	pel	pei *or* pe'	(pello)	(pegli)	(pella)	(pelle)	(pell')
su on	sul	sui *or* su'	sullo	sugli	sulla	sulle	sull'

1. Often the prepositions **con** and, even more frequently,
per are used separate from the article. The forms printed in
parentheses are obsolete.

La Casa

(*See page* 283)

2. Sometimes in poetry, and in a few rarer cases in prose also, other prepositions are used separate from the article.

EXERCISE VIII

America America
Italia Italy

balcone *m.* balcony
camera bedroom
casa house, home
cucina kitchen
legno wood
mattone *m.* floor-tile
pavimento floor
pietra stone

sala da pranzo dining room
salotto parlor
stanza room
stanza da bagno bathroom
studio study

comodo comfortable

passare to pass, spend (*time*);
stop
ma but
quasi almost

A. (1) *Supply the proper Italian form for the words in parentheses:* (*in the*) scuola, (*for the*) scuola, (*from the*) casa, (*of the*) studente, (*to the*) studente, (*by the*) studente, (*in the*) inchiostro, (*to the*) ragazzo, (*to the*) ragazze, (*for the*) stanze, (*on the*) sedia, (*with the*) mano, (*in the*) stanze, (*for the*) professori, (*with the*) penne, (*on the*) libri, (*with the*) mani, (*of the*) inchiostro, (*by the*) studenti, (*on the*) sedie.

(2) *Insert the proper subject pronoun:* 1. —— passiamo. 2. —— studio. 3. —— finite. 4. —— chiamano. 5. —— spiegate. 6. —— pulisci. 7. —— apriamo. 8. —— hanno. 9. —— preferisce. 10. —— siamo.

(3) *Supply the proper form of the present indicative of the verb given in the infinitive:* 1. (*chiamare*) Arturo —— il signor Fantoni. 2. (*partire*) Noi —— dalla scuola. 3. (*pulire*) La ragazza —— la lavagna. 4. (*cominciare*) Gli alunni —— coi verbi. 5. (*chiudere*) Elena —— la porta della classe. 6. (*essere*) I libri del professore —— sulla scrivania. 7. (*insegnare*) La maestra —— agli alunni. 8. (*imparare*) Le alunne —— dalla maestra. 9. (*capire*) Voi —— le parole dello zio. 10. (*guardare*) Noi —— nello specchio.

B. **A casa**

1. Dove siamo? 2. — Siamo nella casa di Carlo. 3. Essa è piccola ma comoda. 4. Il salotto, lo studio, la sala da pranzo e la cucina sono al pian terreno. 5. Le camere e la stanza da bagno sono al piano superiore. 6. La camera del fratello di Carlo è chiusa. 7. Egli è in Italia col fratello d'Elena. 8. Ha molte finestre questa casa? 9. — Ha molte finestre e il salotto ha anche un balcone. 10. Questa finestra·è aperta. 11. Dove sono i ragazzi? 12: — Se non sono nella sala da pranzo, sono a scuola con Arturo. 13. Questa stanza è grande. 14. Nessuna stanza è piccola. 15. Il salotto ha un nuovo pavimento. 16. Dal salotto passo nello studio del padre di Carlo. 17. Egli ha molti libri. 18. Questa stanza non ha nessun balcone. 19. Chi è nella cucina? 20. — La sorella di Carlo è in [1] cucina.

C. 1. Many houses in America are of wood. 2. In Italy the houses are of stone. 3. Are the floors of wood in Italy? 4. — No, they are of tiles. 5. Where are you? 6. — We are on the upper floor. 7. These houses are little but comfortable. 8. Are the windows not open? 9. — No, they are closed. 10. Where is Arthur? 11. — He is at school with the other boys. 12. Where are Mr. Colli and Miss Colli? 13. — They are not at home today. 14. They are not at home every day.

D. 1. You (**voi**) are in the study, and Miss Taylor is in the dining room. 2. No, she is neither in the dining room nor in the parlor; she is in the kitchen. 3. This room has many doors. 4. Almost every room is comfortable, but the bedrooms are small. 5. We prefer the rooms on the ground floor. 6. This is a large bathroom; the bathroom of Mr. Balbi's house is small. 7. You (**Loro**) haven't any balcony. 8. In Italy many houses have balconies. 9. From the study we pass into the parlor. 10. This parlor has two windows. 11. How many doors has it?

---

[1] Note the idiomatic **in cucina** (also **in casa, in sala, in camera,** etc.).

E. *Oral.* *In answering each of the following questions, use
an adjective conveying the opposite idea.* 1. È aperta la
finestra? 2. È piccolo il salotto? 3. Nessuna casa ha una
sala da pranzo? 4. Siamo al piano superiore? 5. Ha ogni
stanza un pavimento di mattoni? 6. È questa la stessa
casa? 7. Sono chiuse le porte? 8. Elena è al pian terreno? 9. È grande la cucina? 10. È questa un'altra
camera? 11. Il fratello di Carlo è studioso? 12. È difficile la traduzione? 13. Sono pigri questi ragazzi? 14. Sono
aperti i libri? 15. È facile la lezione d'oggi? 16. È piccola la scuola?

LESSON IX

40.   **Past Absolute of Model Verbs**

I bought, etc.	*I sold, etc.*	*I finished, etc.*
compr **ai**	vend **ei** (−etti)	fin **ii**
compr **asti**	vend **esti**	fin **isti**
compr **ò**	vend **è** (−ette)	fin **ì**
compr **ammo**	vend **emmo**	fin **immo**
compr **aste**	vend **este**	fin **iste**
compr **arono**	vend **erono** (−ettero)	fin **irono**

1. Note that, with the exception of the 3d person singular
of the verbs in −**are** (compr**ò**), the characteristic vowel of each
conjugation is retained throughout this tense, and that, but
for this characteristic vowel, the endings are the same for all
three conjugations.

2. The 1st person singular, the 3d person singular and the
3d person plural of the past absolute of many, but not all,
verbs of the second conjugation may also end respectively
in −**etti** (vend**etti**), −**ette** (vend**ette**), −**ettero** (vend**ettero**).
This set of forms is less commonly used.

41. Past Absolute of *essere* and *avere*

I was, etc.		*I had, etc.*	
fui	fummo	ɛbbi	avemmo
fosti	foste	avesti	aveste
fu	furono	ɛbbe	ɛbbero

42. Use of the Past Absolute

Iɛri ricevei una lɛttera.	Yesterday I received a letter.
Dante morì in esilio.	Dante died in exile.

This tense is used in stating, without reference to the present, what happened at a certain time in the past. It is always translated by the English simple past or the English emphatic past (= *did sell*).

EXERCISE IX

Ɔlga Olga
Sílvia Sylvia

cartolina post card
francobollo stamp
impiegato, –a clerk
indirizzo address
lɛttera letter
lɛttera raccomandata registered letter
mittɛnte *m. or f.* sender
pacco parcel, package
pɔsta post, post office
postino letter carrier
ricevuta receipt

saluto greeting

lungo long

consegnare to hand
firmare to sign
incontrare to meet
mandare to send
portare to bring, bear, carry
rispondere to answer
trovare to find

fa ago; due giorni fa two days ago
iɛri yesterday

A. (1) *Continue the following throughout the singular and plural:* 1. Io recitai la lezione, etc. 2. Io perdei l'indirizzo, etc. 3. Io capii ogni cosa, etc. 4. Io ebbi una lettera, etc. 5. Io fui alla posta, etc. 6. Io incontrai il postino, etc.

7. Io vendei il violino, etc. 8. Io partii con la sorella di Silvia, etc.

(2) *Insert the proper subject pronoun:* 1. —— ricevesti. 2. —— seguii. 3. —— guardammo. 4. —— foste. 5. —— ebbe. 6. —— mostrai. 7. —— pulirono. 8. —— aprì. 9. —— fummo. 10. —— avesti. 11. —— firmò. 12. —— recitaste. 13. —— ascoltarono. 14. —— ripetei.

(3) *Supply the correct form of the past absolute of the verb given in the infinitive:* 1. (*consegnare*) Voi —— il pacco. 2. (*firmare*) Io —— la ricevuta. 3. (*incontrare*) Essi —— il professore. 4. (*mandare*) Loro —— saluti. 5. (*portare*) Tu —— una cartolina. 6. (*vendere*) Lei —— i libri. 7. (*essere*) Noi —— a scuola. 8. (*avere*) Noi —— cinque lettere. 9. (*passare*) Tu —— insieme con Olga. 10. (*finire*) Egli —— la traduzione. 11. (*consegnare*) Esse —— i quaderni. 12. (*parlare*) Ella —— tedesco. 13. (*capire*) Voi —— il signor Tognini. 14. (*suonare*) Lei —— il violino. 15. (*spiegare*) Noi —— la nuova regola. 16. (*essere*) Essi —— molto attivi. 17. (*avere*) Esse —— sette lettere. 18. (*avere*) Tu —— bisogno d'Arturo. 19. (*essere*) Egli —— in Italia. 20. (*prendere*) Noi —— i francobolli.

B. **Alla posta**

1. Il postino due giorni fa consegnò un pacco a Olga. 2. Olga firmò una ricevuta. 3. E non ricevè nulla Lei? 4. — Io ricevei una lunga lettera e tre cartoline. 5. Silvia mandò un saluto in una delle cartoline. 6. E Lei, signorina, dove fu[1] ieri? 7. — Fui alla posta e comprai dieci francobolli. 8. Parlai con uno degl'impiegati. 9. All'entrata della posta incontrai il professore d'italiano. 10. Dove fu poi? 11. — Poi fui a scuola, ma prima passai a casa d'Elena. 12. Quando mandò Carlo questa lettera raccomandata? 13. — Carlo la mandò sei giorni fa, e rispondemmo ieri.

---

[1] The past absolute of **essere** often renders the English *went, did go.*

14. Ecco il nuovo indirizzo di Carlo. 15. Ha Carlo un nuovo indirizzo? 16. Mi mostri questa lettera. 17. Ogni lettera raccomandata porta l'indirizzo del mittente. 18. Non ricevè Lei anche una cartolina ieri? 19. — Sì, ricevei una cartolina dalla signorina Boschini. 20. Dov'è ora la signorina Boschini? 21. — È in Italia con Maria e la madre di Maria. 22. Dodici giorni fa mandammo un pacco a Maria.

C. 1. Yesterday Sylvia received a registered letter. 2. A letter carrier brought it, and Sylvia signed a receipt. 3. With what did she sign? 4. — She signed with a fountain pen. 5. Didn't you (voi) receive anything? 6. — Yes, sir; I received a long letter and three post cards. 7. Did you (voi) answer the [1] letter? 8. — Yes, we answered the same day. 9. I sent the letter to the post office by (per mezzo di) a boy. 10. The boy brought it to the post office. 11. A clerk sold a stamp to the boy, and the boy handed the letter to the clerk. 12. Here is the receipt; it bears Miss Bardini's address.

D. 1. The letter carrier brought a parcel three days ago. 2. He brought also two letters and five post cards. 3. Who signed the receipt for the parcel? 4. — Olga signed it, sir. 5. Here is the parcel, and here are also the letters and cards. 6. I opened the parcel and looked. 7. Also Mary looked, and we found eight books. 8. Show me the two letters, Mary. 9. One of the letters is in Italian. 10. Mary and I read the letter together and understood almost every word. 11. We answered the same day with a long letter. 12. We sent also many greetings to Miss Nencioni.

E. *Oral.* 1. Dove compriamo i francobolli? 2. Di quanti francobolli abbiamo bisogno per mandare sei lettere? 3. Chi vende i francobolli e le cartoline? 4. Chi porta le lettere? 5. Ricevè Carlo un pacco? 6. Chi mandò il pacco a Carlo? 7. Quando fu Lei alla posta? 8. Che cosa comprò alla posta? 9. Chi incontrò all'entrata della posta? 10. Dove fu Lei poi? 11. A chi consegniamo alla posta le

---

[1] Translate, *to the letter.*

lettere raccomandate? 12. Per mandare un saluto, che cosa scriviamo? 13. Quando rispondemmo alla lettera del signor Tedeschi? 14. Quali saluti portò la lettera del signor Tedeschi? 15. Quando ricevè Lei una lettera? 16. Quando il ragazzo portò la lettera raccomandata alla posta, che cosa consegnò l'impiegato al ragazzo? 17. Se una lettera è in italiano, capisce Lei ogni parola? 18. Che cosa ricevè Lei ieri dal postino? 19. Con che cosa firmiamo una ricevuta?

LESSON X

43.   Past Descriptive of Model Verbs

I bought, was buying, used to buy, etc.	I sold, was selling, used to sell, etc.	I finished, was finishing, used to finish, etc.
compr avo	vend evo	fin ivo
compr avi	vend evi	fin ivi
compr ava	vend eva	fin iva
compr avamo	vend evamo	fin ivamo
compr avate	vend evate	fin ivate
compr avano	vend evano	fin ivano

1. Note that, except for the fact that each conjugation retains its characteristic vowel (a in the first, e in the second, and i in the third), the endings of this tense are the same for all Italian verbs.

2. The first person singular may also end in –a (io comprava, vendeva, finiva), but this form is rapidly becoming obsolete.

44.   Past Descriptive of *essere* and *avere*

I was, was being, used to be, etc.		I had, was having, used to have, etc.	
ero	eravamo	avevo	avevamo
eri	eravate	avevi	avevate
era	erano	aveva	avevano

E

What has been said in § 43, 2 applies also to the verbs essere and avere.

45.   Use of the Past Descriptive

Lavoravo quand'egli entrò.	I was working when he entered.
Parlavano mentre io scrivevo.	They spoke (*or* were speaking) while I wrote (*or* was writing).
Ogni giorno scrivevo una lettera.	Every day I wrote (*or* used to write) a letter.
Egli era ricco.	He was (*or* used to be) rich.
Il cielo era nuvoloso.	The sky was cloudy.

As its name implies, this tense conveys a descriptive idea in the past. It is used also to express an incomplete or habitual action, and to state what was taking place when something else happened or was happening. It corresponds to such English past phrases as *I was doing* or *I used to do* or to a simple past which usually stands for one of these phrases.

While the past absolute generally answers the question *what happened?* the past descriptive tells what was going on or used to happen.

EXERCISE X

credenza sideboard	tavola table
cassettone *m.* chiffonier	
divano divan	magnifico magnificent
lampada lamp	
letto bed	sedere to sit, sit down
mobile *m.* piece of furniture	spolverare to dust
mobilia furniture	coprire to cover [1]
poltrona armchair	
scaffale *m.* bookshelf	davanti a before, in front of
signora lady, madam, Mrs.	dietro a behind
sedia a dondolo rocking-chair	solamente only
tappeto rug	vicino a near

[1] Conjugated like partire.

A. (1) *Continue the following throughout the singular and plural:* 1. Io mostravo una parola sulla lavagna, etc. 2. Io non perdevo mai niente, etc. 3. Partivo io col professore? etc. 4. Io imparavo molte cose, etc. 5. Io non scrivevo a nessuno, etc. 6. Io preferivo imparare, etc. 7. Ero io povero? etc. 8. Io non avevo la traduzione, etc.

(2) *Insert the proper subject pronoun:* 1. —— seguivamo. 2. —— eri. 3. —— preferiva. 4. —— avevate. 5. —— usavano. 6. —— aprivo. 7. —— recitavamo. 8. —— avevano. 9. —— ascoltavi. 10. —— leggeva. 11. —— ripetevate. 12. —— ricevevo. 13. —— guardavano. 14. —— cancellavi. 15. —— coprivano.

(3) *Supply the correct form of the past descriptive of the verb given in the infinitive:* 1. *(passare)* Voi —— le lettere a Giovanni. 2. *(capire)* Essi —— l'italiano. 3. *(seguire)* Tu —— queste ragazze. 4. *(essere)* Io —— diligente. 5. *(suonare)* Lei —— il campanello. 6. *(preferire)* Ella —— sedere. 7. *(avere)* Noi —— bisogno di Carlo. 8. *(essere)* Loro —— attivi. 9. *(vendere)* Tu —— ogni cosa. 10. *(avere)* Io —— un magnifico tappeto. 11. *(spolverare)* Voi —— i mobili. 12. *(prendere)* Egli —— le lettere alla posta. 13. *(imparare)* Essi —— il tedesco. 14. *(insegnare)* Essa —— l'inglese. 15. *(ricevere)* Noi —— molte cartoline. 16. *(coprire)* Tu —— la tavola col tappeto. 17. *(usare)* Voi —— una penna stilografica. 18. *(ascoltare)* Essa —— la maestra. 19. *(guardare)* Io —— la nuova lampada. 20. *(perdere)* Noi —— molte cose.

B. **La mobilia**

1. Alberto mostrava a Carlo la nuova mobilia. 2. Io ero con Alberto e Carlo, e insieme guardavamo ogni mobile. 3. Il cassettone vicino alla finestra aveva uno specchio. 4. Che cosa c'era davanti al letto? 5. —Davanti al letto c'era un piccolo tappeto. 6. Solamente due sedie erano

IL SALOTTO

(*See page* 283)

nella camera. 7. La stanza non era molto grande. 8. Ma ecco il signor Mazzolà. 9. Dov'era Lei, signor Mazzolà? 10. — Ero nel salotto e sedevo sul divano. 11. Parlavo con queste signorine. 12. Passammo insieme nel salotto. 13. Silvia e le altre signore e signorine sedevano nelle poltrone e nelle sedie a dondolo. 14. Una magnifica lampada era sulla scrivania. 15. Dov'era la scrivania? 16. — La scrivania era davanti al balcone. 17. Non ogni libro era sullo scaffale. 18. Tre erano sulla tavola. 19. Una ragazza spolverava i mobili della sala da pranzo. 20. Ogni giorno essa puliva le stanze e spolverava la mobilia. 21. Quando puliva le stanze, apriva le finestre. 22. Le finestre della sala da pranzo erano aperte.

C. 1. Albert's room did not have much furniture. 2. It had only a bed, a chiffonier and two chairs. 3. It was a small room with one window. 4. The window was closed. 5. Where were Albert's sisters? 6. — They were in the dining room, and were dusting the sideboard, the table and the chairs. 7. The dining-room windows were open. 8. We also open the windows when we clean the house. 9. From the dining room we passed into the parlor. 10. It was a large room with much furniture. 11. I sat down in an armchair; and Albert, in a rocking-chair. 12. We began to (a) talk, but, while we were talking, the bell rang.

D. 1. Who rang the bell? 2. — It was Mr. Mazzolà, Albert's uncle. 3. We were sitting in the parlor with Olga and three other ladies. 4. I was near Olga, and you were sitting near this young lady's mother. 5. Mr. Mazzolà sat down in an armchair in front of Olga. 6. When I was in America, I used to prefer the rocking-chairs, but now I prefer the armchairs and the divan. 7. I looked at the furniture. 8. A magnificent rug covered the floor. 9. Behind the divan there was (c'era) a lamp. 10. Another lamp was on the desk; it was green. 11. Is this bookshelf a new piece of furniture? 12. — Yes, sir, and also the mirror behind the large armchair is new.

E. *Oral.* 1. Che cosa mostrava Alberto a Carlo? 2. Che cosa guardavano essi? 3. Dov'era il cassettone? 4. Che cosa aveva il cassettone? 5. Che cosa c'era davanti al letto? 6. Quante sedie c'erano nella camera d'Alberto? 7. Perchè la camera d'Alberto non aveva molta mobilia? 8. Chi suonò il campanello? 9. Dov'eravamo noi? 10. Dove sedeva Lei? 11. Dove sedeva Alberto? 12. Con chi erano nel salotto? 13. Quante lampade c'erano nel salotto? 14. Dov'erano le lampade? 15. Dov'erano i libri? 16. Erano aperte le finestre? 17. Quando Lei pulisce la casa, chiude le finestre? 18. Era chiusa la porta? 19. Dov'era il nuovo specchio? 20. Quali sono i mobili d'una camera? 21. Quali sono i mobili d'una sala da pranzo? 22. Quali sono i mobili d'un salotto? 23. Chi è dietro alla signorina...? 24. Chi è davanti alla signorina...? 25. Chi è vicino al signor...?

LESSON XI

Review

A. *Continue the following throughout the singular and plural:* 1. Io cancello questo sbaglio, etc. 2. Io sono con un ragazzo italiano, etc. 3. Io scrivevo ogni giorno una lettera, etc. 4. Io ebbi sei lettere, etc. 5. Io apro una porta, etc. 6. Io imparai la nuova lezione, etc. 7. Io pulivo la penna stilografica, etc. 8. Io preferii Silvia a Olga, etc.

B. *Review Questions:* 1. When does the letter s take the *unvoiced* sound? 2. When does the letter s take the *voiced* sound? 3. Define and give examples of elision and apocopation. 4. When is the indefinite article written with an apostrophe? 5. Before what words is **uno** to be used? 6. Give a complete list of the subject pronouns. 7. Give all the combinations formed by **in** and the definite article. 8. Do you know of a case in which the definite article is used in Italian and not in English? 9. What negative

expressions are frequently used in connection with negative verbs?
10. What English phrases does the Italian past descriptive usually
render? 11. Count from 12 to 1. 12. What other forms of the
past absolute do you know, which can replace **vendei, vendè,
venderono**?

C. *In each case, supply the correct form of the present indicative,
the past absolute and the past descriptive of the verb given in the infinitive:* 1. (*essere*) Noi — nello studio. 2. (*pulire*) Tu — il
tappeto. 3. (*consegnare*) Voi — la ricevuta al postino. 4. (*vendere*) Essi — la mobilia. 5. (*capire*) I ragazzi — le nuove regole.
6. (*recitare*) Tu — dieci o dodici versi. 7. (*avere*) Ogni alunno
— una penna stilografica. 8 (*prendere*) Voi non — niente.
9. (*partire*) I ragazzi — dalla scuola. 10. (*ascoltare*) Noi non —
le parole dello zio. 11. (*sedere*) Voi — in una sedia a dondolo.
12. (*preferire*) Tu — imparare. 13. (*essere*) Voi non — diligenti.
14. (*avere*) Noi non — libri. 15. (*coprire*) Un tappeto — il
pavimento. 16. (*perdere*) Io — molte cose. 17. (*imparare*) Le
signorine Tedeschi — la lingua inglese. 18. (*cominciare*) Essa —
a suonare il violino. 19. (*vendere*) Arturo — la casa. 20. (*pulire*)
Noi — la lavagna.

D. *Replace the words in parentheses by their correct Italian equivalents:* 1. Egli non scrive (*anything*). 2. Siamo (*at the*) scuola.
3. Parlo (*to*) Arturo. 4. Lei (*used to be*) col professor Bruni.
5. Ecco (*eleven*) pezzi di gesso. 6. Non (*every*) lettera ha l'indirizzo
(*of the*) mittente. 7. Finii questa lezione (*five days ago*). 8. (*First*)
leggiamo la lettera e (*then*) rispondiamo. 9. I ragazzi sono (*on the
upper floor*). 10. La scuola è (*near the*) casa d'Olga. 11. Il
maestro era (*before the*) classe. 12. Essi (*understand*) ogni cosa.
13. Egli portò la lettera (*yesterday*). 14. Ricevei (*a registered
letter*). 15. Egli era (*almost*) povero. 16. Ho (*only*) due matite.
17. Siamo (*on the ground floor*). 18. Egli è a scuola (*now*).
19. Parlò (*while*) ella suonava. 20. Partirono (*because*) avevano
bisogno di partire.

E. *Continue the following:* 1. Uno più tre, quattro (1 + 3 = 4);
due più tre, cinque, etc. 2. Dodici meno due, dieci (12 − 2 = 10),
undici meno due, nove, etc.

F. *Insert the proper subject pronoun:* 1. —— chiamammo.
2. —— avesti bisogno. 3. —— spiegavo. 4. —— suonano. 5. ——
seguivate. 6. —— chiudeva. 7. —— fosti. **8.** —— ebbi. 9. ——
apriste. 10. —— seguirono. 11. —— fui. 12. —— capiscono.
13. —— aveste. 14. —— comprammo. 15. —— spolverarono.

G. *Supply the proper form of a suitable adjective in each case:*
1. La stanza è ——. 2. Alberto e Arturo sono ——. 3. Questa
regola è ——. 4. Egli era un ragazzo ——. 5. Non ho —— libro.
6. Le porte sono ——. 7. La camera di Carlo era ——. 8. Comprai una —— lampada. 9. Ricevemmo una —— lettera. 10. Queste
ragazze non sono ——.

LESSON XII

46. Position of Adjectives

1.

la lingua italiana	the Italian language
l'inchiostro rosso	the red ink
la tavola rotonda	the round table
la lezione seguente	the following lesson
una stanza molto grande	a very large room
un libro molto buono	a very good book

The normal position of an attributive adjective is after
the noun. This is especially the case with those adjectives
which ascribe to the noun a distinctive quality; such as,
nationality, religion, color, material, shape, etc. All adjectives modified by an adverb (such as **molto**) regularly
follow the noun.

2.

una bella rosa	a beautiful rose
un lungo cammino	a long way

Some adjectives of very common use generally precede the
noun, provided they are not modified by an adverb. Such,
among others, are: **bello,** *beautiful;* **brutto,** *ugly;* **buono,**
good; **cattivo,** *bad;* **giovane,** *young;* **nuovo,** *new;* **vecchio,**

old; **antico,** *ancient;* **lungo,** *long;* **breve,** *short;* **grande,** *big;* **piccolo,** *small.*

3.   È un ragazzo cattivo !   He is a bad boy !

But even the adjectives listed above may follow the noun, if used emphatically.

4.   **un povero ragazzo** a poor boy (= an *unfortunate* boy)
      un ragazzo povero a poor boy (= a boy who is *not rich*)

On the other hand, an adjective which normally follows the noun may precede it if prompted by emotion or used in a sense which is not literal.

47.   **Partitive Construction**

Comprai dei libri.	I bought some books.
Mi dia del pane, per favore.	Give me some bread, please.
Ha Lei dei fratelli?	Have you any brothers?
Vuole delle matite?	Do you want any pencils?

The English *some* or *any* is frequently rendered in Italian by di + the definite article.

EXERCISE XII

*a*bito suit of clothes	azzurro blue
calzino sock	bianco white
cam*i*cia shirt	giallo yellow
cappello hat	grigio gray
cappotto overcoat	marrone brown
colletto collar	nero black
colore *m.* color	rosso red
cravatta necktie	verde green
fazzoletto handkerchief	
guanto glove	basso low
p*ai*o pair	duro hard, stiff
sarto tailor	morbido soft
scarpa shoe	stretto narrow

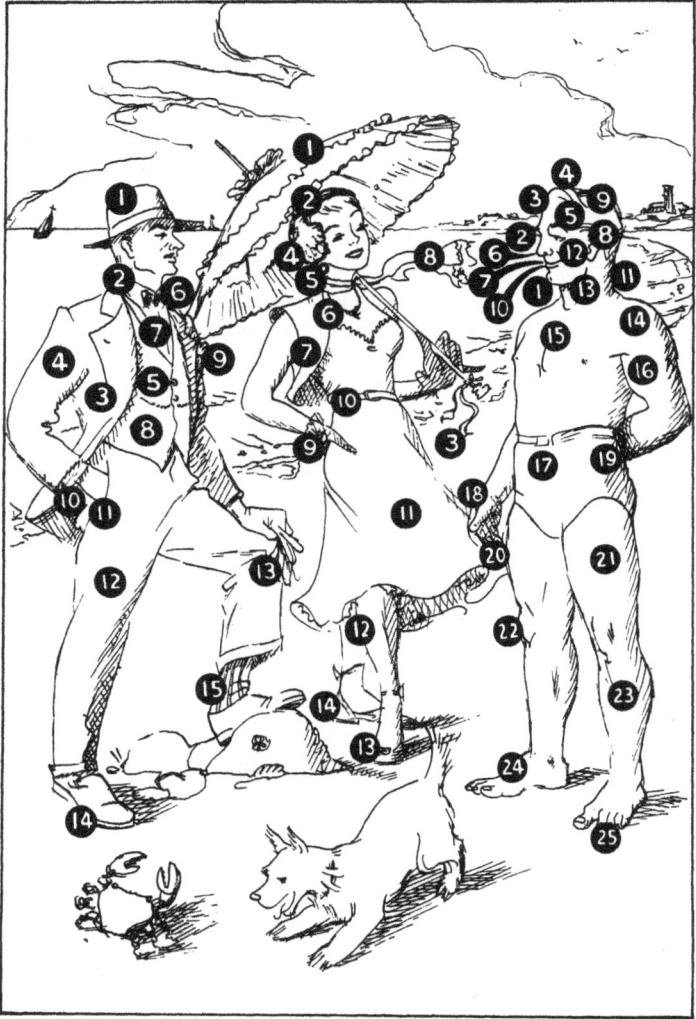

VESTIARIO E PARTI DEL CORPO

(*See page* 284)

A. (1) *Supply in the proper place an adjective* [1] *for each of the following nouns:* 1. Una madre. 2. Un colletto. 3. Le cose. 4. La lettura. 5. Le sedie. 6. I cappelli. 7. La lingua. 8. Il bidello. 9. Una sala. 10. Degli studenti. 11. Le penne. 12. I salotti. 13. I fazzoletti. 14. Il cappotto. 15. Un ragazzo. 16. Le signore. 17. I guanti. 18. La scrivania. 19. La lampada.

(2) *Supply the partitive expression:* 1. Impariamo a memoria — poesie. 2. Scriviamo — lettere. 3. Carlo comprò — colori. 4. Mi mostri — carta. 5. Ci sono — sedie a dondolo. 6. Ecco — nuovi francobolli. 7. Maria comprò — pane. 8. Ha Lei — sorelle? 9. Consegnate — traduzioni. 10. Abbiamo — studenti molto diligenti. 11. Egli vende — mobilia. 12. Ecco — mattoni. 13. La regola aveva — eccezioni. 14. — maestre partirono. 15. Ci sono — campanelli. 16. Ecco — colletti comodi. 17. Preferisco — fazzoletti grandi. 18. Olga dà — gesso ad Arturo. 19. Incontrammo — signorine. 20. Ella firmò — ricevute. 21. Il professore mostrava — nuove parole agli alunni. 22. Ecco — inchiostro.

B.   **Abiti da uomo**

1. Ieri comprai delle scarpe gialle. 2. Sono belle, ma sono strette. 3. Dove sono le altre? 4. — Ecco le altre scarpe; son vecchie, ma son comode. 5. Quando mandò il sarto quest'abito? 6. — Il sarto mandò quest'abito e delle cravatte sei giorni fa. 7. Ieri mandò anche il cappotto. 8. Di che colore è? 9. — È marrone; io preferisco questo colore a ogni altro. 10. Ha Lei dei guanti? 11. — Sì, ho un paio di guanti gialli. 12. Che colletti porta? 13. — Porto dei colletti duri. 14. In America preferiamo dei colletti bassi e morbidi. 15. Quando fui in Italia comprai dei cappelli. 16. Preferisce Lei un cappello duro a un cappello morbido?

---

[1] Do not use bello, bianco, buono, lungo.

17. — No, preferisco un cappello morbido. 18. In Italia comprai anche delle cravatte. 19. Di che colore erano? 20. — Erano di quasi ogni colore: rosse, verdi, azzurre. 21. Dove sono dei fazzoletti? 22. — I fazzoletti, i calzini e i guanti sono sul cassettone. 23. Mi dia una camicia bianca e dei calzini neri. 24. Preferisco questo colore per i calzini.

C. 1. When did you buy some collars? 2. — I bought six collars yesterday. 3. What collars did you buy? 4. — I bought some soft collars; a stiff collar is not very comfortable. 5. I also prefer a soft and low collar. 6. Today I am sending the gray suit to (da) the tailor. 7. Have you any other suits? 8. — Yes, I have also a blue suit and a brown suit. 9. There are some overcoats and some hats in John's room: whose (= of whom) are they? 10. — They are the overcoats and hats of Arthur, Charles and Albert. 11. These gentlemen are in the study with some young ladies. 12. They are looking at some books and John's new bookshelf.

D. 1. Five days ago Charles and Albert bought many things. 2. Charles bought a white shirt and some neckties. 3. What was the color of the neckties? 4. — One was black and yellow, one was gray and green, and the other was red. 5. He bought also some collars and a pair of black shoes. 6. And what did Albert buy? 7. — Albert bought twelve handkerchiefs, some socks and a pair of yellow gloves. 8. Did he buy any shoes? 9. — No, but he bought a suit of clothes from an Italian tailor. 10. By (per) mistake the tailor sent it to Charles' address. 11. Are these shoes narrow? 12. — Yes, they are narrow; they are not comfortable. 13. Red, white and blue, are the American colors; green, white and red, are the Italian colors.

E. *Oral.* 1. Qual è il colore di questa cravatta? 2. Qual è il colore della cravatta dello studente vicino a Lei? 3. Qual è il colore di quest'abito? 4. È marrone quest'abito? 5. Qual è il colore di questa camicia? 6. È nera questa matita? 7. È ogni matita gialla? 8. È rosso il gesso?

9. È verde la lavagna? 10. Quali sono i colori americani?
11. Quali sono i colori italiani? 12. Sono gialle le scarpe
della signorina...? 13. È nera la cravatta del signor...?
14. Qual è il colore delle scarpe del professore? 15. È ogni
fazzoletto bianco? 16. Chi ha una cravatta azzurra?
17. Chi ha un libro nero? 18. È bianco questo muro?

LESSON XIII

48. **Future of Model Verbs**

I shall buy, etc.	*I shall sell, etc.*	*I shall finish, etc.*
comprer ò	vender ò	finir ò
comprer ai	vender ai	finir ai
comprer à	vender à	finir à
comprer emo	vender emo	finir emo
comprer ete	vender ete	finir ete
comprer anno	vender anno	finir anno

Note that the infinitive, less the final vowel, is used as a
stem in forming this tense; a peculiarity of the first conjugation is, however, that the **a** of the infinitive ending –**are**
changes to **e**. Note also that the endings of the future are
the same for all Italian verbs.

49. **Future of *essere* and *avere***

I shall be, etc.		*I shall have, etc.*	
sarò	saremo	avrò	avremo
sarai	sarete	avrai	avrete
sarà	saranno	avrà	avranno

50. **Use of the Future**

Quando venderò i cavalli, com-prerò un'automobile.	When I sell the horses, I shall buy an automobile.
Se parlerò con Silvia, sarai con-tento?	If I speak with Sylvia, will you be satisfied?
Sarà dotto, ma non sembra.	Probably he is a learned man, but he does not seem so.

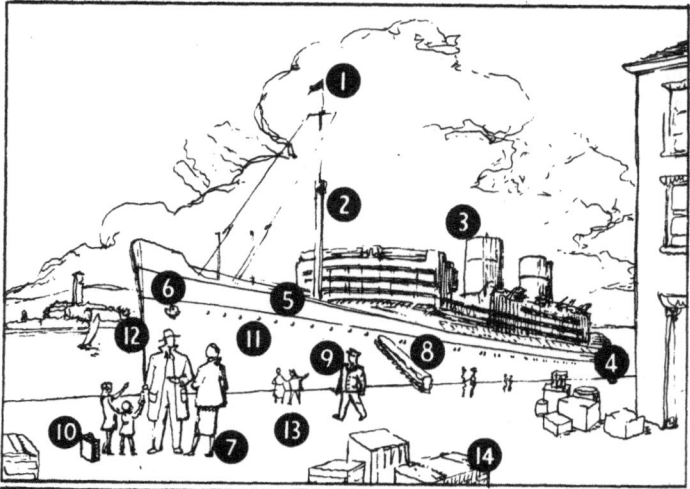

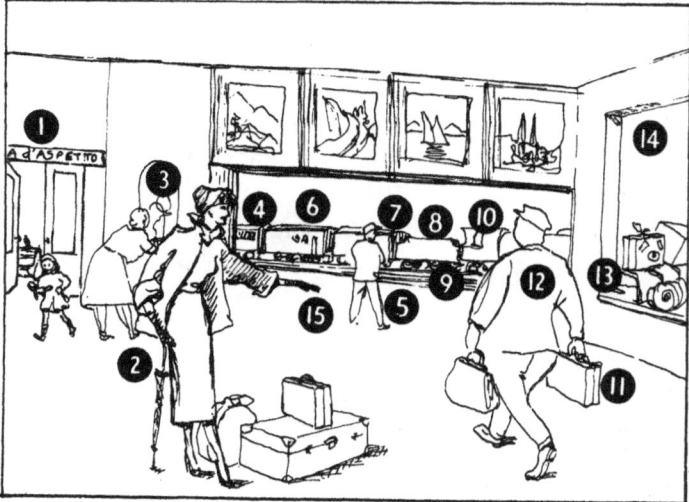

A. IL PIROSCAFO   B. IL TRENO

(See page 284)

Besides being used as in English, the future is employed in Italian also in the following cases: (*a*) In subordinate clauses referring to the future, which are introduced either by a conjunction of time or by se, *if*; (*b*) To express what is probable, even when no idea of future is implied.

51.   *non . . . che*

Non abbiamo che un divano. We have only one divan.

The English *only* is often rendered by placing **non** before the verb and **che** after it.

EXERCISE XIII

bagaglio baggage
baule *m.* trunk
biglietto ticket
carrozza coach, car (*of a train*)
conduttore *m.* conductor
facchino porter
locomotiva locomotive
orario time-table
posto place, seat
sala d'aspetto waiting room
sportello door (*of a car*)
stazione *f.* station
treno train; **treno diretto** express train

uscita exit
valigia valise, suit case
viaggio travel, journey, trip

leggiero light
pesante heavy
primo first
secondo second

aver fretta to be in a hurry
aver ragione to be right
aver torto to be wrong

domani tomorrow

A. (1) *Continue the following throughout the singular and plural:* 1. Se io detterò egli scriverà, etc. 2. Io partirò domani, etc. 3. Io passerò nel salotto, etc. 4. Quando io riceverò la lettera di Silvia, etc. 5. Io sarò diligente, etc. 6. Io non avrò niente, etc. 7. Io firmerò la ricevuta, etc. 8. Io mostrerò la nuova casa, etc.

(2) *Insert the proper subject pronoun:* 1. —— avrete torto. 2. —— troverà. 3. —— sarò. 4. —— apriremo. 5. —— seguiranno. 6. —— leggerai. 7. —— avremo ragione.

8. —— guarderete. 9. —— ascolterò. 10. —— pulirà. 11. —— spolvererete. 12. —— avranno bisogno. 13. —— mostrerai. 14. —— risponderà. 15. —— incontreremo.

(3) *Supply the correct form of the future of the verb given in the infinitive:* 1. (*trovare*) Voi —— Giovanni alla stazione. 2. (*rispondere*) Egli —— con una cartolina. 3. (*mandare*) Tu —— un ragazzo alla posta. 4. (*avere*) Io —— bisogno di una valigia. 5. (*vendere*) Loro —— la casa. 6. (*avere*) Noi —— ragione. 7. (*capire*) Io —— le parole di Carlo. 8. (*avere*) Voi —— torto. 9. (*essere*) Quand'esse —— alla stazione, noi partiremo. 10. (*incontrare*) Lei —— un signore americano. 11. (*prendere*) Voi —— un treno diretto. 12. (*suonare*) Tu —— il campanello. 13. (*studiare*) Noi —— questa lezione. 14. (*essere*) Elena —— in viaggio domani. 15. (*avere*) Maria —— torto. 16. (*scrivere*) Tu —— una lettera ogni giorno. 17. (*leggere*) Voi —— questo racconto. 18. (*passare*) Lei —— dodici giorni in Italia. 19. (*mostrare*) Noi —— la nuova mobilia a Olga. 20. (*ascoltare*) Io —— quando Silvia suonerà.

B. **Alla stazione**

1. Quando partirà Lei? 2. — Partirò domani col signor Fiorentino. 3. Alla stazione compreremo due biglietti di prima classe. 4. Poi passeremo nella sala d'aspetto. 5. Loro non avranno bisogno di facchini se non porteranno molto bagaglio. 6. — Ha ragione; io non porterò che una valigia leggiera. 7. Ha un orario, signor Fiorentino? 8. — Ecco un nuovo orario. 9. Dove sono dei buoni posti, conduttore? 10. — Troveranno dei buoni posti nella seconda carrozza dietro alla locomotiva. 11. Il conduttore ha fretta. 12. Egli chiuderà gli sportelli. 13. Il treno partirà. 14. Una signora americana parla con un facchino. 15. Ecco dei bauli e una valigia, facchino. 16. Sono pesanti questi bauli, signora? 17. — No, sono leggieri. 18. Dov'è l'uscita, facchino? 19. — È vicino alla sala d'aspetto.

20. Ogni grande stazione ha molte entrate e molte uscite.
21. Sarà lungo questo viaggio? 22. — Non sarà lungo perchè questo è un treno diretto.

C. 1. Some American ladies will leave for a long trip in Italy.
2. We shall leave for Washington. 3. When will you leave?
4. — We shall leave tomorrow, for we are in a hurry. 5. Have you a time-table, Miss Fiorentino? 6. — No, I have not any time-table. 7. Do you carry much baggage? 8. — I have only a suit case, but these young ladies have also some trunks. 9. What will Olga carry? 10. — She will carry only a light valise. 11. She is right; a journey with much baggage is not very comfortable.

D. 1. Miss Fiorentino and Miss Giardiello will leave for Chicago tomorrow. 2. What train will they take? 3. — They will take the first express. 4. Mr. Alteri will be at the station when they leave. 5. If the young ladies are in a hurry, he will buy the tickets. 6. Where will he meet the young ladies? 7. — He will be near the exit. 8. No, you are wrong, madam; he will be in the waiting room. 9. Where shall I find the conductor? 10. — He is probably near the train. 11. He will open the door of the car and find some comfortable seats for the two young ladies. 12. They are in a hurry. 13. Which of these two trunks is heavy, porter? 14. — The first [one] is heavy; the second, light.

E. Oral. 1. Quando partirà Lei? 2. Dove compreremo i biglietti? 3. Chi venderà i biglietti? 4. Chi chiuderà lo sportello della carrozza? 5. Chi porterà il bagaglio di questo signore? 6. Quando avremo bisogno di un facchino? 7. Dove troveremo dei posti comodi? 8. È pesante questo baule? 9. Dov'è la prima carrozza? 10. Dov'è la locomotiva? 11. Dov'è la seconda carrozza? 12. Dov'è la sala d'aspetto? 13. Quale classe prenderemo? 14. Un viaggio con molto bagaglio è comodo: ho ragione? 15. Di chi avrò bisogno se partirò con molto bagaglio? 16. Non porterò che una valigia: ho torto? 17. Perchè non ho torto? 18. Se Lei avrà fretta, con qual treno partirà? 19. Ha Lei

F

un orario ? 20. Di quale bagaglio abbiamo bisogno quando partiamo per un lungo viaggio ?

LESSON XIV

52. Possessives

MASCULINE		FEMININE		MEANING
Sing.	*Pl.*	*Sing.*	*Pl.*	
il mio	i miei	la mia	le mie	my, mine
il tuo	i tuoi	la tua	le tue	thy, thine, your, yours
il suo	i suoi	la sua	le sue	his, her, hers, its, your, yours
il nostro	i nostri	la nostra	le nostre	our, ours
il vostro	i vostri	la vostra	le vostre	your, yours
il loro	i loro	la loro	le loro	their, theirs, your, yours

1. The possessives are usually preceded by the definite article.[1]

2. Note that the masculine plural forms of **mio, tuo** and **suo** are irregular, and that **loro** is invariable.

3. As the normal form of address in Italian is the third person, singular or plural (*see* § 26, 3), **il suo** is the possessive of **Ella** or **Lei**; **il loro**, of **Loro**.

53. Use of the Possessives

la mia penna e la mia matita	my pen and pencil
il baule mio e il vostro	my trunk and yours
il suo giardino	his (*or* her, *or* its, *or* your) garden

1. The possessives are repeated before each noun to which they refer.

2. They may be used as adjectives or as pronouns.

[1] For important exceptions to this rule, see § 58.

3. Usually both article and possessive precede the noun, but the article precedes and the possessive follows the noun if possession is emphasized.

4. Possessive adjectives or pronouns agree in gender and number with the object possessed, not, as in English, with the person who possesses. Suo has thus four different meanings, but the context usually makes clear the gender of the possessor.

5. **Ella finisce il suo lavoro.** She finishes her work.
   Ella finisce il lavoro di lui. She finishes his work.

When the possessor is not the subject of the sentence, ambiguity, if there be any, is avoided by the use of di lui, for *his;* di lei, for *her;* di Lei or di Loro, for *your;* and di loro, for *their.* These phrases usually follow the noun.

6.
un mio parente	a relative of mine
questo mio parente	this relative of mine
quattro miei parenti	four of my relatives
molti miei parenti	many of my relatives
dei miei parenti	some of my relatives

Note from the examples above that the possessive may be preceded in Italian by the indefinite article, a demonstrative adjective, a numeral, an adjective indicating quantity, or the partitive. Thus the English *of* is not translated, and the examples given stand literally for *a my relative, four my relatives*, etc. Note also that in these cases the definite article is omitted.

7. **Sacrificò la vita alla Patria.** He sacrificed his life for his country.

The possessive, when not necessary for clearness, is usually replaced by a definite article.

EXERCISE XIV

Napoli *f.* Naples

amico, –a friend
cabina stateroom
cameriere *m.* waiter, steward
capitano captain
destinazione *f.* destination
golfo gulf, bay
gruppo group
mare *m.* sea
oceano ocean
passeggiero passenger

persona person
piroscafo steamer
piroscafo a petrolio oil burner
traversata crossing

incantevole enchanting
lento slow
rapido rapid, fast

occupare to occupy
durante during
presto soon

A. (1) *Replace the words in parentheses by their correct Italian equivalents:* 1. (*My*) finestre sono aperte. 2. (*Our*) studenti sono attivi. 3. (*Their*) porte non son chiuse. 4. (*His*) quaderno è sulla scrivania. 5. (*My*) camera ha un magnifico tappeto. 6. Ecco (*our*) sala da pranzo. 7. Passammo (*into their*) studio. 8. I libri erano (*on her*) scaffale. 9. (*His*) mobilia era nuova. 10. Ecco (*our*) francobolli. 11. Io scrivevo (*her*) indirizzo. 12. Qual è (*his*) indirizzo? 13. Carlo portò (*my*) saluti. 14. Ecco (*their*) orario. 15. Passai (*my*) penna stilografica ad Arturo. 16. Occuparono (*our*) posti. 17. Partì (*with his*) fratelli. 18. Preferisco Napoli e (*its*) golfo. 19. Quali sono (*our*) cabine? 20. (*Their*) camerieri erano italiani.

(2) *Translate into Italian:* 1. A clerk of mine. 2. Many of his post cards. 3. Five of her pencils. 4. Some of their passengers. 5. A new friend of his. 6. Eleven of my letters. 7. Many of my books. 8. Some of our rooms. 9. Eight of their chairs. 10. Every friend of mine.

(3) *Translate in four different ways* (**tu, voi, Lei** *and* **Loro** *forms*): 1. Your house. 2. Your parlor. 3. Your books. 4. Your rooms. 5. Your destination.

PANORAMA OF NAPLES WITH VESUVIUS

Naples is one of the most populous cities in Italy, with more than one million inhabitants.

B.   Sul piroscafo [1]

1. Un gruppo di studenti partì per Napoli. 2. Con gli studenti partì il nostro professore. 3. Avranno una buona traversata perchè il mare è buono. 4. Quando saranno alla loro destinazione? 5. — Presto, perchè il loro piroscafo è molto rapido. 6. Degli amici miei sono sullo stesso piroscafo. 7. Durante la traversata parleranno con dei passeggieri italiani. 8. Impareranno molte cose. 9. Chi è il suo cameriere, signor Giardiello? 10. — È un ragazzo molto intelligente e parla molte lingue. 11. I miei amici occupano una cabina di prima classe. 12. Di˙che classe è la tua cabina, Carlo? 13. — La mia cabina è di seconda classe. 14. Questo piroscafo è lento. 15. Non è un piroscafo a petrolio. 16. Il mare è molto buono. 17. Quando il mare è buono, una traversata sull'oceano è una cosa incantevole. 18. Da Napoli manderemo molte cartoline ai nostri amici d'America. 19. Chi è questo signore? 20. — È il capitano del piroscafo. 21. Quante persone! Chi sono? 22. — Sono dei passeggieri.

C. 1. You and I are departing [2] from New York today. 2. Naples with its enchanting bay is our first destination. 3. Our steamer is large and fast. 4. Is it an English steamer? 5. — No, madam; it is an Italian steamer, and almost every passenger speaks Italian. 6. But in our group not every person speaks Italian. 7. We will learn soon, during our crossing. 8. Some steamers are slow, but ours is very fast because it is an oil burner. 9. Its (= the) captain is a friend of mine. 10. He is a very intelligent person. 11. Is [3] every passenger in your (tu *form*) group [an] American? 12. — No, six are Americans and two are Italians.

D. 1. Your friend Arthur occupies a small stateroom. 2. Is your stateroom also small? 3. — No, our stateroom is large; it

---

[1] For additional Direct-Method exercises, see chart in Lesson XIII.
[2] First person plural.   [3] Place the verb after the word *group*.

is for four passengers. 4. Mine is also very comfortable. 5. Which
seats do you occupy at table? 6. — We sit near our professor,
at the second table. 7. To whom did you (voi) hand your valise?
8. — I handed it to the steward. 9. He is speaking now with some
of our friends. 10. This is my first trip on the ocean. 11. I prefer
a trip on the sea to a trip in a train. 12. The sea of the bay of
Naples is of an enchanting blue.

E. *Oral.* 1. Chi parte da New York? 2. Quale sarà la
loro prima destinazione? 3. Con chi parte il suo amico
Carlo? 4. Ogni passeggiero sul piroscafo è italiano? 5. Chi
è il suo cameriere? 6. Che lingua parla Lei col suo cameriere? 7. Parlano solamente italiano i camerieri di questo
piroscafo? 8. Chi è il capitano? 9. Dov'è la mia valigia?
10. A chi consegnerà Lei la sua valigia? 11. Quali cabine
occupano i signori del nostro gruppo? 12. È grande la
sua cabina? 13. Per quanti passeggieri è la sua cabina?
14. Dove sediamo a tavola? 15. Con chi parlerà Lei durante la traversata? 16. Che lingua parleremo? 17. È lento
questo piroscafo? 18. Perchè è rapido questo piroscafo?
19. Preferisce Lei un viaggio in treno?

LESSON XV

54.   **Some Uses of the Definite Article**

1. L'oro è un metallo.	Gold is a metal.
I libri sono utili.	Books are useful.
La gratitudine è rara.	Gratitude is rare.
Gl'Italiani amano la mu-sica.	Italians love music.

The definite article is required before a noun taken in a
general sense, or an abstract noun.

2. Il Manzoni è un grande scrittore.	Manzoni is a great writer.
Una poesia di Fulvio Testi.	A poem by Fulvio Testi.

Usually a surname, not preceded by a given name, takes the definite article in Italian. (*Review also* § 37.)

55. Nouns in –*i* and in –*u*

la crisi, le crisi	the crisis, the crises
il brìndisi, i brìndisi	the toast, the toasts
la virtù, le virtù	virtue, virtues

Italian nouns may end also in –i or in –u. In both cases, they are invariable. Those ending in –i are feminine if of Greek origin (easily recognizable for, as a rule, they have quite a similar form in English [1]), masculine otherwise. Those ending in –u are all feminine and accented.

56. Other Invariable Nouns

SINGULAR		PLURAL
il re	the king	i re
la città	the city	le città
la serie	the series	le serie
il revolver	the revolver	i revolver

Nouns of one syllable, those ending in an accented vowel or in –ie (except **moglie**, *wife*, pl. **mogli**), the noun **vaglia** (*m.*), *money order*, and the few, usually of foreign origin, which have a consonant ending, do not change in the plural.

57. Nouns and Adjectives in –*io*

SINGULAR		PLURAL
il nostro viaggio	our travel	i nostri viaggi
l'abito grigio	the gray suit	gli abiti grigi
il mormorio	the murmur	i mormorii

Nouns and adjectives ending in –io form their plural simply by dropping the final o, unless the preceding i is stressed (as in **mormorio**), in which case the plural ending is –ii.

---

[1] **Genesi,** *genesis;* **ipotesi,** *hypothesis;* **dieresi,** *dieresis,* etc.

EXERCISE XV

biblioteca library
commedia comedy
dizionario dictionary
esempio example
letteratura literature
novella story, short story
qualità quality
romanzo novel
scrittore *m.* writer
specie *f.* kind
tesi *f.* thesis
tragedia tragedy
università university

vizio vice

contemporaneo contemporary
delizioso delightful, delicious
famoso famous
interessante interesting
inutile useless
utile useful

ammirare to admire
uscire to go out

specialmente especially

A. (1) *Supply the definite article or the partitive as the case may be:* 1. —— romanzi sono —— libri. 2. Ricevei —— lettere. 3. Preferisco —— studenti attivi e diligenti. 4. Questa casa ha —— stanze grandi e comode, ma una è piccola. 5. Abbiamo —— buoni scrittori in America. 6. —— Americani preferiscono —— pavimenti di legno. 7. —— buoni alunni studiano le loro lezioni. 8. Ieri comprai —— cartoline. 9. Incontrammo —— signorine. 10. —— treni hanno una locomotiva e —— carrozze. 11. Gl'Italiani hanno —— università famose. 12. —— novelle del Pirandello sono interessanti.

(2) *Translate into Italian:* These cities, many trips, three revolvers, some good virtues, twelve mirrors, some time-tables, the kings of Italy, the contemporary writers, some mistakes, their wives, these studies, some gray gloves, six qualities of gloves, two money orders.

B.   Nella biblioteca

1. Ieri fui nella biblioteca della nostra università con lo zio di Giovanni. 2. Egli ammirò molto le nuove sale di

lettura. 3. Io avevo bisogno d'un libro italiano per lo studio della mia tesi. 4. In una delle sale incontrammo il professor Anselmi. 5. Egli leggeva una commedia del Pirandello. 6. Trovai il mio libro. 7. Poi uscimmo dalla biblioteca col professore. 8. Parlammo della letteratura contemporanea italiana. 9. Egli ammira molto gli scrittori d'oggi. 10. Ammira Sem Benelli e specialmente il D'Annunzio. 11. Domani comprerò una tragedia di questo famoso scrittore. 12. Comprerò anche un libro di deliziose novelle del Pirandello e un romanzo del Fogazzaro. 13. A casa ho un nuovo dizionario. 14. Ho bisogno del dizionario quando leggo perchè non capisco ogni parola. 15. Un dizionario non è mai inutile. 16. Trovo lo studio della lingua italiana utile e interessante. 17. Quale specie di libri preferisce Lei? 18. — Preferisco le novelle e i romanzi. 19. Molti preferiscono i libri di facile lettura. 20. In letteratura, una delle prime qualità d'un libro è insegnare la virtù con buoni esempi.

C. 1. Where will Arthur finish his studies? 2. — He will finish his studies at, (= in) an Italian university. 3. Italian universities are famous. 4. To whom will these students hand their theses? 5. — They will hand their theses to their professors. 6. Yesterday I met your two uncles in the library. 7. They were reading, and I sat down at their table. 8. They had many kinds of books. 9. When we went out we spoke of Italian literature. 10. I was carrying a new book by (di) Papini. 11. I find his books very interesting. 12. Contemporary Italian writers have many good qualities.

D. 1. We are reading in class a short story by (di) Grazia Deledda. 2. Her stories are very famous. 3. What does Sylvia prefer? 4. — Sylvia prefers poetry to prose, and especially D'Annunzio's poetry in his tragedies. 5. In my little library I have only one book by (di) this great writer. 6. Tomorrow I shall buy the translation of one of Pirandello's novels. 7. His *Il fu Mattia Pascal* is a delightful book. 8. I admire also his comedies.

STREET IN GENOA

9. In his comedies we find many examples of the vices and virtues of our contemporaries. 10. How many of his books have we in our library? — Not many. 11. Have you an Italian dictionary? 12. Dictionaries are very useful books.

E. *Oral.* 1. Lei dove fu ieri? 2. Chi incontrò alla biblioteca? 3. Di quale libro aveva Lei bisogno? 4. Che cosa leggeva il professore? 5. Chi è uno dei grandi scrittori italiani contemporanei? 6. Chi è un altro famoso scrittore? 7. Quanti libri del D'Annunzio abbiamo nella nostra biblioteca? 8. Ha Lei un dizionario italiano? 9. Che cosa comprerà Lei domani? 10. Perchè abbiamo bisogno d'un dizionario? 11. Quando abbiamo bisogno d'un dizionario? 12. Che cosa preferisce Silvia, la prosa o la poesia? 13. Quale poesia? 14. Quale lingua studiamo in questa classe? 15. Quale novella leggiamo oggi? 16. Chi è Sem Benelli? 17. Di chi è " Il fu Mattia Pascal "? 18. Dove troveremo dei libri italiani?

LESSON XVI

58. Omission of Article before Possessives. As a general rule (*see* § 52), the Italian possessives are preceded by the definite article. The article, however, is omitted in some special cases, the most important of which are given below:

1.
mia sorella *or* **la sorella mia**	my sister
le mie sorelle	my sisters
la mia cara sorella	my dear sister
la mia sorellina	my little sister
la loro sorella	their sister
la sua nonna	his grandmother

No article is used when the possessive precedes a noun denoting relationship, provided that the noun is singular and not accompanied by another adjective, nor modified by a suffix. The article is not omitted when the possessive follows the noun (for greater emphasis), when it is loro, or when the noun denoting relationship is one of the following: **babbo,** *daddy;* **mamma,** *mamma;* **nonno,** *grandfather;* **nonna,** *grandmother.* Of the examples given above only the first one (**mia sorella**) meets all of the conditions implied in this rule.

2. **Questo baule è mio.**	This trunk is *mine* (Whose trunk? Mine)
Questo baule è il mio.	*This* trunk is mine (Which trunk? This one)

The article is omitted when the possessive stands alone in the predicate, with the force of an adjective. To determine whether it has the force of an adjective, imagine the sentence as the answer to a question. If the sentence answers a question starting with *whose,* the possessive takes no article; if it answers a question starting with *which,* the article is used.

3. **Mio caro amico, ascolta!**	My dear friend, listen!

No article is used when the possessive modifies a vocative.

NOTE. In § 53, 6 other cases have been given in which the definite article is omitted before a possessive.

59.   **Diminutives**

una ragazzina	a little girl
una cameretta	a small room
i fratellini	the little brothers
delle cosette	some little things

The original meaning of a noun is often modified in Italian by means of a suffix. The suffixes –ino and –etto, both of which convey the idea of *little, small,* are by far the most common. A noun, to which one of these suffixes is added, is called a *diminutive.*

LA FAMIGLIA

(See page 285)

EXERCISE XVI

cognata sister-in-law	**suocera** mother-in-law
cognato brother-in-law	**suocero** father-in-law
cognome *m.* surname	
cugino, –a cousin	**caro** dear, expensive
famiglia family	**giovane** young
figlia daughter	**lontano** distant, far
figlio son, child	**vero** true, real
genero son-in-law	
nipote *m. or f.* nephew, niece,	**amare** to love, like
grandson, granddaughter	**conoscere** to know, be ac-
nuora daughter-in-law	quainted with
parente *m. or f.* relative	**lodare** to praise
	rispettare to respect

A. (1) *Replace the words in parentheses by their correct Italian equivalents:* 1. (*My*) fratelli. 2. (*My*) giovane sorella. 3. (*His*) padre 4. (*Her*) mamma. 5. (*Her*) madre. 6. (*Her*) cara madre. 7. (*Their*) cugino. 8. (*My*) cuginetti. 9. (*Our*) zia. 10. (*His*) cognate. 11. (*Our*) cari cognati. 12. (*My*) zietta. 13. Questa matita è (*mine*). 14. Queste sorelle (*of his*).

(2) *Translate in four different ways:* 1. Your father. 2. Your young daughter-in-law. 3. Your daughter. 4. Your aunts. 5. Your little granddaughter.

(3) *Read aloud the following sentences, replacing the singular subject by its plural form and making the necessary changes:* 1. Mio cognato non parla italiano. 2. Tuo cugino conosce questa signorina. 3. Questa ragazza ha lo stesso cognome. 4. Suo nipote comprò dei guanti. 5. Nostra madre è americana. 6. Conosce Lei mia suocera? 7. Qual libro preferisce vostra cognata? 8. Mia figlia è una ragazza intelligente. 9. Questo mio parente sarà a Chicago domani. 10. Questo tappeto è suo

(4) *Translate the following diminutives :* cognatina, sorelline, ziette, cuginetto, fratellino, lettino, casetta, cosina.

B. La famiglia

1. Mia zia passerà cinque giorni coi suoi suoceri. 2. Ella
ha molti parenti; un fratello, quattro sorelle e due cognati.
3. Non ha figli? 4. — Sì, ha tre figlie, le mie cugine.
5. Anche noi abbiamo una grande famiglia. 6. Quanti ni-
poti ha Lei? 7. — Non ho che una nipote, la figlia di mia
sorella Emma. 8. Porto i suoi saluti a Lei e ai suoi parenti.
9. Conosce Lei la cognata del signor Zumpetti? 10. È una
giovane signora molto intelligente e una vera amica. 11. Ella
partirà domani con mia sorella. 12. Prenderanno un treno
diretto. 13. Chi è suo suocero? 14. — Non ho nè suocero
nè suocera. 15. Ho un nonno, e non ha lo stesso mio
cognome perchè egli è il padre di mia madre. 16. Ogni
nonna ama e loda i suoi nipotini. 17. Conosce Lei questo
signore? 18. È un parente lontano di mia nuora. 19. Mio
caro amico, loderò la tua virtù se amerai e rispetterai tua
madre! 20. Chi firmerà questa lettera? 21. — La firmerà mio genero. 22. La lettera è sua.

C. 1. In Mrs. Narni's home they speak Italian. 2. Does her
mother-in-law also speak Italian? 3. — No, she does not know
Dante's language. 4. How many children has she? 5. — She
has only three children, but she has twelve grandchildren. 6. She
is a good friend of my grandmother. 7. Yesterday many of your
relatives were in my house. 8. Is this house yours? 9. — Yes,
madam; this house is mine. 10. Who is this little boy? 11.—He is
a nephew of mine. 12. Do you love (tu *form*) your father and
mother, Johnny? 13. Good children love and respect their
fathers and mothers.

D. 1. My uncles send their greetings to your family.
2. Mr. Narni, is Charles a real friend of yours? 3. — No, he is
not a real friend of mine. 4. He has not many good qualities.
5. But I respect his family; his relatives are very good. 6. Do
you know his aunt, Mrs. Narni? 7. She will leave tomorrow for

Chicago together with her young daughter. 8. How many days
will they spend in (a) Chicago? 9. — They will spend eleven days
in Chicago, in the home of Mrs. Narni's brother-in-law. 10. Tomorrow I shall meet four persons at the station. 11. Who are
they? 12. — They are my father-in-law, one of my cousins and
two distant relatives of mine.

E. *Oral. In answering the following questions, use nouns
denoting relationship whenever possible.* 1. Chi passerà undici giorni nella mia casa? 2. Quanti fratelli ha Lei?
3. Non ha Lei una sorella? 4. Chi è il padre di suo padre?
5. Chi è la moglie di suo fratello? 6. Chi sono le mogli dei
figli d'una persona? 7. Qual è il suo cognome, signorina?
8. Qual è il cognome dell'alunno vicino al signor...?
9. Qual è il cognome dell'alunno dietro al signor...?
10. Ha Lei molti parenti stretti? 11. Quali sono? 12. Chi
è la madre della moglie del signor Scotti? 13. Chi è la
figlia di suo zio? 14. Chi è il figlio di suo zio? 15. La sua
famiglia di quante persone è? 16. Quali sono le persone
della sua famiglia? 17. A chi scriverà una lettera oggi?
18. A chi manderà dei saluti? 19. Conosco io suo padre?
20. Dov'è suo padre?

LESSON XVII

60.   Some Conjunctive Personal Pronouns

SINGULAR	PLURAL
Masc. lo him, it	li them, you
Fem. la her, it, you	le them, you

L'ammiro e lo lodo.	I admire and praise him.
La salutai.	I greeted her (*or* you).
L'aspetteremo.	We shall wait for him (her, it *or* you).
Li chiamavamo.	We were calling them (*or* you).
Le osservo.	I observe them (*or* you).

1. These pronouns denote the direct object in the third person, and, as the third person is the normal form of address in Italian, they translate also the English *you*. Note their similarity with the definite article.

2. They are used only in connection with a verb, and regularly precede it.

3. Lo and la usually elide before a vowel.

4. In rendering the English *you*, while la is used in addressing either a man or a woman, a distinction of gender occurs in the plural, and li is used in addressing men only or men and women; le, in addressing women only.

61. *Some* or *Any*

Hɔ qualche valigia.	I have some valises.
Ha Lei qualche amico?	Have you any friends?
Osservai alcuni ragazzi.	I observed some boys.
Hɔ un pɔ' di pane.	I have some (*or* a little) bread.
Abbiamo libri *u*tili.	We have (some) useful books.
Ɛcco libri, penne e matite.	Here are books, pens and pencils.

The partitive idea, which is usually rendered by the preposition di and the definite article (*see* § 47), may be expressed in Italian also in one of the following ways:

1. By qualche or alcuno, whenever *some* or *any* stands for *a few*. Note, however, that qualche (together with the noun it modifies) is always singular, even when the meaning is plural, while alcuno agrees in gender and number with the noun to which it refers.

2. By un pɔ' di, in case *some* or *any* has the meaning of *a little*.

3. By the noun alone, whenever such construction is correct in English. The latter way is to be preferred in case of enumeration.

For *any* with negative verbs, see § 33, 2. For *some* or *any*, used as pronouns (*some of it, some of them*, etc.) see § 97, 1.

EXERCISE XVII

bagno bath, bathing	**andare** to go
barca boat	**invitare** to invite
esca bait	**nuotare** to swim
estate *f.* summer	**pescare** to fish
pescatore *m.* fisherman	**pigliare** to catch
pesce *m.* fish	**remare** to row
rete *f.* net	**sembrare** to seem, look like
spiaggia shore	**tirare** to pull, haul
stabilimento di bagni bath	
stagione *f.* season [house	**a mezzogiorno** at noon
volta time, turn	**come** as, like, how
	così so
calmo calm	**di solito** usually
scorso last, past	**volentieri** gladly, willingly

A. (1) *Substitute for each direct object the proper conjunctive pronoun* (lodo mia sorella = la lodo): 1. Spolverai la credenza.   2. Consegno le lettere.   3. Vendo dei libri. 4. Cancello delle parole.   5. Perdo dieci minuti.   6. Mandiamo un saluto.   7. Ammiro questa ragazza.   8. Trovo delle cravatte.   9. Conosciamo questi signori.   10. Invitiamo la signorina Lazzi.   11. Compriamo delle reti.   12. Ammiravano la mia barca.   13. Piglio molti pesci.   14. Amo questa stagione.

(2) *Translate into Italian, rendering* some *or* any *with one of the forms studied in* § 61: 1. We have some passengers. 2. Have you any chalk? 3. They received some parcels. 4. I need some paper.   5. Do you speak any other language? 6. You find some places.   7. I buy shoes, gloves and hand-kerchiefs.   8. I need some trunks.   9. They admired some Italian houses.   10. She signed some receipts.   11. Here is some bait.   12. I speak to some fishermen.

(3) *Answer the following questions:* 1. Quante stanze ha la sua casa? 2. Quali stanze ha la sua casa? 3. Quali sono i mobili d'una camera? 4. Quali sono i mobili d'una sala da pranzo? 5. Quali sono i mobili d'uno studio? 6. Quali sono i mobili d'un salotto?

B. **Sulla spiaggia**

1. Non ama l'estate Lei? 2. — Sì, l'amo per molte cose. 3. L'amo specialmente perchè è la stagione dei bagni di mare. 4. L'estate scorsa ero in Italia con alcuni miei parenti. 5. Li incontrai a Napoli e passammo qualche giorno insieme. 6. Nella buona stagione di solito il mare è molto calmo. 7. I miei parenti amavano nuotare e quasi ogni giorno andavamo al mare. 8. Andavamo a uno stabilimento di bagni non lontano da casa. 9. Non nuota Lei? 10. — Nuoto e remo volentieri. 11. È una cosa deliziosa andare in barca quando il mare è calmo. 12. Noi andavamo in barca qualche volta, e mio cugino e io remavamo. 13. Non pescavano? 14. — Sì, pescavamo alcune volte, ma non pigliavamo molti pesci. 15. L'esca non era buona. 16. Io preferisco sedere sulla spiaggia e guardare i pescatori quando tirano le reti. 17. Essi sono molto interessanti. 18. A chi non sembra incantevole il golfo di Napoli nell'estate?

C. 1. Are we going to (a) fish today? 2. — Yes, we are going to (a) fish if the sea is calm. 3. I met Mr. Sacchi yesterday, and invited him to (ad) go in our boat. 4. He likes to row. 5. Where shall we meet him? 6. — He will be on the shore, near the bath house. 7. Have you some bait? 8. — No, but I shall buy it, and shall also bring a net. 9. We shall leave at noon, together with your friend. 10. This time we shall catch some fish. 11. Last time I didn't catch anything.

D. 1. Who are these young ladies? 2. I find them every day on the shore. 3. — I don't know them, but they look like Americans. 4. Will you swim today, Arthur? 5. — No, I prefer to go bathing

MONT BLANC FROM THE ITALIAN SIDE

(al **bagno**) some other day. 6. The sea is so calm and blue, and the bath house is so near! You are lazy. 7. We pass by (= before) some fishermen. 8. I look at them while they are hauling their net. 9. How interesting they are! (= How they are interesting!) 10. They will catch some fish and will sell them. 11. Do you know this gentleman, Helen? 12. — Yes, I know him.

E. *Oral.* *In answering the following questions, use conjunctive personal pronouns whenever possible.* 1. Ama il mare Lei? 2. In quale stagione il mare è di solito molto calmo? 3. Invitai io il signor Sacchi a pescare nella mia barca? 4. Nuota Lei? 5. Tirano la rete i pescatori? 6. Pigliano sempre pesci i pescatori? 7. Chi incontriamo sulla spiaggia? 8. Guarda Lei queste ragazze? 9. Sono americane? 10. Mostrerà Lei lo stabilimento di bagni a questi signori? 11. Ha una rete? 12. Chi ha un po' d'esca? 13. Che pigliamo con l'esca? 14. Quale stagione è buona per i bagni di mare? 15. Di che colore è il mare quando è calmo? 16. Conosce Lei questo signore? 17. Chi è? 18. Conosce Lei questa signorina? 19. Chi è? 20. Ha un po' di carta?

LESSON XVIII

62. Past Participles

I	II	III
compr ato bought	vend uto sold	fin ito finished
stato been	avuto had	

63. Compound Tenses. 1. Compound tenses are formed from the past participle and one of the auxiliaries, **avere** or **essere**.

2. Each of the four simple tenses already studied has a corresponding compound tense. They are respectively: the Present Perfect, the Past Perfect, the Second Past Per-

fect and the Future Perfect. These eight tenses are called
the tenses of the *Indicative Mood*.

3. The auxiliary **avere** is used in conjugating all transitive
and many intransitive verbs; the auxiliary **essere** is used in
conjugating: (*a*) the passive voice (*see* § 134); (*b*) the reflexive verbs (*see* § 127, 2); (*c*) some intransitive verbs (*see*
§ 135); and (*d*) the verb **essere**.

64. **Agreement of Past Participle**

1. **Ella è stata qui stamani.**   She was here this morning.
   Siamo arrivati.   We have arrived.

A past participle used with **essere** agrees with its **subject**
in gender and number.

2. **Ho comprato** (*or* **comprata**)   I have bought the house.
   la casa.
   La casa che ho comprata (*or*   The house I bought.
   comprato).
   L'ho comprata.   I bought it.

A past participle used with **avere** may or may not agree
with its *direct object*. It usually does not agree when the
object follows; it nearly always agrees when the object precedes; and it always agrees when the object is a personal
pronoun preceding the verb.

3. **Tu sei arrivato.**   You have arrived (*addressing a
   Voi siete arrivato.   man*)
   Lei è arrivato.

   Tu sei restata.   You have remained (*addressing
   Voi siete restata.   a woman*).
   Lei è restata.

   L'abbiamo chiamato.   We have called you (*addressing
                             a man*).

   L'ho riconosciuta.   I recognized you (*addressing a
                             woman*).

IL RISTORANTE

(*See page* 285)

The pronouns used in direct address are considered masculine or feminine according to the sex of the person addressed, and the past participle agrees accordingly.

65. Present Perfect

I have bought, *I bought, etc.*	*I have sold,* *I sold, etc.*	*I have finished,* *I finished, etc.*
hɔ comprato hai comprato, etc.	hɔ venduto hai venduto, etc.	hɔ finito hai finito, etc.

I have been, I was, etc.	*I have had, I had, etc.*
sono stato, –a sɛi stato, –a, etc.	hɔ avuto hai avuto, etc.

66. Use of the Present Perfect

Stamani hɔ comprato un romanzo.	This morning I bought a novel.
Quest'anno non hɔ studiato.	This year I have not studied.
Ella ha imparato a cantare.	She has learned to sing.

This tense, which is translated either by the English present perfect or by the simple past, is used in stating what happened at a certain time in the past, with reference to the present. Such action may have occurred: (*a*) since midnight, as in the first example; (*b*) in a period of time not yet completed, as in the second example; (*c*) in a time not determined, but with effects still lasting, as in the third example.

The student should carefully distinguish the use of this tense from that of the past absolute, and refrain from using the present perfect after such expressions of concluded periods of time, as **iɛri, due giorni fa, l'anno scorso,** etc.

EXERCISE XVIII

bicchiere *m.* glass	accettare to accept
cameriera maid	aiutare to help
coltello knife	apparecchiare to set
cucchiaino teaspoon	arrivare to arrive [1]
cucchiaio spoon	dimenticare to forget
cuoco, –a cook	lavare to wash
forchetta fork	mettere to put
invito invitation	preparare to prepare
ordine *m.* order	sorvegliare to watch
piatto dish	
pranzo dinner	adesso now
tazza cup	spesso often
tovaglia tablecloth	stamani this morning
tovagliolo napkin	tra poco soon, in a little while

A. (1) *Continue the following:* 1. Io ho parlato con **mia** cognata, tu hai parlato con **tua** cognata, etc. 2. Ho io ripetuto lo stesso sbaglio? etc. 3. Io non ho pulito la **mia** stanza, etc. 4. Io ho avuto torto, etc. 5. Io non sono stato alla stazione, etc.

(2) *Supply the correct form of the present perfect of the verb given in the infinitive:* 1. (*mostrare*) Io —— lo stabilimento di bagni ad Alberto. 2. (*avere*) Noi —— torto. 3. (*essere*) Lei —— nella cucina. 4. (*studiare*) Voi non —— stamani. 5. (*incontrare*) Egli —— degli Americani. 6. (*suonare*) Tu —— il campanello. 7. (*essere*) Noi —— alla casa d'Olga. 8. (*capire*) Tu non —— niente. 9. (*vendere*) Loro —— i biglietti. 10. (*essere*) Voi —— diligenti. 11. (*dimenticare*) Egli —— i suoi amici. 12. (*essere*) Essa —— a scuola stamani. 13. (*apparecchiare*) Maria —— la tavola. 14. (*sorvegliare*) Mia madre —— la cuoca. 15. (*essere*) Loro —— a pranzo. 16. (*essere*) Noi —— buoni. 17. (*avere*) Egli —— fretta. 18. (*avere*) Voi —— bisogno d'un coltello. 19. (*accettare*) Essi —— l'invito mio. 20. (*essere*) Esse —— spesso a New York.

---

[1] Conjugated with **essere.**

(3) *Substitute pronouns for the object nouns, making the necessary changes* (ho studiato la lezione = l'ho studiata): 1. Abbiamo lavato i piatti. 2. Hai apparecchiato la tavola. 3. Avete preparato il pranzo. 4. Hanno dimenticato le parole. 5. Ho accettato gl'inviti. 6. Ella ha aiutato sua sorella. 7. Ho sorvegliato le ragazze. 8. Abbiamo comprato dei libri. 9. Hanno chiamato i fratelli. 10. Ha spiegato la lezione.

B. **Un pranzo**

1. Stamani Elena ha invitato delle sue cugine a pranzo. 2. Le cugine hanno accettato l'invito. 3. Il pranzo sarà a mezzogiorno. 4. La cuoca è in cucina. 5. Ella prepara il pranzo. 6. Tra poco la cameriera apparecchierà la tavola. 7. Ella ha lavato i piatti e i bicchieri. 8. Ha pulito le forchette, i cucchiai e i coltelli. 9. Ha portato ogni cosa dalla cucina nella sala da pranzo. 10. Ecco una tovaglia e otto tovaglioli. 11. La tovaglia è sulla tavola e i tovaglioli sono sulla credenza. 12. Elena è stata spesso in cucina a sorvegliare la cuoca. 13. Sua sorella è nella sala da pranzo. 14. Aiuta la cameriera ad apparecchiare la tavola. 15. Per quanti posti apparecchiano? 16. — Apparecchiano per otto posti; quattro per le cugine, uno per Elena e tre per gli altri della famiglia. 17. La cameriera ha dimenticato di mettere le tazze. 18. Ecco le tazze; i cucchiaini sono nella credenza. 19. È mezzogiorno. 20. Ogni cosa è in ordine.

C. 1. This morning we forgot to (di) buy some napkins. 2. We have invited some ladies for (a) dinner. 3. Has Miss Alessandri accepted your invitation? 4. — No, she has not accepted it because her aunt arrives today. 5. The maid and the cook are in the kitchen. 6. Yesterday they washed the dishes and glasses. 7. This morning they cleaned the knives, forks and spoons. 8. Now they are preparing our (= the) dinner. 9. I don't need to watch these girls. 10. Where is my sister? 11. — She is on the upper floor. 12. She will soon be in this room.

D. 1. My sister-in-law is in her room now. 2. In a little while I shall help her to (a) set the table. 3. I have often been in the dining room to (per) put everything in order. 4. The new table-cloth and the napkins are on the sideboard. 5. We need other chairs because we have invited many persons. 6. We sent eleven invitations yesterday. 7. This morning we invited another lady: Mrs. Romano. 8. They have often been in our house. 9. Here is the maid with the cups and teaspoons. 10. Everything will be in order at noon.

E. *Oral.* 1. Quante persone ha Lei a pranzo? 2. Ha la signorina Alessandri accettato l'invito? 3. Perchè non l'ha accettato? 4. Dov'è la cuoca? 5. Chi l'aiuta? 6. Chi è stato spesso in cucina? 7. Ha bisogno Lei di sorvegliare la sua cuoca? 8. Chi è nella sala da pranzo? 9. Chi l'aiuta ad apparecchiare la tavola, signorina? 10. Che cosa mettiamo sulla tavola? 11. Dove sono i tovaglioli? 12. Dove sono i bicchieri? 13. Che cosa ha dimenticato Lei? 14. Chi lava i piatti? 15. Ha invitato Lei suo cugino? 16. Ha Carlo invitato sua cugina? 17. Abbiamo noi invitato i nostri cugini? 18. Per quanti posti apparecchieremo? 19. Quando sarà in ordine ogni cosa?

LESSON XIX

67. Present Indicative of Some Irregular Verbs

The verbs **dovere**, *to be obliged*, **potere**, *to be able*, and **volere**, *to want*, have the following irregular present indicative:

I must, am obliged, have to, etc.	I can, may, am able, etc.	I want, etc.
dɛvo	pɔsso	vɔglio
dɛvi	puɔi	vuɔi
dɛve	puɔ	vuɔle

dobbiamo	possiamo	vogliamo
dovete	potete	volete
devono	possono	vogliono

68.   Further Cardinal Numerals

13	tredici	17	diciassette
14	quattordici	18	diciotto
15	quindici	19	diciannove
16	sedici	20	venti

EXERCISE XIX

albergo hotel	accompagnare to accompany
appuntamento appointment	aspettare to wait, wait for
automobile *f.* automobile, car	desiderare to desire, wish
minuto minute	essere in ritardo to be late
museo museum	rimanere to remain [1]
quadro picture, painting	ritornare to return [1]
statua statue	telefonare to telephone
tavolino little table, stand	vedere to see
telefono telephone	visitare to visit, call on

impaziente impatient	*faccia pure* please do
pronto prompt, ready	*fino a* until

in tutto il mondo the world over

A. (1) *Continue the following:* 1. Io devo studiare adesso, etc. 2. Non posso io aprire la finestra? etc. 3. Non voglio io la stessa cosa? etc. 4. Io devo mandare le lettere alla posta, etc. 5. Posso io occupare questo posto? etc. 6. Io voglio seguire il suo esempio, etc.

(2) *Give for each verb in parentheses the correct form of the present indicative:* 1. Egli (potere). 2. Noi (volere). 3. Essi (dovere). 4. Tu (potere). 5. Essa (volere). 6. Voi (dovere). 7. Noi (potere). 8. Essi (volere). 9. Io (dovere). 10. Voi (potere). 11. Voi (volere). 12. Noi (dovere). 13. Io (potere). 14. Io (volere). 15. Tu (dovere). 16. Loro (potere). 17. Tu (volere). 18. Ella (aovere).

Conjugated with essere.

(3) *Supply the correct form of the present perfect of the verb given in the infinitive:* 1. (*remare*) Egli —— volentieri. 2. (*essere*) Noi —— sulla spiaggia stamani. 3. (*invitare*) Ecco la signora Fiore; io l'—— a pranzo. 4. (*ritornare*) L'automobile —— dalla stazione. 5. (*essere*) Gli alunni —— in ritardo. 6. (*occupare*) I posti che noi —— sono buoni. 7. (*accompagnare*) Le signore ch'io —— sono pronte. 8. (*essere*) Le mie cugine —— impazienti. 9. (*telefonare*) Io —— al mio professore. 10. (*comprare*) I mobili che tu —— sono magnifici.

(4) *Continue the following:* 1. Dieci più uno, undici; undici più uno, dodici, etc. 2. Venti meno uno, diciannove; diciannove meno uno, diciotto, etc.

B.   Al museo

1. Siamo nell'albergo insieme col signor Tozzi. 2. Il signor Tozzi è un caro amico mio e di mio fratello. 3. Dove vogliamo andare stamani? 4. — Mio fratello desidera di visitare il museo; se Lei vuole, l'accompagneremo. 5. — Volentieri, ma devo prima telefonare a casa. 6. — Faccia pure; ecco il telefono. 7. Mentre egli telefona, io posso scrivere una cartolina a mia madre. 8. Manderò dei saluti anche al babbo e alle sorelline. 9. La penna e l'inchiostro sono sul tavolino vicino alla finestra. 10. Qualche minuto passa. Ora siam pronti. 11. Il signor Tozzi ha finito di telefonare, e possiamo andare. 12. Il museo è lontano dall'albergo. 13. Dobbiamo prendere un'automobile. 14. Che automobile è questa? — È una Lancia, signori. 15. La Lancia è una famosa automobile italiana. 16. Rimaniamo nel museo fino a mezzogiorno. 17. Mio fratello vuol visitare ogni sala. 18. Egli ama molto i quadri e le statue, ma io sono impaziente perchè ho un appuntamento. 19. Devo ritornare all'albergo se non voglio essere in ritardo. 20. Prendiamo un'altra automobile e partiamo.

SELF-PORTRAIT BY MICHELANGELO
Galleria Uffizi, Firenze.
Michelangelo was the greatest artist of the Italian Renaissance,
at once a painter, sculptor, architect, and poet.

C. 1. We have an appointment with Miss De Palma and her sister this morning. 2. We are in a hurry because we are late. 3. We must take an automobile to (**per**) go to their hotel. 4. If you want an automobile, you must telephone. 5. Have you (**voi**) a telephone in this house? 6. — Yes, sir; it is on the stand in my father's study. 7. Where do you want to go with the two young ladies? 8. — They want to visit our museum, and we shall accompany them. 9. May I use your telephone? — Please do. 10. When will the car arrive? 11. — It will arrive in fifteen minutes. 12. We must be ready to (**a**) go out if we don't want to be late for our appointment.

D. 1. We take an automobile and go to Miss De Palma's hotel. 2. It is a " Fiat," an Italian car famous the world over. 3. In eighteen minutes we shall be in front of the hotel. 4. If you want to wait in the car, I shall return in a little while. 5. I want to call the young ladies, and then we shall leave together. 6. They must be impatient because we are late. 7. You may go; I shall gladly wait for you. 8. Here are the two Misses De Palma; now we can go to the museum. 9. These young ladies want to see everything, but I have often been in this museum and I want only to see some new paintings. 10. You must see also the statues on the ground floor; they are very interesting. 11. Can't you remain until noon? 12. — No, we can't remain; we must return to our hotel because we have another appointment.

E. *Oral.* 1. Con chi ha Lei un appuntamento? 2. Perchè ha fretta? 3. Che cosa dobbiamo prendere per non arrivare in ritardo a un appuntamento? 4. Posso telefonare? 5. Dov'è il telefono? 6. A chi vuol telefonare? 7. Perchè vuol telefonare? 8. Dove vogliamo andare? 9. Chi aspettiamo? 10. Che cosa ammiriamo in un museo? 11. Fino a quando resteremo nel museo? 12. Dove andiamo poi? 13. Può rimanere nel museo fino a mezzogiorno? 14. Perchè non può rimanere? 15. Quale automobile italiana è molto famosa? 16. Perchè la signorina De Palma vuol rimanere nel museo fino a mezzogiorno?

17. Vuol rimanere anche Lei? 18. Perchè deve ritornare all'albergo? 19. Posso uscire? 20. Quando abbiamo bisogno di un'automobile?

LESSON XX

69. **Past Perfect**

I had bought, etc.	*I had sold, etc.*	*I had finished, etc.*
avevo comprato	avevo venduto	avevo finito
avevi comprato, etc.	avevi venduto, etc.	avevi finito, etc.

I had been, etc.	*I had had, etc.*
ero stato, –a	avevo avuto
eri stato, –a, etc.	avevi avuto, etc.

70. **Second Past Perfect**

I had bought, etc.	*I had sold, etc.*	*I had finished, etc.*
ebbi comprato	ebbi venduto	ebbi finito
avesti comprato, etc.	avesti venduto, etc.	avesti finito, etc.

I had been. etc.	*I had had, etc.*
fui stato, –a	ebbi avuto
fosti stato, –a, etc.	avesti avuto, etc.

71. **Use of the Past Perfect Tenses**

Avevo ammirato quell'uomo. I had admired that man.
Quand'egli ebbe finito, partì. When he had finished, he left.

Both tenses denote what had happened, like the English past perfect, but the second past perfect is used only in subordinate clauses introduced by a conjunction of time, such as **quando,** *when,* **appena** or **appena che,** *as soon as,* **dopo che,** *after,* **subito che** *immediately after,* etc. A subordinate clause in the second past perfect is regularly followed by a principal clause in the past absolute.

H

LA CAMERA

(*See page* 285)

72.   **Future Perfect**

I shall have bought, etc.	*I shall have sold, etc.*	*I shall have finished, etc.*
avrò comprato	avrò venduto	avrò finito
avrai comprato, etc.	avrai venduto, etc.	avrai finito, etc.

I shall have been, etc.	*I shall have had, etc.*
sarò stato, –a, etc.	avrò avuto
sarai stato, –a, etc.	avrai avuto, etc.

73.   **Use of the Future Perfect**

The rules given for the use of the future (*see* § 50) apply also to this tense.

EXERCISE XX

bronchite *f.* bronchitis	**alto** high, tall
dieta lattea milk diet	**ammalato** ill
febbre *f.* fever	
guarigione *f.* recovery	**dormire** to sleep [1]
medicina medicine	**guarire** to recover [2]
medico physician	**ordinare** to order
notte *f.* night	**pensare** to think
prescrizione *f.* instruction	
principio beginning, touch	**allora** then, at that time
riposo rest	**che** that
temperatura temperature	**o** or

A. (1) *Continue the following:* 1. Io l'avevo dimenticato, etc. 2. Quando li ebbi imparati, etc. 3. Non ero stato utile, etc. 4. Dopo che l'ebbi capito, etc. 5. Io avrò ricevuto qualche lettera, etc. 6. Sarò io stato in Italia? etc. 7. Quando l'ebbi conosciuta, etc. 8. Io le avevo aiutate, etc.

(2) *Replace the words in parentheses by their correct Italian equivalents:* 1. Noi (*shall have sold*) la nostra automobile. 2. Ella (*had known*) il cugino di Carlo. 3. Dopo che tu

---

[1] Conjugated like **partire**.   [2] Conjugated like **finire**.

(*had occupied*) il suo posto, egli arrivò. 4. Voi (*had been*) a casa del professore. 5. Essi (*had been in a hurry*). 6. Quando Silvia (*had found*) il libro, lo consegnò a suo fratello. 7. Voi (*will have finished*) tra poco. 8. Tu (*had been*) ogni giorno alla scuola. 9. Quand'ella (*had invited*) Olga, preparò ogni cosa. 10. Lei (*probably have fished*) fino a mezzogiorno.

(3) *Translate into Italian:* 1. The physician had ordered a medicine. 2. My sister is probably asleep. 3. When Arthur had finished his lesson, he went to school. 4. As soon as I shall have caught some fish, I shall return home. 5. My friend Lodini had occupied my seat. 6. He must have (= probably) invited his friends (*f.*). 7. While he was taking the medicine, the physician entered (into) the room. 8. At first he had been swimming (**andare** [1] **a nuotare**), then he rowed. 9. When she had set the table, Olga and Sylvia arrived. 10. I shall have prepared the dinner in a little while.

B.   **Un ragazzo ammalato**

1. Non ero stato a casa d'Alberto da molti giorni. 2. Nè mio fratello nè io l'avevamo veduto a scuola. 3. Pensai allora d'andare a vedere se era ammalato. 4. Lo trovai a letto. 5. Appena l'ebbi veduto, capii che aveva un po' di febbre. 6. Aveva avuto una temperatura molto alta durante la notte. 7. Sedei e parlai con sua madre. 8. Il medico l'aveva visitato il giorno prima. 9. Aveva trovato che Alberto aveva un principio di bronchite e aveva ordinato alcune medicine e dieta lattea. 10. Alberto guarirà presto se seguirà le prescrizioni del medico. 11. Se non le seguirà, la sua guarigione sarà lenta. 12. Egli ha adesso bisogno di riposo. 13. Il riposo aiuta molto, e il medico l'ha ordinato. 14. Alberto ritornerà a scuola quando il medico penserà ch'egli sarà guarito. 15. Il mio amico ha perduto molte lezioni. 16. Al principio troverà lo studio un

_____
[1] Conjugated with **essere.**

po' difficile, ma egli è intelligente e imparerà presto.
17. Quando ritornerà a scuola, l'aiuterò. 18. Anche il professore l'aiuterà.

C. 1. I had received a letter from Albert's mother. 2. Albert
was ill. 3. As soon as my brother and I had finished our lessons,
we went to his house. 4. Charles also had called on him. 5. We
found him in (a) bed with a high fever. 6. His temperature had
not been so high the day before. 7. He had slept during the night.
8. A physician visited him every day. 9. He had found that the
poor boy had a touch of bronchitis. 10. May I speak to Albert?
— No, he must sleep now.

D. 1. I had seen some medicines on a stand near Albert's bed.
2. The physician had ordered them. 3. He had also ordered [a]
milk diet and rest. 4. After we had spoken to Albert's mother,
we left. 5. How many days must Albert spend in (a) bed? 6. He
must spend ten or twelve days in (a) bed, if the physician orders it.
7. Will he take the medicines? 8. He will take them willingly if
he wants a prompt recovery. 9. Will Albert follow the physician's
instructions? 10. When he has followed them, he will recover and
return to school.

E. *Oral. In answering these questions, use conjunctive
personal pronouns whenever possible.* 1. Chi aveva ricevuto
una lettera? 2. Di chi era la lettera? 3. Perchè era a
letto Alberto? 4. Quando andò Lei a casa sua? 5. Con
chi andò? 6. Aveva qualche altro amico visitato Alberto?
7. Aveva febbre Alberto? 8. Era bassa la sua temperatura?
9. Chi lo visitava ogni giorno? 10. Che aveva trovato il
medico? 11. Che aveva ordinato? 12. Guarirà presto Alberto? 13. Quanti giorni deve passare a letto? 14. Sarà
rapida la sua guarigione se egli non seguirà le prescrizioni
del medico? 15. Quando ritornerà a scuola? 16. Alberto
troverà facile lo studio quando ritornerà a scuola? 17. Chi
l'aiuterà al principio? 18. Perchè imparerà presto?

LESSON XXI

74.   Cardinal Numerals

1	uno	17	diciassette	38	trentotto
2	due	18	diciotto	40	quaranta
3	tre	19	diciannove	50	cinquanta
4	quattro	20	venti	60	sessanta
5	cinque	21	ventuno	70	settanta
6	sɛi	22	ventidue	80	ottanta
7	sɛtte	23	ventitrè	90	novanta
8	otto	24	ventiquattro	100	cɛnto
9	nove	25	venticinque	101	cɛnto uno
10	diɛci	26	ventisɛi	102	cɛnto due
11	undici	27	ventisɛtte	180	cɛnto ottanta
12	dodici	28	ventotto	200	duecɛnto
13	tredici	29	ventinove	1000	mille
14	quattordici	30	trenta	2000	due mila
15	quindici	31	trentuno	100,000	cɛnto mila
16	sedici	32	trentadue	1,000,000	un milione

Note that **venti, trenta, quaranta,** etc. drop the final vowel in combining with **uno** or **otto.**

75.   Use of the Cardinal Numerals

1.   **un signore**   one gentleman
                 una signora   one lady

Uno has a feminine, **una,** and when used adjectively has the forms of the indefinite article (*see* § 19).

2.   **quarantuna lira** ⎫
                 lire quarantuna ⎭   forty-one lire

If the noun modified by **ventuno, trentuno,** etc. follows the numeral, it is preferable to put it in the singular.

3.   **mille novecɛnto**   nineteen hundred

Eleven hundred, twelve hundred, etc. are translated *one thousand one hundred,* etc.

4. Contrary to English usage, **uno** is omitted before **cento** and **mille**. The plural of **mille** is **mila**.

5. **due milioni d'abitanti** two million inhabitants

Milione is a masculine noun; its plural is **milioni**. It requires the preposition **di** before the noun to which it refers.

6. In compound numbers no conjunction is used.

7. **tutti e due i cugini** both cousins

Both is **tutti e due**; *all three*, **tutti e tre**, etc. If a noun follows, it takes the definite article (*see also* § 133, 2).

76. Months of the Year. The names of the months are: **gennaio, febbraio, marzo, aprile, maggio, giugno, luglio, agosto, settembre, ottobre, novembre, decembre.** They are all of masculine gender and are usually written with small letters.

77. **Dates**

il primo febbraio	on February first
l'otto marzo 1548	March eighth, 1548
il 1916	1916
nel 1921	in 1921
nel marzo del 1670	in March, 1670

1. The cardinal numerals are used to express the days of the month, with the single exception of **primo**, *first*.

2. A date is generally preceded by the masculine definite article (**giorno, mese** or **anno** being understood), and is written in the following order: day, month, year. The English *on* is never translated.

Milano Milan	**regno** kingdom
Roma Rome	**soldato** soldier
Torino Turin	**terremoto** earthquake
	ufficiale *m.* officer
abitante *m.* inhabitant	
anno year	**austriaco** Austrian
censimento census	**francese** French
fronte *f.* front	
governo government	**aver luogo** to take place
guerra war	**dichiarare** to declare
impero empire	**durare** to last
mese *m.* month	**morire** to die
perdita loss	**nacque** was born
popolazione *f.* population	**secondo** according to

A. (1) *Read aloud in Italian:* 60, 71, 88, 191, 219, 754, 888, 999, 1884, 1898, 1902, 1906, 1913, 1916, 2456, 9322, 10,357, 268,436, 4,785,691.

(2) *Continue the following:* 1. Due per due, — quattro (i.e. 2 × 2 = 4); due per tre, —— etc. *as far as* due per venticinque. 2. Tre per due, — sei; tre per tre, —— etc. *as far as* tre per dodici. 3. Quattro per due, —— otto; quattro per tre, —— etc. *as far as* quattro per dodici.

(3) Le quattro stagioni dell'anno sono: **la primavera, l'estate, l'autunno, e l'inverno.** (*a*) Quali sono i mesi della primavera? dell'estate? dell'autunno? dell'inverno? (*b*) Qual è il primo giorno della primavera? etc. (La primavera comincia il . . .)

(4) *Give the dates of the following events:* 1. La scoperta dell'America. 2. La dichiarazione dell'indipendenza. 3. La fine della Guerra Mondiale. 4. La sua data di nascita. 5. La fine dell'anno scolastico.

B. **I numeri**

1. I mesi dell'anno sono dodici. 2. Alcuni mesi hanno trenta giorni; altri, trentuno. 3. Il mese di febbraio ha di

solito ventotto giorni. 4. Qualche volta febbraio ha ventinove giorni. 5. In Italia il censimento ha luogo ogni dieci anni. 6. Anche noi, in America, lo abbiamo ogni dieci anni. 7. Nel 1921 Torino aveva 502,274 abitanti. 8. La popolazione di Palermo era nello stesso anno di 400,348 abitanti. 9. Nel terremoto di Messina morirono 76,483 persone. 10. Solamente 452 persone morirono nel terremoto di San Francisco. 11. Il governo americano dichiarò guerra il 6 aprile 1917. 12. La guerra durò un anno, sette mesi e cinque giorni. 13. Essa finì l'11 novembre 1918. 14. Dante nacque nel maggio del 1235. 15. Secondo alcuni, nacque il 14 maggio. 16. Un altro grande scrittore italiano è il Manzoni. 17. Egli nacque nel 1785 e morì nel 1873. 18. Specialmente famoso è il suo romanzo *I Promessi Sposi*.

C. (*All numerals in C and D are to be written out.*) 1. A year has 365 days. 2. April, June, September and November have 30 days. 3. The month of February has 28 days, but once every four years it has 29 days. 4. The other months have 31 days. 5. According to the census of 1921, the kingdom of Italy had a population of 38,835,941. 6 The same census shows that Naples had 780,220 inhabitants; Milan, 718,304; and Rome, 691,314. 7. How many inhabitants has now the kingdom of Italy? 8. — It has almost 42,000,000 inhabitants. 9. On May 24, 1915, the Italian government declared war on (a) the Austrian empire. 10. The war ended on November 4, 1918.

D. 1. The Italian war lasted 3 years, 5 months and 10 days. 2. In November 1918, the Italians occupied Trento and Trieste. 3. The Italian losses in the war were 16,382 officers and 480,787 soldiers. 4. On the French front 4,375 Italians died; on the other fronts, 7,384. 5. Carducci was born in 1835. 6. Who does not admire his poems? 7. We read and admire Pirandello and Zuccoli; they are both contemporary writers. 8. Dante's *journey* through (attraverso) the Inferno took place in the year 1300. 9. Dante died September 14, 1321. 10. His surname was Alighieri.[1]

---

[1] Omit the definite article before this name.

E. *Oral.* 1. Che anno è questo? 2. Che giorno è oggi? 3. Quanti sono i mesi dell'anno? 4. Che mese è questo? 5. Quali sono i mesi dell'estate? 6. Quali sono i mesi di trenta giorni? 7 Quanti giorni ha febbraio in quest'anno? 8. Qual è il primo mese dell'anno? 9. In che anno nacque Dante? 10. In che anno morì? 11. Qual era il suo cognome? 12. Quali scrittori contemporanei italiani conosce Lei? 13. Di chi sono " I Promessi Sposi "? 14. Quanti abitanti ha Roma? 15. Quanti abitanti abbiamo in America? 16. In che anno il governo italiano dichiarò guerra all'impero austriaco? 17. In che anno andammo in guerra noi? 18. In che giorno finì la guerra? 19. Su quale fronte erano i nostri soldati? 20. In che mese finiranno le nostre lezioni?

LESSON XXII

Review

A. *Continue the following:* 1. Io sorveglierò i **miei** cugini, tu sorveglierai i **tuoi** cugini, etc. 2. Io l'avevo ricevuta, etc. 3. Domani avrò finito questo romanzo, etc. 4. Quando li ebbi visitati, etc. 5. Io chiuderò la **mia** porta, tu chiuderai la **tua** porta, etc. 6. Sarò io stato in Italia? etc. 7. Io devo dichiarare, etc. 8. Io voglio dormire, etc.

B. *Review Questions:* 1. Mention six adjectives which usually precede the noun. 2. In what cases is the future used in Italian, contrary to English usage? 3. How are *his* and *her* translated in Italian when the form **suo** may be ambiguous? 4. Mention a few cases in which the definite article is used in Italian while omitted in English. 5. Explain the different usage of the present perfect and past absolute, and give examples. 6. When does the past participle in a compound tense agree with the subject? 7. When is the article omitted before the possessives? 8. In how many ways can the word *some* be rendered in Italian? 9. Explain the different usage of the past perfect and the second past perfect, and give examples. 10. Give the names of the months in Italian. 11. Give the six possible translations of the possessive **suo**. 12. How would you translate *some of his novels?* 13. Of what gender are the nouns which end in –i? 14. Of what gender are the nouns which end in –u? 15. What nouns are invariable? 16. Which are the suffixes most commonly used in forming a diminutive? Give two examples. 17. What is the normal position of a conjunctive personal pronoun? 18. When is the verb **avere** used as an auxiliary? 19. When is the verb **essere** used as an auxiliary? 20. Does a past participle used with **avere** always agree with its direct object?

C. *Give the plural of the following nouns:* la servitù, la via, il ronzio, la tesi, l'azione (*f.*), la sera, l'analisi, il re, lo sportello, la beltà, l'ordine (*m.*), la qualità, l'ora, l'individuo, il pascià.

D. *Replace the words in parentheses by their correct Italian equivalents:* 1. Ecco (*your*) biglietti, ed ecco (*mine*). 2. Comprai (*some*) specchi. 3. Ritornerò (*if you send*) anche a Maria un invito. 4. Egli aveva (*seven books of yours*). 5. Trovarono (*my*) cugini a casa. 6. Ricevemmo (*nineteen*) lettere. 7. Ieri (*I sold*) la mia mobilia. 8. Stamani (*I sold*) la mia scrivania. 9. Appena (*they had spoken*) con Carlo, partirono. 10. Quest'anno Elena (*was not*) studiosa. 11. Egli parla ora (*with some relatives of his*). 12. L'anno scorso (*I went*) a Napoli. 13. Ella non visita che Olga perchè (*she is in a hurry*). 14. Le nostre lezioni finiranno (*in June*). 15. Ha Lei i suoi libri? — (*I have them.*) 16. Egli ha (*four million*) lire. 17. (*Both*) partiranno domani. 18. Arrivò (*on July 1st.*). 19. Arturo e Mario (*want*) uscire tra poco. 20. (*May I*) prendere questo quaderno? — (*Please do.*)

E. *Translate in four ways, using the pronouns* **tu, voi, Lei** *and* **Loro**: 1. You will praise this little boy. 2. You have not understood her. 3. You have been ill. 4. Will you answer? 5. You may go out. 6. You had respected them. 7. You must sleep. 8. You recited yesterday 9. Do you want to be useful? 10. You are wrong.

F. *Insert a noun in each of the following phrases:* 1. Una —— verde. 2. Un —— povero. 3. La —— bianca. 4. Le —— gialle. 5. Un —— pigro. 6. Le —— raccomandate. 7. I —— duri.

8. Una —— comoda. 9. Il —— azzurro. 10. Un —— leggiero.
11. La —— pesante. 12. Il —— incantevole. 3. Una —— utile.
14. Le —— possibili. 15. I —— ammalati.

G. *Add an adjective to each of the following nouns:* 1. Una guerra
——. 2. Una lezione ——. 3. La fronte ——. 4. Le finestre ——.
5. La lingua ——. 6. Le persone ——. 7. Una novella ——.
8. Un ragazzino ——. 9. Una guarigione ——. 10. Gli scrittori
——.

H. *For each of the following verbs give the required form of all the
simple and compound tenses of the indicative mood:*

occupare — 2d person singular	avere — 1st person plural
essere — 3d person singular	ripetere — 1st person singular
pulire — 3d person plural	seguire — 2d person plural

LESSON XXIII

78.   Masculine Nouns in –*a*

SINGULAR		PLURAL
il **programma**	the program	i **programmi**
il **poeta**	the poet	i **poeti**

Not all nouns ending in –a are of feminine gender. A
certain number of them, ending in –ca, –ga, –ma or –ta, and
mostly of Greek origin, are masculine, and form their
plural in –i.

79.   Nouns in –*a* of Both Genders

SINGULAR		PLURAL
il *or* la **suicida**	the suicide	i **suicidi**, le **suicide**
il *or* la **violinista**	the violinist	i **violinisti**, le **violiniste**

Some nouns ending in –cida or –ista, the latter generally
denoting professions, are of both genders and have a masculine plural in –i and a feminine plural in –e.

80.   Nouns and Adjectives in *–ca* or *–ga*

SINGULAR		PLURAL
l'amica	the friend	le amiche
il collega	the colleague	i colleghi
bianca, lunga	white, long	bianche, lunghe

In forming the plural of nouns and adjectives ending in –ca or –ga, an **h** is inserted before the final e or i. This is done in order to keep the guttural sound of the **c** or **g**.

81.   Nouns and Adjectives in *–cia* or *–gia*

	SINGULAR		PLURAL
	la faccia	the face	le facce
	grigia	gray	grige
BUT	la farmacia	the drug store	le farmacie
	la bugia	the lie	le bugie

Nouns and adjectives ending in –cia or –gia usually drop the i before the ending –e of the plural, provided that the i is unstressed; they keep it if it is stressed.

82.   Present Indicative of *andare* and *fare* (*irregular*)

I go, etc.	*I do* or *make, etc.*
vado *or* vɔ	faccio *or* fɔ
vai	fai
va	fa
andiamo	facciamo
andate	fate
vanno	fanno

EXERCISE XXIII

artista *m. or f.* artist	**moda** fashion; **di moda** fashionable
calza stocking	
camicetta shirt waist	**modista** milliner
giacca coat	**pelliccia** fur, fur coat
gonnella skirt	**profeta** *m.* prophet
manica sleeve	**sarta** dressmaker

seta silk	**corto** short
sistema *m.* system	**elegante** elegant
veste *f.* dress	**passato** past, last
	poco little, not much (*pl.* few)
che who, which, that	**ricco** rich
	unico only
capriccioso capricious	**venturo** next, coming
far caso di to pay attention to	

A. (1) *Continue the following:* 1. Io non vado con delle amiche, etc. 2. Io faccio ogni cosa, etc. 3. Io non vado mai alla casa di questo signore, etc. 4. Io non faccio mai nulla, etc.

(2) *Give the plural of the following nouns:* il monarca, il pianista, la biblioteca, la guancia, la foca, il profeta, la provincia, il collega, l'artista (*m.*), l'artista (*f.*), la nostalgia, il duca, la barca, la ciliegia.

(3) *Give for each verb in parentheses the correct form of the present indicative:* 1. Noi (*andare*) alla scuola. 2. Tu (*fare*) molte cose. 3. Io (*andare*) col maestro. 4. Loro (*fare*) una traduzione. 5. Egli (*andare*) alla stazione. 6. Noi (*fare*) una buona traversata. 7. Non (*andare*) voi in un treno diretto? 8. Lei (*fare*) un altro appuntamento. 9. Perchè (*andare*) tu allo stabilimento di bagni? 10. Essi (*fare*) un censimento ogni dieci anni. 11. Ella (*andare*) dov'è suo fratello. 12. Che cosa (*fare*) io? 13. Lei non (*fare*) nulla in questo salotto. 14. Perchè (*andare*) esse nella loro cabina?

B.   **Abiti da donna** [1]

1. Ieri mia sorella ricevè dalla sarta la sua nuova veste. 2. È di seta grigia, il colore di moda. 3. La moda non è la stessa ogni anno. 4. L'anno passato le signore portavano abiti con giacca e gonnella. 5. Anche le camicette con

For additional Direct-Method exercises, see chart in Lesson XII.

maniche corte eran di moda. 6. Facciamo una buona cosa
se compriamo poche vesti ogni anno. 7. È anche un sistema
utile per le persone che non sono ricche. 8. Io non fo caso
della moda. 9. — Lei è un'eccezione. 10. Gli artisti amano
gli abiti eleganti. 11. Adesso la modista d'Elena va in
Italia. 12. Noi preferiamo andare in Italia l'anno venturo.
13. In America abbiamo buone pellicce. 14. Esse non
sono così care come in Italia. 15. Domani compreremo
delle calze. 16. Porto solamente calze di seta. 17. La
seta italiana è famosa. 18. Quale moda avremo l'anno
venturo? 19. — L'anno venturo la moda non sarà così
capricciosa come quest'anno. 20. — Lei è un profeta!

C. 1. Now ladies wear long dresses with short sleeves. 2. Last
year short skirts with white shirt waists were fashionable. 3. What
will be fashionable next year? 4. — We are not prophets; fashion
is so capricious! 5. My milliner and my dressmaker are real
artists. 6. Don't you admire this hat? 7. My dressmaker makes
also my sister-in-law's dresses. 8. Today we are going to (a) buy
some white skirts. 9. I am going with Sylvia and Helen. 10. They
are my only real friends.

D. 1. I need also some stockings. 2. I shall buy gray stockings.
3. This color is fashionable now. 4. My young friends (f.) are
very rich and they go to (in) Italy almost every year. 5. Sylvia has
two magnificent fur coats. 6. I am doing as almost every lady
now does; I am wearing long skirts. 7. Few ladies wear short
skirts this year. 8. They do not pay any attention to fashion.
9. Here are two coats and some elegant silk dresses (= dresses of
silk). 10. They are not mine; they are my cousin's.

E. *Oral.* 1. Sono di moda le vesti corte? 2. Sono di
moda le camicette? 3. Di qual colore preferisce Lei le
camicette? 4. Chi fa le vesti di sua sorella? 5. Chi fa i
cappelli delle signore? 6. Dove vanno Silvia ed Elena quasi
ogni anno? 7. Sono molte le signore che non fanno caso
della moda? 8. Con una veste bianca quali calze sono di

moda? 9. Quale colore era di moda l'anno passato?
10. Quale colore è di moda quest'anno? 11. Quale colore
sarà di moda l'anno venturo? 12. Preferisce Lei una giacca
corta a una lunga? 13. Ha ogni ragazza una pelliccia?
14. Quali ragazze hanno delle pellicce? 15. Sono di seta
le sue calze? 16. Di quale colore sono? 17. Di qual colore
è la veste di questa ragazza? 18. Che cosa faccio io adesso?
19. Che cosa fanno gli alunni? 20. Capisce Lei ogni mia
parola?

LESSON XXIV

83.   Nouns and Adjectives in *—co*

SINGULAR		PLURAL
il fuɔco	the fire	i fuɔchi
ciecc	blind	ciechi
il mɔnaco	the monk	i mɔnaci

Nouns and adjectives ending in —co form their plural in
—chi if the stress of the word is on the syllable before the
last; otherwise, in —ci.

This rule, however, has several exceptions, the most important of
which are: (a) **amico,** *friend,* **grɛco,** *Greek,* **nemico,** *enemy,* and
pɔrco, *pig,* which form their plural in —ci; (b) **carico,** *load, loaded,* and
stɔmaco, *stomach,* the plural of which is in —chi.

84.   Nouns and Adjectives in *—go*

SINGULAR		PLURAL
il lago	the lake	i laghi
il dialogo	the dialogue	i dialoghi
vago	vague	vaghi

Nouns and adjectives ending in —go form their plural
in —ghi.

85. Present Indicative of *dare* and *stare* (*irregular*)

I give, etc.	*I stay or am, etc.*
dɔ	stɔ
dai	stai
dà	sta
diamo	stiamo
date	state
danno	stanno

1. Note that the third person singular of **dare** is accented. The accent serves to distinguish this verbal form from the preposition **da**.

2. The verb **stare** means *to be*, but it implies a temporary condition, as: **come sta ?** *how are you* (*now*) ?

EXERCISE XXIV

autunno autumn
borgo hamlet, village
bɔsco wood
campagna country; in cam-
  pagna in *or* to the country
campo field
carro wagon
città city; in città in *or* to the
  city
contadino farmer
fiɛno hay
fiore *m.* flower
grano wheat
inverno winter

primavɛra spring
rigo line
svago amusemɛnt

bɛllo beautiful, handsome
carico loaded
selvatico wild
vicino neighboring

lavorare to work

come sta? how are you?
stɔ bɛne, grazie I am well,
  thanks.

A. (1) *Continue the following:* 1. Io do questa valigia al mio amico, tu dai questa valigia al tuo amico, etc. 2. Io sto coi miei parenti, tu stai coi tuoi parenti, etc. 3. Io non do niente adesso, etc. 4. Io non sto comodo, etc.

(2) *Give the plural of the following nouns:* il pacco, il distico, il parco, il lastrico, l'amico, lo storico, il porco, lo svago, il parroco, il catalogo.

I

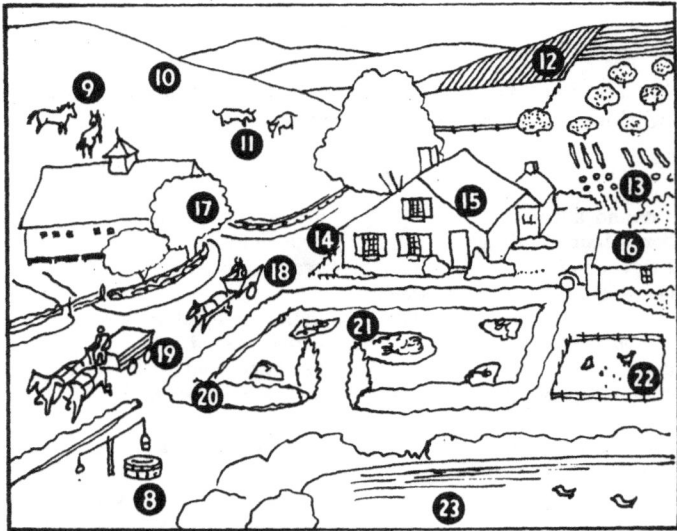

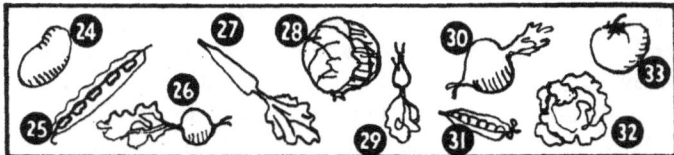

LA CAMPAGNA

(See page 285)

(3) *Give for each verb in parentheses the correct form of the present indicative:* 1. Tu (*dare*) una ricevuta al signor Ferri. 2. Egli (*stare*) nello studio. 3. Io non (*dare*) il mio indirizzo. 4. Come (*stare*) voi? 5. Voi (*dare*) il biglietto al conduttore. 6. Noi non (*stare*) alla stessa tavola. 7. Silvia e Olga (*dare*) un pranzo alle loro amiche. 8. Io (*stare*) in un buon albergo. 9. Il signor Guidi (*dare*) un appuntamento a suo cugino. 10. Tu (*stare*) a dieta lattea. 11. Noi (*dare*) dei libri alla biblioteca. 12. Loro non (*stare*) comodi.

B.   **In campagna**

1. Nella primavera e nell'autunno preferisco la campagna alla città. 2. Mio fratello sta in campagna adesso. 3. Ri-

Photo R. P. L. Ledésert

SANTA MARGHERITA

cevei una sua lettera otto giorni fa. 4. Come sta? — Sta
bene, grazie. 5. Noi andiamo in campagna nell'estate.
6. Perchè non andate anche voi in campagna? 7. — Perchè
nell'estate lavoriamo in città. 8. Dove andiamo, conosco
una famiglia di contadini. 9. La loro casa non è lontana
dal borgo. 10. Hanno molti figli. 11. Il primo, quando
non va alla scuola, lavora con suo padre nei campi. 12. È
un ragazzo molto intelligente. 13. Se voi date dei libri a
questo ragazzo, fate una cosa molto buona. 14. Egli ama
la lettura. 15. Quando sono in campagna, vado quasi ogni
giorno al bosco vicino. 16. È un posto selvatico ma molto
bello. 17. Nel bosco trovo molti fiori, fiori d'ogni colore.
18. La casa dove stiamo è nel borgo. 19. È una casa piccola
ma comoda. 20. Dalle finestre vediamo il bosco e i campi
vicini.

C. 1. Some farmers are working in a field of wheat. 2. Two
wagons loaded with (di) hay pass in front of their house. 3. On
the first wagon I see a little boy. 4. Where are you (voi) going
today? 5. — We are going to the city, sir. 6. We want to sell
this hay. 7. Some friends of mine also are going to the city.
8. They find few amusements in the country, especially in the
winter. 9. They are right; but the country is so beautiful in the
spring or in the autumn! 10. Also in the summer, I prefer the
country to the city.

D. 1. In the woods you (tu) find many kinds of wild flowers.
2. Don't you like flowers? 3. We want to spend twenty days in
the country this summer. 4. Where I go, I know almost every
person in the neighboring hamlets. 5. Is this place very distant
from the city? 6. — No, madam; the journey is short. 7. What
are you doing now, Miss Cotillo? 8. Are you writing a letter?
9. — Yes, I am writing to my father and mother. 10. I am writing
only [a] few lines because I must go out and am in a hurry. 11. I
shall write a long letter tomorrow. 12. How are they? — They
are very well, thanks.

E. *Oral.* 1. Quando preferisce Lei la campagna alla città?
2. Quando preferisce la città? 3. Che cosa fanno i contadini nei campi? 4. E Lei che cosa fa quando è in campagna? 5. Scrive molte lettere? 6. Quando scrive, a chi
scrive? 7. Ha Lei dei parenti in campagna? 8. Che cosa
troviamo nei boschi? 9. Dove troviamo molti svaghi?
10. Quanti giorni vuol suo padre passare in campagna?
11. Il borgo è lontano dal bosco? 12. Di chi è il carro carico
di fieno? 13. Chi sta sul carro? 14. Dove va il ragazzo?
15. Perchè va in città? 16. Dove andiamo noi? 17. Con
chi andiamo? 18. Chi lavora nei campi? 19. E lungo il
viaggio dalla città al borgo? 20. Come stanno i suoi
fratelli?

LESSON XXV

86.   Irregular Nouns

1.

| il mio braccio sinistro | my left arm |
| le sue braccia | his arms |

A certain number of nouns in –o have an irregular plural in
–a, which is feminine. The most important of them are:

braccio arm	membro member (*of the body*)
centinaio about a hundred	migliaio about a thousand
dito finger	miglio mile
frutto fruit	osso bone
ginocchio knee	paio pair
labbro lip	riso laughter
lenzuolo sheet	uovo (*or* ovo) egg

2. The following nouns have an entirely irregular plural:

SINGULAR		PLURAL
il bue	the ox	i buoi
la moglie	the wife	le mogli
l'uomo	the man	gli uomini

87.   Irregular Adjectives

1. un bɛl cielo   a beautiful sky
    i bɛi monti   the beautiful mountains
    un bɛllo specchio   a fine mirror
    i bɛgli *alberi*   the beautiful trees
    una bɛlla dɔnna   a beautiful woman
    le bɛlle case   the beautiful houses
    un bɛll'uɔmo   a handsome man
    una bɛll'*anima*   a beautiful soul

The adjectives **bɛllo,** *beautiful, handsome, fine;* **buɔno,** *good;* **grande,** *big, large, great;* and **santo,** *saint, saintly,* while perfectly regular when placed after a noun, or when used as predicates, are subject to the following changes whenever they precede a noun:

Bɛllo takes forms similar to those of the definite article, and **bɛl, bɛi, bɛllo, bɛgli, bɛlla, bɛlle, bɛll'** are used according to the rules given for **il, i, lo, gli, la, le, l'.**

2. un buɔn cavallo   a good horse
    un buɔn amico   a good friend
    un buɔno stipendio   a good salary
    una buɔna cena   a good supper
    una buɔn'azione   a good action

Buɔno has, in the singular, forms similar to those of the indefinite article, and **buɔn, buɔno, buɔna, buɔn'** are used the same way as **un, uno, una, un'.**

3. un gran filɔsofo   a great philosopher
    un grande scandalo   a great scandal
    un grand'*albero*   a large tree
    San Luigi, Santo Stefano   St. Louis, St. Stephen
    Sant'Andrea, Sant'Anna   St. Andrew, St. Anne

Grande and **santo** become **gran** and **san** before a masculine noun beginning with any of the consonants except **s** impure and **z,** and elide before a noun, whether masculine or feminine beginning with a vowel.

EXERCISE XXV

appetito appetite	**patata** potato
arrosto roast	**pisello** pea
burro butter	**pomeriggio** afternoon
caffè *m.* coffee	**resto** rest
cena supper	**sera** evening; **di sera** in the
colazione *f.* breakfast, lunch	evening
desinare *m.* dinner	**vitello** veal
insalata salad	
latte *m.* milk	**far colazione** to take breakfast
mattina morning; **di mattina**	**mangiare** to eat
in the morning	
panino roll	**di buon'ora** early

dopo after, afterward

A. (1) *Complete the following phrases by inserting in each of them the proper form of* **bello, buono** *or* **grande**: un ... alunno, un ... fiore, un ... profeta, una ... maestra, la ... Italia, dei ... studi, un ... signore, delle ... tesi, un ... treno, una ... virtù, un ... baule, dei ... scaffali, un ... sistema, un ... vizio, un ... violino, delle ... qualità, un ... salotto, dei ... specchi, un ... romanzo, dei ... bicchieri.

(2) *Place the proper form of "santo" before the following names*: Isabella, Alberto, Federico, Caterina, Giovanni, Elena, Pio, Giorgio, Elisabetta, Saverio, Arturo, Stanislao.

B. ### Mangiamo

1. Fo colazione di buon'ora, ma mangio poco. 2. Di mattina non ho molto appetito. 3. Di solito prendo una tazza di latte e caffè, e due panini con burro. 4. Poi vado alla scuola, dove passo il resto della mattina. 5. Ho dei buoni professori e imparo molto, specialmente quando preparo bene le mie lezioni. 6. A mezzogiorno ritorno a casa. 7. Mia madre ha apparecchiato la tavola e il desinare è pronto. 8. Siamo cinque persone a tavola: mio padre, mia madre, le mie sorelle e io. 9. Oggi abbiamo mangiato

La Cucina

(*See page* 286)

dell'arrosto di vitello con patate e piselli. 10. Poi la cameriera ha portato a tavola l'insalata. 11. Abbiamo finito il nostro desinare con frutta e caffè nero. 12. Nel pomeriggio, quando non ho lezioni, vado di solito in città. 13. Oggi sono stato alla posta. 14. Ho mandato una lettera raccomandata. 15. Poi ho comprato dei libri e un paio di guanti. 16. Questa sera avevamo degli amici di mio padre a cena. 17. Erano due signori italiani. 18. Essi hanno parlato a tavola di cose molto interessanti. 19. Io ho passato il resto della sera nello studio. 20. Ho preparato le lezioni per domani.

C. 1. Good morning, sir ! How are you? 2. — Good morning, Albert ! Our breakfast is ready. Have you a good appetite this morning? 3. — Every morning I have a good appetite. 4. We go into the dining room now. 5. We take breakfast with Arthur, Charles and their wives. 6. On the table we find some beautiful flowers. 7. Here is the maid. — What will you take? 8. — I shall take some fruit and two eggs. 9. Usually I don't eat eggs in the morning, but today I shall follow your example, I shall take them. 10. Here are rolls and butter.

D. 1. Do you take milk in your coffee? 2. — No, thanks. I prefer black coffee. 3. We have finished our breakfast, and we are going to the city with the other men. 4. We shall return early because we have not much to (da) do. 5. I must buy a large rug for the parlor, and Albert wants to buy six pairs of socks. 6. While we have been in the city, the cook has prepared our dinner. 7. For dinner we have today a roast of veal, potatoes, peas, salad and fruit. 8. In the afternoon Albert will learn his lessons, and I shall write a letter to a good friend of mine. 9. Afterward I shall read a fine novel by (del) Fogazzaro. 10. This evening, after supper, I shall send Albert to the post office.

E. *Oral.* 1. Quando facciamo colazione? 2. Ha molto appetito Lei, di mattina? 3. Che cosa prende di solito per colazione? 4. Preferisce il caffè nero al caffè e latte?

5. Prende il caffè in un bicchiere? 6. Dove vanno gli studenti dopo colazione? 7. E Lei dove va? 8. Che cosa fa nella scuola? 9. Quando ritorniamo a casa? 10. Troviamo il desinare pronto? 11. Chi apparecchia la tavola a casa sua? 12. Chi prepara il suo desinare? 13. Che mangia Lei di solito a mezzogiorno? 14. Che cosa fa Lei nel pomeriggio? 15. Nel pomeriggio d'ieri dov'erano i suoi fratelli? 16. E Lei dov'era? 17. Che cosa compreremo oggi in città? 18. Chi sarà a cena a casa nostra questa sera? 19. Di che parleremo? 20. Dove passeremo il resto della sera?

LESSON XXVI

88. **Demonstrative Adjectives**

Quest'indirizzo è *u*tile.	This address is useful.
Mi dia codesto libro, per favore.	Give me that book, please.
Quelle piante e quegli *a*lberi sono in fiore.	Those plants and trees are in bloom.

1. **Questo,** *this,* refers to somebody or something near the person who speaks. **Codesto,** *that,* (spelled also **cotesto**) refers to somebody or something near the person addressed. **Quello,** *that,* refers to somebody or something far from both the person speaking and the one addressed.

2. **Questo** and **codesto** elide before a singular word beginning with a vowel; **quello** is inflected like **bɛllo** (*see* § 87, 1).

3. With a series of nouns, the demonstrative adjective must be repeated before each of them.

89. Adverbs of Place. Parallel to the above given demonstrative adjectives, the following adverbs of place should be noted:

qua or qui, *here*, — near the person who speaks;
costà or costì, *there*, — near the person addressed;
là or lì, *there*, — far from both.

90.   **Relative Pronouns**

Il libro che è sulla tavola.	The book which is on the table.
Gli amici che abbiamo.	The friends we have.
L'uomo con cui parlo.	The man with whom I speak.
Il marito di Maria, il quale scrive che verrà domani.	Mary's husband, who writes that he will come tomorrow.
Uno scrittore i cui libri sono buoni.	A writer whose books are good.
Chi tace, afferma.	He who keeps silent, consents (Silence gives consent).

1. The relative pronouns are:

che — invariable, used only as a subject or a direct object;

cui — invariable also, and used either as an indirect object or after a preposition;

il quale — which is inflected (**la quale, i quali, le quali**) and agrees in gender and number with its antecedent. It may be used as a subject, as a direct object, or after a preposition. A preposition preceding it combines in one word with the article.

As each of these pronouns may refer to either persons or things they stand, according to the meaning, for the English *who, whom, that,* or *which.*

2. As seen in the second example, the relative pronoun (direct object), often omitted in English, is never omitted in Italian.

3. The form **il quale** is rather sparingly used, except for emphasis or to avoid ambiguity, as shown in the fourth example.

4. The English *whose* is usually rendered by **il cui, la cui, i cui, le cui**, according to the gender and number of the word which follows. *He who* or *him who* is translated by **chi,** and sometimes by **colui che.**

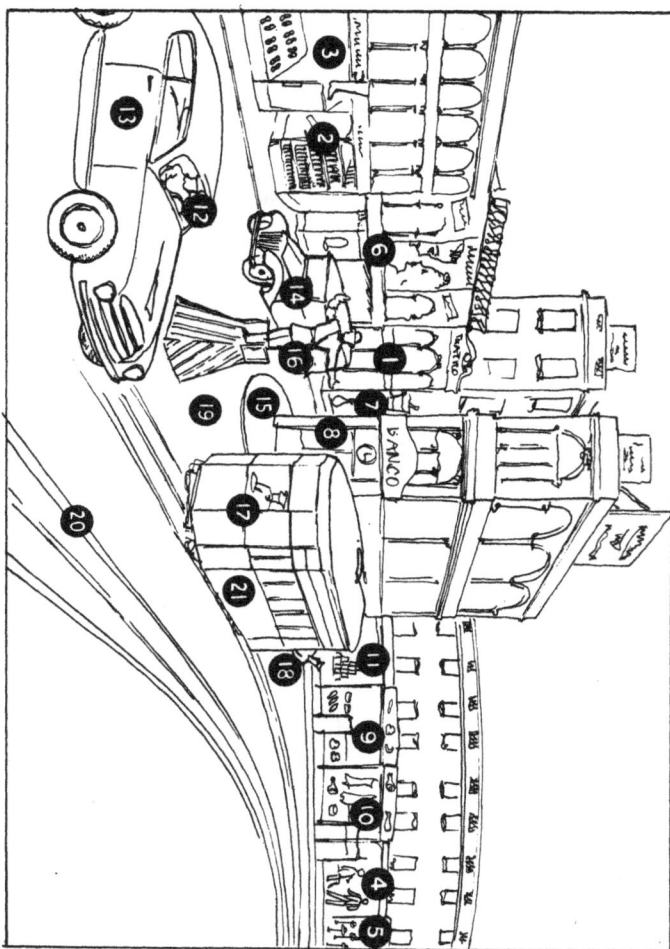

La Via

(See page 286)

5. **Non possiamo far sempre quel che vogliamo.**   We cannot always do what we want.

The English relative pronoun *what*, when equivalent to *that which*, is translated quel che, or quello che, or ciò che.

EXERCISE XXVI

cammino walk, way	**contento** glad, satisfied
cantonata corner (*of a street*)	**stanco** tired
chiesa church	
gente *f.* people	**camminare** to walk
lira lira (*Italian money*)	**osservare** to observe
minuta bill of fare	**scendere** to descend, get down
negozio store	**mi dia** give me
piazza square	**scusi** I beg your pardon
ristorante *m.* restaurant	
vettura carriage	**per** through
vetturino driver	**per favore** please
via street	

A. (1) *Place the proper form of* quello *before each of the following nouns:* artista, boschi, burro, camicia, dizionari, eccezioni, fieno, giorni, impiegati, inverno, modiste, novella, orario, pomeriggio, righi, signori, svaghi, uomo, uomini, viaggio, zio, zii.

(2) *Form a sentence with each expression.*

(3) *Supply the proper relative pronoun and the demonstrative adjective, if one is lacking:* 1. Il caffè —— prendo è buono. 2. La signora con —— parlavo era mia madre. 3. —— ragazzo, e la ragazza con —— uscì, sono fratello e sorella. 4. Il professore preferisce —— alunni —— sono diligenti. 5. —— ama lo studio, impara. 6. La lettera —— scrivo non sarà lunga. 7. Un ragazzo —— quaderni sono in ordine è diligente. 8. La stanza in —— lavoro non è grande. 9. Ecco le cento lire di —— avrai bisogno. 10. Faccio —— posso. 11. Passeremo per la piazza di —— ella parlava. 12. —— dorme non piglia pesci. 13. Osserviamo —— essi hanno

comprato. 14. La via per — passiamo adesso è Via Cavour.

B. In città

1. Scusi, signore, dov'è la posta? 2. — È a Piazza Dante, a venti minuti di cammino da qui. 3. — Siamo stanchi! Vogliamo prendere una vettura? 4. — Se desiderano una vettura, chiamerò quella che è là, alla cantonata. 5. I miei due amici e io prendiamo la vettura e partiamo. 6. Per le vie per le quali passiamo, osserviamo molte cose interessanti. 7. Quanti bei negozi e quanta gente! 8. Ecco una magnifica chiesa. 9. È la chiesa in cui fummo ieri. 10. Quando siamo alla posta, diamo quattro lire al vetturino e scendiamo. 11. Conosco quella signora che adesso parla con l'impiegato. 12. È una signora americana che ha una stanza nel nostro albergo. 13. Dopo pochi minuti usciamo dalla posta. 14. Ho ricevuto una lettera che aspettavo da alcuni giorni e sono così contento! 15. Risponderò oggi stesso. 16. Che cosa facciamo adesso? 17. — Adesso andiamo a mangiare. 18. Ogni mattina facciamo colazione di buon'ora e a mezzogiorno abbiamo appetito. 19. Ecco un ristorante che sembra buono. 20. Sediamo a una tavola apparecchiata per tre persone. 21. Mi dia codesta minuta, per favore.

C. 1. He who is in a hurry needs a carriage. 2. We are not in a hurry and prefer to walk and look at the stores. 3. The ladies with whom Charles and I are walking, are Olga and Sylvia. 4. They are the ladies whose brother plays the violin so well. 5. Fifteen minutes ago we were in a large store where Olga bought some beautiful gloves. 6. Sylvia bought nothing; probably she does not need anything. 7. The square through which we are passing now, has a church into which my friends want to go. 8. I shall wait for them there, at the corner. 9. I beg your pardon, sir: do you know a good restaurant not far from here? 10. — You will find a good restaurant in almost every hotel on (di) this street.

D. 1. While my friends are in church, I observe the people.
2. Those men who are getting down from that carriage look like
Americans. 3. They are talking to the driver now. 4. If they do
not speak Italian, that man will not understand them. 5. But
here are my two friends, Olga and Sylvia. 6. We want to go to one
of the restaurants of which that man spoke. 7. We are glad to (di)
find that he was right. 8. The dinner is good and not very expensive: twelve lire a person (a testa). 9. Please give me that
cup; 1 wish some coffee. 10. We shall call a carriage to (per)
return to the hotel, for we are tired.

E. *Oral.* 1. Chi ha bisogno d'una vettura? 2. Che cosa
preferisce Lei a una vettura? 3. Vuole andare in una
vettura o in un'automobile quando non ha fretta? 4. Dov'è
la posta in questa città? 5. Che cosa riceviamo alla posta?
6. Che cosa osserviamo mentre camminiamo? 7. Quando
Lei è stanco di camminare, che cosa fa? 8. Che fa chi va
in un negozio? 9. Ha Olga comprato dei fazzoletti?
10. Perchè Silvia non ha comprato nulla? 11. Dove a-
spettava il loro amico? 12. Chi scendeva da una vettura?
13. Con chi parlavano? 14. Che cosa facciamo quando
andiamo in un ristorante? 15. Perchè andiamo in un
ristorante? 16. Dov'è un buon ristorante in questa città?
17. È lontano da qui? 18. Che cosa vuol Lei mangiare a
mezzogiorno? 19. Cammineremo per ritornare all'albergo?

LESSON XXVII

91. Imperative of Model Verbs

Sing.	compr **a**	buy	vend **i**	sell
Plur.	compr **iamo**	let us buy	vend **iamo**	let us sell
	compr **ate**	buy	vend **ete**	sell
Sing.	fin **isc i**	finish	part **i**	depart
Plur.	fin **iamo**	let us finish	part **iamo**	let us depart
	fin **ite**	finish	part **ite**	depart

Note that there is no 3d person of the imperative in Italian. When the 3d person is needed, it is borrowed from the present subjunctive.

Note also that the larger part of the verbs of the 3d conjugation add –isc to their stem in the 2d person singular (*see* § 30).

92.   Imperative of *essere* and *avere*

SING.	sii	be	abbi	have
PLUR.	siamo	let us be	abbiamo	let us have
	siate	be	abbiate	have

93.   Imperative of the Four Irregular Verbs
of the 1st Conjugation

SING.	va' go, etc.	da' give, etc.	fa' do, etc.	sta' be, etc
PLUR.	andiamo	diamo	facciamo	stiamo
	andate	date	fate	state

94.   Negative Imperative

non comprare	do not buy
non compriamo	let us not buy
non comprate	do not buy

A peculiarity of the imperative is that the negative form of the 2d person singular is made by **non** and the *infinitive*.

95.   Hours of the Day

È l'una.	It's one o'clock (A.M.).
Sono le tredici.	It's one o'clock (P.M.).

In Italy it is customary to count the hours from midnight to midnight, and therefore the hours after noon are counted from 12 to 24. The numeral indicating the time is preceded by the definite article, and both article and verb agree with **ora,** *hour,* or **ore,** understood.

Study the following expressions:

Che ora è? *or* Che ore sono?	What time is it?
È mezzanotte.	It's midnight.
Sono le tre meno un quarto.	It's a quarter to three (A.M.).
Sono le venti e un quarto.	It's a quarter past eight (P.M.).
È l'una e quaranta.	It's forty minutes past one (A.M.).
Sono le cinque meno dieci.	It's ten minutes to five (A.M.)
A che ora?	At what time?
Alle due e mezzo (*or* mezza).	At half past two (A.M.).
Stamani; stasera	This morning; this evening
Stanotte	Last night (until noon; after noon it means *tonight*)

96.   Age

Quanti anni ha Lei? }	
Che età ha Lei? }	How old are you?
Ho ventidue anni.	I am twenty-two years old.
Questo bimbo ha tre mesi.	This baby is three months old.

Age is expressed by means of the verb **avere**.

EXERCISE XXVII

abilità ability	**tempo** time, weather; **a tempo**
atto act	on time
attore *m.* actor	
attrice *f.* actress	**pieno** full
fila row	**vuoto** empty
fine *f.* end	
occasione *f.* occasion	**applaudire** to applaud [1]
palco box (of a theater)	**recitare** to act
palcoscenico stage	**udire** to hear
platea parquet	
prima donna leading lady	**al massimo** at the most
spettacolo show	**giusto** just
teatro theater	**mirabilmente** admirably

A. (1) *Supply the 2d person singular imperative, affirmative and negative, of the verb given in the infinitive:* 1. (*tirare*)

[1] Conjugated like **partire**.

K

IL TEATRO

(See page 286)

—— la rete. 2. (*scendere*) —— al pian terreno. 3. (*andare*)
—— nella cucina. 4. (*stare*) —— nel salotto. 5. (*chiudere*)
—— le finestre. 6. (*fare*) —— caso della moda. 7. (*pulire*)
—— questa stanza. 8. (*dettare*) —— questa poesia. 9. (*firmare*) —— la lettera. 10. (*partire*) —— domani. 11. (*dare*)
—— il romanzo a Elena. 12. (*imparare*) —— queste parole.

(2) *Supply the 1st and 2d persons plural imperative, affirmative and negative, of the verb given in the infinitive:* 1. (*ritornare*) —— di buon'ora. 2. (*mangiare*) —— a casa. 3. (*vedere*)
—— chi sono. 4. (*andare*) —— al teatro. 5. (*seguire*) ——
il suo esempio. 6. (*dare*) —— dei libri a questo ragazzo.
7. (*essere*) —— contenti. 8. (*fare*) —— quel che vuole
Alberto. 9. (*prendere*) —— il violino d'Elena. 10. (*coprire*)
—— questo pavimento con un tappeto. 11. (*stare*) —— con
queste ragazze. 12. (*applaudire*) —— gli attori.

(3) *Translate into Italian:* 1. It is noon. 2. It is 9 : 37.
3. It is 1 : 45. 4. The train leaves at 2 : 15. 5. Our lesson
starts at 9 : 10. 6. It ends at 10. 7. It was midnight.
8. We shall leave tonight. 9. At what time did you return
home? 10. —— We returned at 7 : 30.

(4) *Answer the following questions:* 1. Quanti anni ha
Lei? 2. Che età ha suo padre? 3. Quanti anni avrà suo
fratello fra tre anni? 4. Quanti anni avrà (*fut. of probability*)
il suo professore? 5. Quanti anni aveva Lei otto anni fa?
6. Che età hanno alcuni suoi amici?

B. Al teatro

1. Mangiaste di buon'ora ieri sera? 2. — Sì, mangiammo
alle diciotto e mezzo, perchè desideravamo d'andare al
teatro. 3. Mio fratello aveva comprato un biglietto per
un palco di prima fila al Teatro Argentina. 4. Il Teatro
Argentina è uno dei primi di Roma. 5. Uscimmo dall'-
albergo alle venti, e arrivammo giusto a tempo. 6. Lo
spettacolo cominciava alle venti e un quarto. 7. Era la

prima volta che udivo attori italiani. 8. Davano una bella commedia del Giacosa. 9. Capii quasi ogni parola ed ebbi occasione d'ammirare l'abilità degli artisti di teatro italiani. 10. La prima donna recitava mirabilmente. 11. Era la Stoppano. La conosci? 12. Il teatro era pieno. 13. Nella platea ogni posto sembrava occupato, e solamente qualche palco era vuoto. 14. Dal nostro palco noi udivamo molto bene perchè non stavamo lontani dal palcoscenico. 15. Applaudimmo molte volte. 16. Alla fine del secondo atto la Stoppano ricevè anche dei fiori. 17. Lo spettacolo finì alle ventitrè e dieci. 18. Dopo il teatro andammo a fare una piccola cena. 19. Poi prendemmo un'automobile per ritornare all'albergo. 20. A mezzanotte andammo a letto.

C. *In translating these sentences, use the 2d person singular, in direct address.* 1. Have you never been in an Italian theater, Olga? 2. Let's eat early this evening and go to a show. 3. Where can we buy the tickets? 4. — If you want, we shall buy them at the theater. 5. Invite your friend Sylvia also. 6. — No, don't invite her, for her mother is ill. 7. At what time does the show begin? — At twenty minutes after eight. 8. Call a driver, please. We must take a carriage because the theater is far from here. 9. — Don't be in a hurry. It is only a quarter to seven. 10. In [a] few minutes I shall be ready to (a) go out.

D. *Unless instructed otherwise, use the 2d person singular, in direct address, also in these sentences.* 1. We are in the theater now; we have two good seats in (di) [the] parquet. 2. Do you know (2d person plural) that lady in that box in (di) [the] second row? 3. — I know her; she is the sister of a friend of mine. 4. How old is she? — She is twenty-seven years old, at the most. 5. The theater is full; only [a] few seats are empty. 6. The first act starts; here is the leading lady. 7. She is a famous actress and acts admirably. 8. At the end of the act we applaud; every person in the theater applauds. 9. The first actor, the leading lady's father, has shown great ability. 10. Listen! A bell rings; the second act starts. 11. The stage is empty; but see! two actors arrive at the same time.   12. The show lasts almost three hours; it will end at a quarter after eleven.

E. *Oral.*   1. Quanti anni ha Lei?   2. Quanti anni ha suo fratello?   3. Che età ha suo zio?   4. Che ora è? 5. A che ora comincia la nostra lezione?   6. A che ora finisce?   7. A che ora mangiò Lei ieri sera?   8. Ha mai udito attori italiani?   9. Quanti teatri abbiamo in questa città?   10. Hanno molti palchi i teatri americani? 11. Quale posto preferisce Lei, in un teatro?   12. Sono pieni i teatri dalle diciassette alle diciannove?   13. A che ora sono pieni, di solito?   14. Chi udiamo in un teatro? 15. Che cosa udiamo?   16. Qual è un'attrice americana che recita bene?   17. Dopo il teatro, dove andiamo? 18. A che ora arriviamo a casa?   19. A che ora va Lei a letto, di solito?   20. A che ora fa colazione?

LESSON XXVIII

97.   **Conjunctive Personal Pronouns**

The pronouns here given are called *conjunctive* because they are used only in connection with a verb, serving as direct objects, indirect objects, or reflexive objects.

DIRECT OBJECTS	INDIRECT OBJECTS	REFLEXIVE OBJECTS
mi me	mi to me	mi myself
ti thee, you	ti to thee, to you	ti thyself, yourself
lo him, it	gli to him, to it	si himself, herself, itself
la her, it, *you*	le to her, to it, *to you*	*yourself*
ci us	ci to us	ci ourselves
vi you	vi to you	vi yourself, yourselves
li them, *you* (*m.*)	loro to them, *to you*	si themselves, *your-*
le them, *you* (*f.*)		*selves*

1. Ne avevo quattro.   I had four (of them).
    Ne hɔ avuti molti.   I have had many of them.

Another conjunctive pronoun is **ne**, *of it, of them.* It translates also *some* or *any*, whenever these words stand for *some of it, some of them, any of it,* or *any of them.* It is often used pleonastically, and is never omitted when a numerical adjective or similar word stands after the verb without the noun.

When **ne** is used with a compound tense, the past participle agrees with it as if it were a direct object form.

2. Note, from the table above, that:

(*a*) In the 1st and 2d persons, singular and plural, the same forms are used for the three different functions, while only the 3d person offers different forms.

(*b*) The 3d person, being the normal form of address in Italian, renders also the English *you*, as follows:

Addressing one person:	la ⎫		le ⎫			si	yourself
Addressing more than one							
man, or men and women:	li ⎬ you		loro ⎬ to you			si	yourselves
Addressing more than one							
woman:	le ⎭		loro ⎭			si	yourselves

    3. M'ha veduto.   He has seen me.
       L'hɔ usato.   I have used it.

Most of the conjunctive personal pronouns may drop the final vowel and take an apostrophe, before a verb beginning with a vowel. The elision, however, occurs more frequently with **mi, ti, si,** and nearly always with **lo, la.**

    4. Ci rispettiamo.   We respect ourselves. We respect one another.
      Ci rispettiamo l'un l'altro.   We respect one another.

The plural reflexive pronouns are used also as reciprocal pronouns. The sense is usually clear, but ambiguity can be avoided by adding to the verb **l'un l'altro,** *one another,* which emphasizes the reciprocal meaning.

98. Use of the Conjunctive Personal Pronouns

1. **Egli mi conosce.** — He knows me.
   Non ne abbiamo. — We haven't any.
   Gli dirà tutto. — He will tell him everything.
   Scriverò loro. — I shall write to them.
   Gli ho parlato. — I have spoken to him.

The conjunctive personal pronouns, except **loro**, immediately precede the verb. If the verb is a compound tense, the pronoun precedes the auxiliary, as shown in the last example.

2. **Desideravo di vederlo.** — I wished to see him.
   Imparandolo. — In learning it.
   Parlatene loro. — Speak of it to them.
   Dammi codeste lettere. — Give me those letters.
   Digli tutto. — Tell him everything.
   Eccoli. — Here they are or There they are.

But when the verb is an infinitive,[1] a present participle, a past participle used without auxiliary, or an affirmative imperative,[2] the pronoun follows the verb, and is written as one word with it.

Note that:

(*a*) In combining with a pronoun, the infinitive loses its final **e**.

(*b*) An imperative ending in a stressed vowel causes the doubling of the initial consonant of the pronoun which is attached to it, **gli** being the only exception to this rule.

(*c*) **Loro** is never attached to the verb.

(*d*) The stress of the verb remains unchanged, in spite of the addition of the pronoun.

(*e*) The interjection **ecco** takes the pronouns appended just as if it were an imperative.

---

[1] Not the infinitive used, with a negative, as imperative (*see* § 94).

[2] Not the negative imperative, nor the subjunctive used as an imperative (*see* § 91).

GLI ANIMALI

(See page 287)

99. Conjunctive Adverbs

Ci andai ieri.	I went there yesterday.
Vi ritornai.	I returned there.
Ne arrivano.	They arrive from there.
C'è un buon teatro.	There is a good theater.

Here and *there*, when they denote a place already mentioned, and no particular stress is laid upon them, are rendered by **ci** or **vi**. In the same way, *thence* is rendered by **ne**. These adverbs are used only in connection with a verb, and precede or follow it, according to the same rules given for the pronouns **ci, vi, ne**. *There is*, *there are*, etc. are translated **c'è** or **v'è**, **ci sono** or **vi sono**, etc.

EXERCISE XXVIII

angolo corner	ruscello brook
anitra duck	stalla stable, barn
arca di Noè Noah's ark	vacca cow
cane *m.* dog	
capra goat	orgoglioso proud
cavallo horse	tutto all, whole; tutto il libro
gallina hen	the whole book; tutti i libri
gallo rooster	all books
gattino kitten	
gatto, −a cat	abbaiare to bark
maiale *m.* pig	aver paura to be afraid
pollaio chicken yard	divertirsi to amuse oneself,[1]
pollo chicken	have a good time
puledro colt	domandare to ask

pagare to pay, pay for

A. (1) *Continue the following:* 1. Io mi guardo nello specchio, etc. 2. Io mi mostrerò diligente, etc. 3. Io mi trovai solo, etc. 4. Io mi mettevo a lavorare, etc. 5. Egli **mi** aiuta, egli **ti** aiuta, etc. 6. Egli **mi** fa un favore, egli **ti** fa

---

[1] Conjugated like **partire**.

un favore, etc. 7. Essi **mi** guardano, essi **ti** guardano, etc.
8. Essi **mi** danno torto, essi **ti** danno torto, etc.

(2) *Translate into Italian:* 1. Here I am. 2. Here you
are (*five ways*). 3. Here he is. 4. Here she is. 5. Here it
is (*two ways*). 6. Here they are (*two ways*). 7. He speaks
to her. 8. We speak to each other. 9. I shall visit him.
10. You will sell the house to them.

(3) *Supply the conjunctive pronoun of the person indicated,
and where the 3d person is indicated give both the masculine
and the feminine forms:* 1. Arturo —— (1*st person plural*)
parla. 2. Io —— (3*d p.s.*) offro dei biglietti. 3. Essi ——
(2*d p.s.*) osservano. 4. Egli —— (2*d p.p.*) spiega la lezione.
5. Tu detti —— (3*d p.p.*) una poesia. 6. Noi —— (3*d p.s.*)
chiamiamo. 7. Voi —— (1*st p.s.*) conoscete bene. 8. Olga
—— (3*d p.s.*) risponderà.

(4) *Substitute* ci, vi, *or* ne *for the prepositional phrases with*
in, a, di, *or* da *according to sense:* 1. Usciamo dal teatro.
2. Saremo a casa alle diciotto. 3. Egli è nello studio adesso.
4. Desideravo un po' di carta. 5. Offrii delle frutta. 6. Ritornerò a scuola domani. 7. Arrivano da Napoli. 8. La-
vorai in quella stanza. 9. Eravamo a Roma. 10. Parlai
della casa di mio zio. 11. Stavano in una stalla. 12. Carlo
e io andavamo al teatro tutte le sere. 13. Egli scendeva
dal piano superiore. 14. Prenderò delle medicine.

B.   **Animali domestici**

1. La primavera è arrivata, ed eccoci in campagna!
2. Vi passeremo tutto il giorno e ritorneremo in città
stasera. 3. Tutto quello che vediamo è interessante.
4. Prima andiamo alla stalla perchè lo zio che visitiamo
desidera di mostrarci un nuovo cavallo. 5. L'ha comprato
da poco tempo e l'ha pagato molto caro. 6. Nella stalla
c'è anche un puledro, e in un angolo vedo una gatta con dei
gattini. 7. Guardali, Alberto! Uno è bianco e nero, e

gli altri son tutti grigi. 8. Ma non siamo in campagna per passare il tempo in una stalla: usciamone. 9. Andiamo nei campi, dove tutto è così bello! 10. Avete delle vacche, zio? 11. — Ne ho una che ci dà il latte per la famiglia. 12. Dov'è? Non la vedo. 13. — Eccola. È là, dove sono quelle anitre, non lontano da quel ruscello. 14. Gli domando se ha dei maiali, e mi risponde che ne ha tre. 15. Ma egli va orgoglioso del suo pollaio e desidera di mostrarlo ad Alberto. 16. Nel pollaio ci sono da cinquanta a sessanta galline e alcuni galli. 17. Udiamo un cane che abbaia, e mio fratello ha paura. 18. Abbaia perchè una vettura passa davanti alla casa di mio zio. 19. Ci divertiamo così tutta la mattina e a mezzogiorno andiamo a mangiare di buon appetito. 20. Non si diverte anche Lei quando va in campagna?

C. 1. Yesterday my sister and I went to the country. 2. We went together to (a) visit our uncle. 3. I go there very often. 4. We left at six o'clock so as (per) to arrive early. 5. My uncle was waiting for us at the station with his carriage. 6. He had bought a new horse and was very proud of it. 7. I asked him how much he had paid for it. 8. How much do you think (voi form)? — Eight thousand lire! 9. We arrived at his house in about half [an] hour. 10. A dog met us and started to (ad) bark at the horse.

D. 1. Don't be afraid (tu form), Olga: it is a good dog. 2. But my sister was not afraid; she is twelve years old now. 3. My aunt was very glad to (di) see us. 4. We spent almost the whole day in the fields. 5. Uncle, show me (voi form) where the cows are.[1] 6. — There they are! Don't you see (tu form) them, near that brook, where some ducks are swimming? 7. My sister likes chickens and wished to see them. 8. Then my uncle showed her the chicken yard, in which he had eighty or ninety hens and three roosters. 9. I went into the barn to (a) see a new colt

[1] Translate, *where are the cows.*

and I also found there two pigs and a goat. 10. In a corner there was a cat with five kittens: that barn was a real Noah's ark! 11. My sister and I had a very good time the whole day. 12. [We] both returned to the city in the evening and were very tired when we went to bed.

E. *Oral.* 1. Dove andò quol ragazzo ieri? 2. Ci va spesso? 3. A che ora partì da casa? 4. Con chi andò? 5. A che ora arrivarono? 6. Chi aspettava alla stazione? 7. Perchè era orgoglioso lo zio? 8. Chi ebbe paura? 9. Perchè ebbe paura? 10. Perchè abbaiava il cane? 11. Dov'era il puledro? 12. Dov'erano le vacche? 13. Che cosa sembrava un'arca di Noè? 14. Perchè? 15. Chi si diverte in campagna? 16. Perchè si diverte? 17. A che ora ritornarono in città i due ragazzi? 18. A che ora andarono a letto? 19. Ritornarono dalla campagna in una vettura? 20. Quante volte è stato Lei in campagna quest'anno?

LESSON XXIX

100. Use of the Conjunctive Personal Pronouns
(Continued)

Me lo restituirai?	Will you return it to me?
Parlatecene.	Speak of it to us.
Glieli daremo.	We shall give them to him, (to her, to you).
Lo daremo loro.	We shall give it to them.

1. When two conjunctive personal pronouns are used with the same verb, the indirect object precedes the direct object (contrary to English usage), and both precede, or follow the verb, as in the case of a single pronoun (*see* § 98).

2. **Loro,** as always, follows the verb.

3. Before **lo, la, li, le** and **ne,**

(*a*) **mi, ti, si, ci** and **vi**[1] change i into e, and become respectively **me, te, se, ce** and **ve;**

(*b*) **gli** and **le** alike become **glie,** which is written as one word with the following pronoun, giving these forms:

> **glielo**
> **gliela** } it to him, *or* it to her, *or* it to you
>
> **glieli**
> **gliele** } them to him, *or* them to her, *or* them to you
>
> **gliene**   some to him. *or* some to her, *or* some to you

EXERCISE XXIX

anello ring	**smeraldo** emerald
braccialetto bracelet	**sposalizio** wedding
compleanno birthday	
corallo coral	**esatto** exact
dono gift, present	**forte** strong
gioielliere *m.* jeweler	**prezioso** precious
gioielleria jewelry	**splendido** splendid
oggetto object	
orecchino earring	**consigliare** to advise
oro gold	**offrire** to offer [2]
orologio watch	**presentare** to present, introduce
perla pearl	duce
prezzo price	**ricordare** to remember
rubino ruby	
scatola box	**abbastanza** enough

A. (1) *Translate each of the following phrases in two ways:* glielo mostro, glieli mostro, gliene mostro due, gliela presenterò, gliele passeremo, gliene passai due, dateglielo, non glielo vendete, parlategliene, glielo dichiarai.

(2) *Translate into Italian in four different ways* (you as tu, voi, Lei *and* Loro): 1. I shall teach it to you. 2. He will send them to you. 3. She did not repeat it to you.

---

[1] Also the adverbs **ci** and **vi** (*see* § 99).   [2] Conjugated like **partire.**

4. He will respect you. 5. I called you. 6. We shall read
it to you. 7. She will show them to you. 8. Has she
brought it to you?

(3) *Rewrite, using where possible direct and indirect conjunctive pronouns instead of the object nouns:* 1. Carlo consegnò una lettera a sua madre. 2. Presentai i miei cugini
al signor Conti. 3. Offro dei fiori a mia cugina. 4. Por-
teremo questi libri ai nostri amici. 5. Manderai dei saluti
a suo suocero. 6. Parlavo di queste cose al professore.
7. Passerete i quaderni agli altri alunni. 8. Spiegai la
lezione ad Arturo. 9. Egli parlò a Silvia del suo viaggio in
Italia. 10. Venderemo questa casa.

B.   **Dal gioielliere**

1. Tra alcuni giorni avrà luogo lo sposalizio di mia cugina.
2. Mia sorella e io desideriamo di darle un dono. 3. Lo
compreremo oggi, e glielo manderemo per il giorno dello
sposalizio. 4. Guido ci presenterà a un gioielliere suo
amico, che ha un negozio a via Cavour. 5. Là troveremo
quello che desideriamo. 6. Via Cavour è lontana, ma
prenderemo una vettura. 7. Che cosa desiderano, signori?
— Qualche oggetto per un dono a una signora. 8. Il
gioielliere ha degli anelli magnifici, e ce ne mostra alcuni.
9. Sono belli, ma son anche cari. 10 Mia sorella ne ammira molto uno con un rubino e due perle. 11. Io ne
preferisco un altro con uno splendido smeraldo. 12. Vediamo anche dei braccialetti: son tutti d'oro con pietre
preziose. 13. Ma finiamo col comprare un paio d'orecchini
di corallo e piccole perle. 14. Il gioielliere ce li offre a un
prezzo non caro. 15. Son così belli, e nostra cugina sarà
così contenta! 16. Anche la scatola in cui il gioielliere ce
li ha venduti è bella. 17. Ritornerò in quel negozio tra pochi
giorni. 18. Ho veduto un orologetto d'oro a buon prezzo e

desidero di comprarlo. 19. L'offrirò a mia sorella per il suo compleanno. 20. Quello ch'ella ha adesso non è d'oro.

C. *Use the* voi *form in rendering the direct address whenever it occurs in these sentences.* 1. Has my sister-in-law shown you her new bracelet? 2. — Yes, she showed it to me, and I found it very beautiful. 3. She received it from my brother [a] few days ago. 4. The seventh of this month was her birthday. 5. It is a splendid gift: where did he buy it? 6. — He bought it from a jeweler who is a friend of our family. 7. If you want to buy some precious objects, I advise you to (di) go to that store. 8. — Thanks! I wish to (di) go there now. 9. If you remember the exact address of it, please write it for me (= to me) on this piece of paper. 10. — Here it is. If you want. I shall telephone to the jeweler.

D. 1. I must go to (a) buy a present for my sister, whose wedding will take place the first of the month. 2. I want to go now to the store of which you have spoken. 3. — Well, then let's go there together. 4. I also wish to (di) see my friend and shall introduce him to you. 5. Here we are in the jewelry store (= store of jewelry). 6. The jeweler has some magnificent earrings and shows them to us. 7 Some are with pearls, some with rubies, and here is a splendid pair (of them [1]) with emeralds. 8. He also shows us some Italian rings with corals and offers them to me at a good price. 9. But my sister will be glad to (di) have a watch, and I ask to (di) see some of them. 10. Please show (voi *form*) some of them to us. 11. May I see some other watches? 12. He shows them to me, and I buy a very beautiful gold watch (= watch of gold). 13. I pay, and the jeweler hands it to me in a little box. 14. Is this box strong enough? 15. My sister is in Italy, and I must send it to her by mail (per posta).

E. *Oral.* 1. Che cosa vende un gioielliere? 2. Conosce Lei un gioielliere? 3. Dove sta il suo negozio? 4. Ricorda il suo esatto indirizzo? 5. Qual è l'indirizzo di casa sua? 6. Che cosa diamo a una persona cara il giorno del suo compleanno? 7. Qual è il giorno del suo compleanno?

[1] To be translated.

8. Diamo dei doni solamente per un compleanno? 9. È stato Lei mai a uno sposalizio? 10. Allo sposalizio di chi? 11. Quale oggetto prezioso preferisce Lei? 12. Qual è la pietra preziosa che Lei preferisce? 13. Di che colore è un rubino? 14. E una perla? 15. E uno smeraldo? 16. Conosce Lei una pietra preziosa che è famosa in Italia? 17. Un gioielliere vende solo anelli, orecchini e braccialetti? 18. Chi ha un orologio in questa classe? 19. Quanto lo ha pagato? 20. Che ora è?

LESSON XXX

101.   **Present Participle**

Buying	*Selling*	*Finishing*
compr ando	**vend endo**	**fin endo**

Being	*Having*
essendo	**avendo**

102.   **Perfect Participle**

Having bought	*Having sold*	*Having finished*
avendo comprato	**avendo venduto**	**avendo finito**

Having been	*Having had*
essendo stato	**avendo avuto**

103. Use of the Present Participle.[1] 1. The present participle is invariable in form; that is, it does not undergo any change on account of gender, number or person.

2. It translates the English present participle whenever the latter has a verbal function. For the translation of the English present participle used as a noun or an adjective, see respectively § § 148, 2 and 158.

---

[1] No attempt is here made to distinguish between the present participle and the gerund, either in English or in Italian.

3. **Sbagliando impariamo.**   We learn by erring.
   Copiando feci uno sbaglio.   In copying I made a mistake.
   Arrivando ci salutò.   On arriving he greeted us.

Besides rendering the English present participle used alone with a verbal force, the Italian present participle translates also the English present participle preceded by the prepositions *by*, *in*, *on* or *through*.

4. **Parlando di lui, arrivammo**   While we were speaking of him,
   a casa.   we arrived home.
   Essendo ricco, può viaggia- Since he is rich, he can travel.
   re.
   Vendendo a tal prezzo, non   If I sold at such a price, I would
   guadagnerei nulla.   earn nothing.

The present participle may replace a clause of time, cause, or condition.

104.   Progressive Construction

Stava ancora dormendo.   He was still sleeping.
Stava lavorando.   He was working.
Andava imparando.   He was learning.

The present participle of a verb may be combined with a form of **stare** or **andare** to form a progressive construction. **Stare** is more commonly used, but **andare** is preferred to convey an idea of motion or growth.

As has already been explained (*see* § 23, 1 *and* § 45), the progressive idea can be expressed by both the simple present (**compro**, *I am buying*) and the past descriptive (**compravo**, *I was buying*). Because of this the progressive construction is less frequently used in Italian than in English, and when used it implies more emphasis. **Sto comprando** = *I am in the act of buying.*

105.   Adverbs of Manner

1. **generoso** generous   **generosamente** generously
   cortese courteous   **cortesemente** courteously

Adverbs of manner are usually formed by adding **–mente** to the feminine singular of the adjective.

L

2.	leale	loyal	lealmente	loyally
	regolare	regular	regolarmente	regularly
But:	folle	mad	follemente	madly
	mediocre	mediocre	mediocremente	moderately

Adjectives ending in –le or –re drop the final vowel in adding –mente, provided that no consonant precedes those endings.

EXERCISE XXX

le Alpi the Alps
Vittorio Emanuele Victor Emmanuel

duce *m.* leader
gloria glory
indipendenza independence
lotta struggle
nazione *f.* nation
nemico enemy
patria country, fatherland
periodo period
popolo people
potenza power

storia history
trono throne
uomo di stato statesman
vita life
vittoria victory

destare to arouse
rischiare to risk
sacrificare to sacrifice
scacciare to drive, expel

a capo di at the head of
circa about
oltre beyond

sempre più more and more

A. (1) *Give for each verb in parentheses the present or perfect participle according to sense:* 1. (*Imparare*) quella lezione, ne studiò un'altra. 2. (*Dare*) dei libri a quel ragazzo, faccio una buona cosa. 3. (*Uscire*) dalla scuola, incontrò il maestro. 4. (*Osservare*) le ragazze, le trovò intelligenti. 5. Stiamo (*leggere*) un romanzo della Serao. 6. (*Camminare*) per Via XX Settembre, trovai un mio amico. 7. (*Conoscere*) quei signori, egli desiderò di star con loro. 8. (*Aver bisogno*) d'Elena, le telefonai. 9. (*Aprire*) la porta, entrerai. 10. (*Preparare*) la sua lezione, imparò molte cose nuove.

(2) *Give the adverbs of manner corresponding to the following*

adjectives: capriccioso, incantevole, pesante, ricco, selvatico, forte, esatto, difficile, comodo, alto, contemporaneo, splendido, elegante, inutile, lungo, lontano, povero, grande, facile, giusto.

(3) *Replace the pronouns in parentheses by their correct Italian equivalents:* 1. Telefonando (*to her*) alle sedici, ero in ritardo. 2. Mangiando (*them, m.*), ella mi guardava. 3. Ordinando (*me*) di far queste cose, avrete torto. 4. Parlò mostrando (*to him*) la porta. 5. Sarò contento invitando (*her*). 6. Osservando (*them*), le trovò strette. 7. Lasciando (*to them*) quel che desideravano, egli mostrò che non era capriccioso. 8. Imparò quella poesia recitando (*it*) molte volte. 9. Sacrificando (*to him*) il suo posto, egli seguì il mio consiglio. 10. Scrivendo (*to her*), si ricordò d'Elena.

B. **Storia d'Italia**

1. Tutta la storia d'Italia, da quella di Roma a quella dei giorni nostri, è ricca di glorie. 2. Adesso stiamo studiando il periodo che va dal 1821 al 1919. 3. È la storia delle guerre d'indipendenza. 4. Stiamo leggendo alcuni libri che il nostro professore ci ha consigliati. 5. Essi sono molto interessanti. 6. Egli ci ha parlato stamani di Vittorio Emanuele II, il Padre della Patria. 7. Vittorio Emanuele rischiò tutto, il trono, la vita sua e quella dei suoi figli, per l'indipendenza italiana. 8. Ma nella dura lotta egli non fu solo. 9. Altri grandi uomini lo aiutarono a scacciare gli Austriaci dalla patria. 10. Mazzini[1] occupa il primo posto tra quelli che prepararono gl'Italiani alla vittoria. 11. Egli insegnò loro ad amar la loro patria com'egli stesso l'amava. 12. Cavour fu il grande uomo di stato che consigliò Vittorio Emanuele negli anni di lotta.

---

[1] Certain names of men, such as **Mazzini**, **Cavour**, etc., are used preferably without the definite article, on account of their very familiar usage.

13. Dal 1850 al 1861, anno in cui morì, egli fu al governo, ammirato e amato da tutto il popolo. 14. Egli portò la nazione alla vittoria del 1859, dalla quale ebbe principio il regno d'Italia. 15. Ma l'uomo che gl'Italiani ameranno sempre più con l'andar degli anni, è Garibaldi. 16. Chi non conosce qualche cosa della vita di questo famoso duce? 17. A capo dei suoi soldati dalla[1] camicia rossa, egli passò di vittoria in vittoria. 18. Dalle Alpi al mare tutti gl'Italiani vanno orgogliosi, e con ragione, di questi loro grandi uomini.

C. 1. I am studying Italian history now. 2. I am learning something about the great men of Italy. 3. Our professor often speaks of them to us in class. 4 By speaking of them to us, he teaches us many interesting things. 5. Yesterday, on finishing his lesson, he advised us to (di) read some books on the Italians' struggle for independence. 6. I am reading one of these books now. 7. This period of Italian history starts in (da) eighteen hundred twenty-one and ends with the Great War. 8. With the victory of Vittorio Veneto — October 24th–November 4th,[2] nineteen hundred eighteen — the Italians drove the Austrians beyond the Alps. 9. In reading Italian history, I admire more and more the Italian people.

D. 1. Italians are justly proud of the great men who helped them to (a) drive the enemy from their country. 2. Victor Emmanuel II, risking throne and life, was at the head of the struggle. 3. Cavour was the statesman who advised him and prepared the victory. 4. Mazzini, arousing the Italians with his books and his example, taught them to (ad) love their country and to (a) sacrifice everything to it. 5. In Garibaldi the Italians had a leader who brought them to victory. 6. In reading the history of the Great War, we see that Victor Emmanuel III, by taking his place at the head of his soldiers, followed the example of his grandfather. 7. Italians love and respect him as a father. 8. Great men are

---

[1] The preposition **da** has sometimes a descriptive meaning; in this case it should be translated by *with*. [2] No article before these dates.

now at the head of the government. 9. They are showing the people the path to (**da**) follow in order to give their country new glory.

E. *Oral.* 1. Che cosa abbiamo imparato in questa lezione? 2. Di chi ci parla spesso il nostro professore? 3. Che cosa ci ha egli consigliato di fare? 4. Qual è un interessante periodo della storia d'Italia? 5. Da che anno comincia la lotta degl'Italiani per l'indipendenza della loro patria? 6. Con quale vittoria gl'Italiani scacciarono gli Austriaci oltre le Alpi? 7. Quando ebbe luogo questa vittoria? 8. Chi fu Vittorio Emanuele II? 9. Chi fu l'uomo di stato che preparò la vittoria? 10. In quale anno morì? 11. Per quanti anni fu egli al governo? 12. Chi destò il popolo italiano coi suoi libri e col suo esempio? 13. Chi fu Garibaldi? 14. Di che colore erano le camice dei suoi soldati? 15. Chi è Vittorio Emanuele III? 16. Perchè gl'Italiani lo amano come un padre? 17. Quale esempio ha egli seguito? 18. Chi è adesso a capo del governo italiano? 19. Che cosa mostra egli al popolo italiano? 20. Chi è a capo del governo americano?

LESSON XXXI

106. Disjunctive Personal Pronouns. While the conjunctive personal pronouns (see § 97) are used only in connection with a verb, the pronouns listed below are used independently of it. Their most common usage is as objects of prepositions.

	SINGULAR			PLURAL	
1st *person*	me	me		noi	us
2d *person*	te	thee, you		voi	you
	lui	him		loro	them (*m. and f.*)
	lei	her			
3d *person*	esso	him, it		essi	them (*m.*)
	essa	her, it		esse	them (*f.*)
	Lei	you		Loro	you
	sè	himself, herself, itself, themselves, yourself, yourselves.			

Note that lui, lei and their plural, loro, are used only
with reference to persons, while esso, essa, essi and esse may
refer to persons, animals, or things.

107. Use of the Disjunctive Personal Pronouns. The
disjunctive personal pronouns are used in the following cases:

1.	**Lavoriamo con loro.**	We work with them.
	Studia da sè	He studies by himself.

After prepositions.

Note that instead of con me, con te, and con sè, the forms
meco, teco and seco are sometimes used.

2.	**Sei più alto di me.**	You are taller than I.

After comparatives.

3.	**Visiterò te ed essi.**	I shall visit you and them.
	Parla a lui e a lei.	He speaks to him and to her.

In place of the conjunctive, when the verb has two or more
direct or two or more indirect objects.

4.	**Seguirò voi.**	I shall follow *you*. (The un-emphatic form would be **Vi seguirò**)
	Amo te, non amo lui.	I love you, I don't love him.

In place of the conjunctive, for emphasis, clearness, or
contrast.

5.	**Io partirò, ma non lui.**	I shall depart, but not he.
	L'ha scritto lui stesso.	He himself has written it.
But:	**L'ho scritto io stesso.**	I myself have written it.

In place of the subject pronouns, for emphasis, but
only if the pronoun to be used is of the third person, singular
or plural. For greater emphasis, the adjective stesso may
be added .

6. Beato lui!   Happy he!

In exclamations.

7. Se io fossi lui.   If I were he.

When the pronoun stands in the predicate after the verb
essere. But note that *it is I, it is you,* etc. are **sono io, sei
tu, è lui, è lei, siamo noi, siete voi, sono loro.**

EXERCISE XXXI

Sicília Sicily

affari *m. plur.* business
assistente *m.* assistant
azione *f.* stock
banca (*or* banco) bank
cambiale *f.* note
cassa di risparmio savings department
cassiere *m.* cashier
conto corrente checking account
danaro money
depòsito deposit
informazione[1] *f.* information
interesse *m.* interest

obbligazione *f.* bond
sportello window (*of an office*)
ufficio office
usciere *m.* usher
vaglia *m.* money order

commerciale commercial
speciale special

depositare to deposit
emettere to issue
lasciare to leave (*something*)
menare to lead
prestare to lend
ritirare to draw, draw out
trattare to transact

A. (1) *Translate into Italian:* 1. I go with him. 2. I
respect you, not them. 3. He needs us. 4. I shall meet
him and her. 5. He does it for us. 6. It is I. 7. We
observed *you.* 8. She herself wishes it. 9. I myself returned there. 10. It was he. 11. He will read with us.
12. He sacrificed himself for her.

(2) *Give eight possible answers to each question:* 1. Chi
era là? 2. Chi l'ha ordinato? 3. Chi ha perduto
quest' orologio?

(3) *Fill in each blank with the present, present perfect,
past absolute and future (four forms) of the verb in paren-*

---

[1] Plural when more than one "piece of information" is meant.

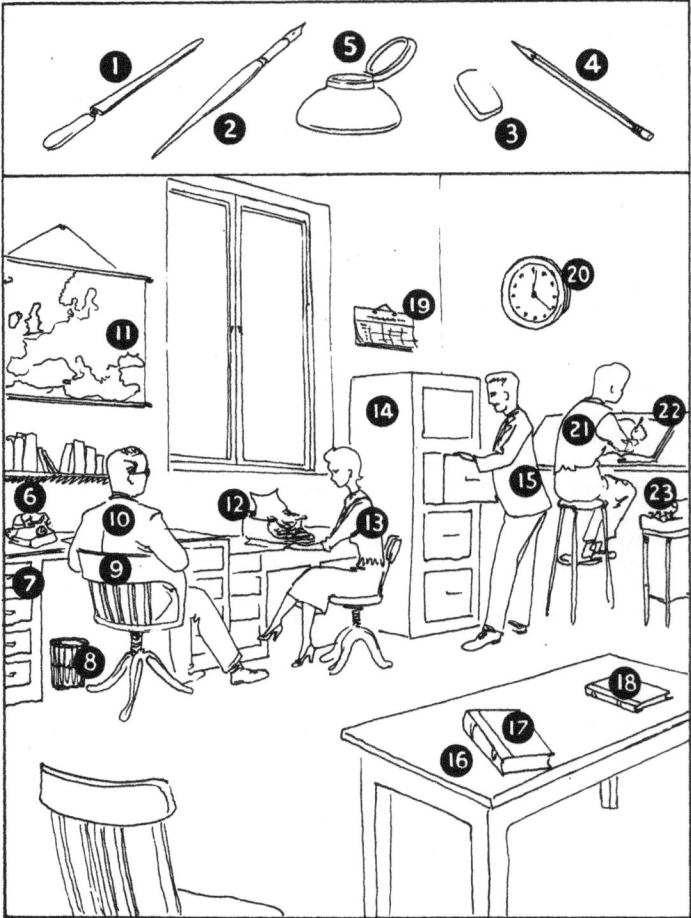

L'UFFICIO

(See page 287)

theses: 1. (*pulire*) Carlo —— la lavagna. 2. (*ripetere*) Mia cugina —— lo stesso sbaglio. 3. (*telefonare*) Noi —— ai nostri amici. 4. (*osservare*) Arturo e Alberto —— dei bei negozi. 5. (*applaudire*) Io —— solamente i buoni attori. 6. (*essere*) Tu —— in una cabina. 7. (*destare*) Elena —— il suo fratellino. 8. (*incontrare*) Voi —— ogni giorno qualche amico. 9. (*essere*) Carlo e io —— in campagna. 10. (*guarire*) Il medico —— quel povero ragazzo.

B. **Alla banca**

1. Vai alla banca adesso? 2. — Sì; vado tra qualche minuto. 3. — Andiamoci insieme allora! Mi presenterai al cassiere, che non conosco. 4. Che desideri da lui? 5. — Desidero di comprare delle obbligazioni. 6. — Io ho bisogno di vederlo per pagare del danaro per una cambiale che firmai tre mesi fa. 7. — Bene, così sarà utile a me e a te di parlargli; egli mi consiglierà quali obbligazioni comprare. 8. — Hai con te il danaro? 9. — No; sta depositato alla cassa di risparmio, ma lo ritirerò perchè non son contento dell'interesse che ricevo. 10. — Quanto ti danno? — Mi danno il tre e mezzo per cento. 11. Andando alla banca, Arturo mi parla delle banche italiane. 12. In Italia ci sono molte grandi banche, come la Banca d'Italia, il Banco di Napoli, il Banco di Sicilia, e la Banca Commerciale. 13. Alcune di queste banche hanno uffici anche in America. 14. Esse comprano e vendono azioni e obbligazioni, ricevono depositi a conto corrente e a interesse, fanno affari d'ogni specie. 15. Gl'Italiani che stanno in America vanno di solito a una di queste banche se desiderano di mandare del danaro in Italia. 16. Ma eccoci alla banca. 17. Davanti a ogni sportello vediamo signori e signore. 18. Degl'impiegati emettono vaglia, altri ricevono depositi, altri danno informazioni. 19. Un usciere mena Arturo e me all'ufficio

del cassiere. 20. Ma egli è occupato, e noi trattiamo i nostri affari con un suo assistente.

C. 1. Do you wish to (di) go with us to your bank this morning? 2. — I have nothing to (da) do, and shall be glad to (di) go with you. 3. I myself wish to (di) go there. 4. — Then let's go now. It's two o'clock, and they will close at three. 5. My cousins, Victor and Sylvia, go with me to the bank. 6. We take a carriage in order to arrive there in time. 7. Neither he nor she has ever been in this city. 8. I shall introduce them to the cashier, who is a friend of mine. 9. He wishes to (di) open a checking account, and she has some money to (da) deposit in (a) the savings department. 10. We arrive at the bank, and an usher leads us to the cashier's office.

D. 1. The bank is now full of people. 2. Some are there to (per) deposit money, others to (per) draw it out. 3. There are special windows for ladies. 4. But while other clerks are at the windows, special business is transacted by the cashier and his assistants. 5. They lend money on notes, issue money orders, and sell stocks and bonds. 6. Victor, isn't it you who wish to (di) open a checking account? 7. — Yes, it is I. 8. Victor and Sylvia are in the office with me. 9. I introduce him and her to the cashier, and the cashier gives them the information they need. 10. He gives him a paper to (da) sign, and leads her to (da) the clerk who receives deposits on (a) interest. 11. What interest do you give in this bank? 12. — We give (the)[1] four per cent.

E. *Oral.* 1. Qual è la sua banca? 2. Chi conosce Lei alla banca? 3. Quando va Lei alla banca? 4. Riceviamo interesse se depositiamo il nostro danaro a conto corrente? 5. Dove depositiamo il nostro danaro se desideriamo d'avere un interesse? 6. Che cosa vende una banca? 7. Conosce Lei qualche banca italiana? 8. Che hanno in America alcune di queste banche? 9. Che affari fanno? 10. Perchè vanno a una di queste banche gl'Italiani che stanno in

[1] the = il.

America? 11. Chi troviamo alla porta d'una banca?
12. Che cosa fa l'usciere d'una banca? 13. A che ora
aprono le banche in America? 14. A che ora chiudono?
15. A che ora finiscono di lavorare gl'impiegati d'una
banca? 16. Quando desideriamo di mandare del danaro,
che cosa facciamo? 17. Che cosa trattiamo nell'ufficio del
cassiere d'una banca? 18. È solo il cassiere nel suo ufficio?
19. Chi ci mena nel suo ufficio? 20. Che interesse danno
le banche di questa città?

LESSON XXXII

108. The Irregular Verb *sapere*

PRESENT INDICATIVE	PAST ABSOLUTE
I know, etc.	*I knew, etc.*
so	*seppi*
sai	sapesti
sa	*seppe*
sappiamo	sapemmo
sapete	sapeste
sanno	*seppero*

The irregularity of the past absolute should be carefully
noted. It affects three forms only: the 1st and 3d singular
and the 3d plural. These forms have in common an irregular
stressed stem and they have respectively the endings –i, –e,
–ero. The three other forms are perfectly regular, both in
stem and endings.

109. Irregular Past Absolute. What has been stated in
the preceding paragraph applies not only to the verb **sapere**,
but also to all irregular past absolutes in Italian, except
three: those of the verbs **essere, dare,** and **stare.**

110. The Past Absolute of Some Irregular Verbs

conoscere — *conobbi*		rispondere — *risposi*	
	conoscesti, etc.		rispondesti, etc.
mettere — *misi*		vedere — *vidi*	
	mettesti, etc.		vedesti, etc.
emettere — *emisi*		volere — *volli*	
	emettesti, etc.		volesti, etc.

111.   Meaning of *sapere* and *conoscere*

Sa questa parola?	Do you know this word?
Sa chi parlerà?	Do you know who will speak?
Sa cantare?	Do you know how to (Can you) sing?
Conosce la signora Marzetti?	Do you know Mrs. Marzetti?
Conosce quel ristorante?	Do you know that restaurant?

1. **Sapere** means *to know* a thing or a fact. It also renders the English *can* in the sense of *to know how*.

2. **Conoscere** means *to know, to be acquainted with*.

EXERCISE XXXII

assegno check	**aver l'abitudine di** to be used to
biglietti di banca paper money	**firmare** to endorse
dorso back	**identificare** to identify
firma signature	**passeggiare** to take a walk
moneta coin	**riconoscere** to recognize
tasca pocket	**rifiutare** to refuse
	riscuotere to cash
diverso different (*plur.* several)	**temere** to fear
nazionale national	
obbligato obliged	**affermativamente** affirmatively
vecchio old	**se** whether
	subito at once

A. (1) *Continue the following:* 1. Io so chi egli è, etc.
2. Io seppi chi egli era, etc. 3. Io misi la lettera alla
posta, etc. 4. Io non volli partire, etc. 5. Io risposi con

una cartolina, etc. 6. Non vidi io la vettura che passava? etc. 7. Io emisi un vaglia, etc. 8. Io so questa regola, etc.

(2) *Give for each verb in parentheses the correct form of the past absolute:* 1. Noi (*sapere*) dove andare. 2. Il signor Cusano (*volere*) ritornare subito. 3. Silvia non (*rispondere*) mai alle mie cartoline. 4. Essi (*mettere*) dei francobolli sulle lettere. 5. L'impiegato (*emettere*) un vaglia. 6. Io (*vedere*) quei signori al teatro. 7. Voi (*volere*) divertirvi. 8. I miei amici (*rispondere*) al mio saluto. 9. Arturo e Carlo (*sapere*) sorvegliarli. 10. Noi (*mettere*) i libri sullo scaffale. 11. Io (*volere*) far come lui. 12. Tu (*rispondere*) subito. 13. Egli non (*riconoscere*) sua sorella. 14. Io (*mettere*) la lampada sul tavolino. 15. Olga e Silvia mi (*vedere*) dopo molti anni. 16. Esse non mi (*riconoscere*). 17. Io non (*sapere*) la mia lezione. 18. La signorina Alessandri (*vedere*) ogni cosa. 19. I ragazzi (*volere*) andare in campagna. 20. Io (*riconoscere*) che avevo torto.

(3) *Insert the correct form of the present indicative of* sapere *or* conoscere *according to sense:* 1. Elena —— molte signore. 2. Noi —— a che ora il treno arriverà. 3. Essi non —— quel che fanno. 4. Io —— la lingua italiana e la francese. 5. —— voi quante persone arriveranno stasera? 6. Chi non —— che Roma è chiamata la Città Eterna? 7. Egli mi —— bene. 8. Noi non —— nessun teatro in questa città. 9. Noi —— che ogni regola ha qualche eccezione. 10. Tu —— che Dante è il primo poeta d'Italia.

B.   **Affari di banca**

1. Devo andare alla Prima Banca Nazionale per riscuotere un assegno. 2. Sa a che ora apriranno? 3. — Apriranno alle nove. 4. Bene, allora abbiamo venti minuti di tempo. 5. Conosce il cassiere? 6. — No, non lo conosco, ma conosco diversi impiegati in quella banca. 7. Vuole accompagnarmi, se non ha niente da fare? — Volentieri.

8. Passeggiando insieme, il signor Cini e io arriviamo alla banca. 9. — Sa a quale sportello dobbiamo andare, usciere? 10. L'usciere mi risponde che, per riscuotere un assegno, dobbiamo presentarci al secondo sportello. 11. Ha una penna stilografica, signor Cini? 12. Devo firmare il mio assegno e ho dimenticato la mia penna a casa. 13. Egli me la dà, e io metto la mia firma sul dorso dell'assegno. 14. Grazie, le sono molto obbligato. 15. L'impiegato riceve l'assegno e mi consegna il danaro. 16. Son cinquecento lire in biglietti di banca. 17. Non ho avuto bisogno d'essere identificato perchè alla banca mi conoscono. 18. Metto il danaro in tasca, e usciamo. 19. Alle dieci abbiamo un appuntamento, al nostro albergo, con degli amici americani. 20. Abbiamo ancora mezz'ora di tempo, e non sappiamo come occuparla. 21. L'albergo non è lontano, e possiamo arrivarci in pochi minuti. 22. Invito allora il signor Cini a prendere una tazza di caffè con me.

C. 1. Two days ago I saw on (per) the street my friend Arthur whom I had not met for (da) several years. 2. He did not recognize me, but I recognized him at once. 3. Where have you been all this time? 4. — My brother and I have been in Italy; we returned to (in) America this month. 5. He asked me where I was going, and I answered him [1] that I was taking a walk. 6. — I must go to the bank to (per) draw out some money. Do you know the cashier of the First National Bank? 7. — Yes, I know him very well; he is an old friend of mine. 8. Will you go [2] with me to the bank to (per) identify me? 9. I shall be greatly obliged to you. 10. I did not know how to refuse, and thus we went together.

D. 1. After a few minutes we were at the bank. 2. I saw the usher and called him. 3. Do you know whether the cashier is in his office? 4. He answered me affirmatively and led us to the cashier's office. 5. First I wanted to introduce Arthur to him, then we spoke of what my friend needed. 6. He wished to cash

---

[1] Translate, *to him.*   [2] Not a future.

a check he had received from home. 7. — Very well, sir; but you
(**voi**) forgot to (**di**) endorse it. Please sign here. 8. Arthur put
his signature on the back of the check. 9. — Do you want gold
or paper money? 10. I shall be very glad if you let (**farà**) me have
paper money. 11. I am not used to carrying (**portare**) gold coins
in [my] pocket and I fear to (**di**) lose them. 12. When we went
out, an automobile passed in front of us; my sisters were in it,
but they didn't see us.

E. *Oral.* 1. Chi incontrai per la via alcuni giorni fa?
2. Mi riconobbe egli? 3. Perchè non mi riconobbe? 4. Da
quanti anni non m'aveva veduto? 5. Dov'era stato in
questi anni? 6. Quand'egli mi domandò dove andavo, che
cosa gli risposi? 7. Dove voleva egli andare? 8. Per far
che cosa? 9. Conosceva egli il cassiere della Prima Banca
Nazionale? 10. Lo conosco io? 11. Lei chi conosce alla
sua banca? 12. Se io non conosco nessuno alla banca,
posso riscuotere un assegno? 13. Che cosa faccio allora?
14. Che cosa risponde Lei a chi le fa un favore? 15. Sa a
che ora le banche chiudono in questa città? 16. Sa chi è
l'impiegato che sta allo sportello dove riscuotiamo gli as-
segni? 17. Che cosa mettiamo sul dorso d'un assegno per
riscuoterlo? 18. Con che cosa firmiamo? 19. Non di-
mentica Lei mai di portar la sua penna stilografica? 20. Preferisce biglietti di banca a monete d'oro? 21. Perchè?
22. Ha Lei l'abitudine di portare oro con sè?

LESSON XXXIII

Review

A. *Continue the following:* 1. Io faccio ogni cosa da **me**, tu fai
ogni cosa da **te**, etc. 2. Io do delle frutta a lui e a lei, etc. 3. Io
vado con la signorina Ricci, etc. 4. Io sto lavorando per loro, etc.
5. Io so di che parlerà, etc. 6. Io non volli uscire, etc. 7. Non
risposi io subito? etc. 8. Io seppi la lezione d'ieri, etc.

B. *Review Questions:* 1. Are there masculine nouns ending in –a ? Mention some and tell how their plural is formed. 2. Are there nouns in –a of both genders ? Give a few examples. 3. Mention some nouns in –o which have a feminine plural in –a. 4. How are quello and bello inflected before a noun ? 5. What difference of meaning is there between codesto and quello ? 6. Give the three most important adverbs of place. 7. When is the relative pronoun che used ? 8. When is the relative pronoun cui used ? 9. What meaning has chi as a relative pronoun ? 10. How do you form the negative imperative, second person singular ? 11. Give in Italian the hours from noon to midnight. 12. Give the conjunctive pronouns used as direct objects. 13. Give the conjunctive pronouns used as indirect objects. 14. Give the rules concerning their usage. 15. Which are the conjunctive adverbs ? 16. Explain the Italian progressive construction. 17. How is an adverb of manner formed from an adjective ? 18. Give a complete list of the disjunctive personal pronouns. 19. Which is their most general usage ? 20. In what other cases are they used ? 21. What difference of meaning is there between sapere and conoscere ? 22. Explain the conjugation of an irregular past absolute and give an example.

C. *Supply the correct form of the past absolute of the verb given in the infinitive:* 1. (*sapere*) Io non —— che fare. 2. (*volere*) Essi —— andare allo stabilimento di bagni. 3. (*rispondere*) Noi —— affermativamente. 4. (*sapere*) Tu —— perchè ell'era con noi. 5. (*sapere*) Caterina non —— quel che era buono per lei. 6. (*vedere*) Io —— il piroscafo che partiva. 7. (*riconoscere*) Egli lo —— presto. 8. (*mettere*) Esse —— ogni cosa in ordine. 9. (*volere*) Arturo —— rifiutare. 10. (*rispondere*) Io —— due giorni dopo. 11. (*sapere*) I ragazzi non —— la loro lezione. 12. (*vedere*) Carlo e Arturo —— che avevano torto. 13. (*mettere*) Io —— i libri sulla scrivania. 14. (*vedere*) Non —— tu chi era nel salotto ?

D. *Place the definite article before each of the following nouns, then give the plural of both article and noun:* programma, banca, farmacia, medico, frutto, uomo, moglie, uovo, cuoco, cuoca, bue, labbro, centinaio, occhio, faccia, violinista, amico, sposalizio, oca, zio.

E. *Replace the words in parentheses by their correct Italian equivalents:* 1. Ammiro il (*beautiful*) mare d'Italia. 2. Egli è un (*great*) maestro. 3. (*That*) libro (*which*) Lei ha, è mio. 4. La signora (*to whom*) Lei offrì la sedia, è mia sorella. 5. (*He who*) dorme, non piglia pesci. 6. (*Be*) calmo, fratello mio! 7. Arriverà (*tonight*). 8. La lettera che (*I am copying*) è lunga. 9. Parlava (*to me and to her*). 10. Questa è la chiesa di (*Saint Victor*). 11. Ecco il ragazzo (*whom*) chiamerai. 12. Non ho nessuna penna (*with which*) scrivere. 13. Il signore (*whose*) sorella Lei conosce, sarà qui tra due giorni. 14. Partirò (*this morning*). 15. Presterò del danaro (*to you, but not to him*). 16. Un (*good*) anello costa molto. 17. Egli ha comprato (*some beautiful*) cavalli. 18. Mi ricordo dei (*beautiful*) anni passati.

F. *Explain the meaning of the following table, and give examples:*

GENDER	F. (M.)	M. F.	M. F.	M.	F.
NOUN ENDINGS *Sing.*	–a	–e	–i	–o	–à
Plur.	–à –e –i	–è –i	–i	–ò –i –a	–à

G. *Translate into Italian:* 1. He will sit with you (*four ways*). 2. I shall introduce him to her. 3. Let's close the door. 4. Don't write to him (**tu** *form*). 5. It was she. 6. He himself signed that paper. 7. They will sell it to you (*four ways*). 8. He was speaking of it to me. 9. I need him and you (*four ways*). 10. He is afraid of us. 11. I am inviting him and her. 12. If I help you, will you help me (*four ways*)? 13. Be glad (**tu** *and* **voi** *forms*). 14. It is they. 15. Don't be capricious (**tu** *and* **voi** *forms*). 16. You give it to them. 17. He was washing himself. 18. She herself dusted it this morning.

H. *Give the present participle and the perfect participle, and then the positive and negative imperative, of each of the following verbs:*

scacciare	vedere	finire	essere
avere	preferire	presentare	perdere

M

LESSON XXXIV

112. **Conditional of Model Verbs**

I should or *would buy, etc.*	*I should* or *would sell, etc.*	*I should* or *would finish, etc.*
comprer ɛi	vender ɛi	finir ɛi
comprer esti	vender esti	finir esti
comprer ɛbbe	vender ɛbbe	finir ɛbbe
comprer emmo	vender emmo	finir emmo
comprer este	vender este	finir este
comprer ɛbbero	vender ɛbbero	finir ɛbbero

Compare the stem of this tense with that of the future. As for the endings, note that they are the same for all Italian verbs and that, in the first singular, the third singular and the third plural, the stressed e has the open sound. Note also that the first person plural differs from the first person plural of the future by having a double m.

113. **Conditional of *essere* and *avere***

I should or *would be, etc.*		*I should* or *would have, etc.*	
sarɛi	saremmo	avrɛi	avremmo
saresti	sareste	avresti	avreste
sarɛbbe	sarɛbbero	avrɛbbe	avrɛbbero

114. **Conditional Perfect**

I should or *would have bought, etc.*	*I should* or *would have sold, etc.*	*I should* or *would have finished, etc.*
avrɛi comprato	avrɛi venduto	avrɛi finito
avresti comprato, etc.	avresti venduto, etc.	avresti finito, etc.

I should or *would have been, etc.*	*I should* or *would have had, etc.*
sarɛi stato, –a	avrɛi avuto
saresti stato, –a, etc.	avresti avuto, etc.

115. Use of the Conditional. The conditional is used in the following cases:

1. **Non glielo mostrerebbe.**	He would not show it to him.

To express what is uncertain or indefinite in the principal clause.

2. **Dissero che partirebbero.**	They said they would leave *(and they did)*.
Dissero che sarebbero partiti.	They said they would leave *(and they did not)*.

To express future time in relation to a past tense of a verb of thinking, believing, saying, etc.[1] When the statement made has failed to come true, the conditional perfect is used.

3. **Amerei uscire.**	I should like to go out.

In a statement or request expressed with deference.

4. **Secondo lui, il presidente sarebbe ammalato.**	According to him, the president is ill.

To express what is reported by hearsay, or on the authority of somebody else.

5. In the conclusion of conditional sentences (*see* § 152).

116.   Idiomatic Use of *a*

I miei amici sono a Pisa.	My friends are in Pisa.
BUT: **Questi eventi ebbero luogo in Napoli.**	These events took place in Naples.

Before names of cities, the English *in* is generally rendered by **a**, but it may be rendered by **in** if the meaning is *within*.

---

[1] **Dicono che partiranno** expresses future time in relation to the present.

EXERCISE XXXIV [1]

A. (1) *Continue the following:* 1. Io lavorerei ogni giorno, etc. 2. Io prenderei una vettura, etc. 3. Non mi divertirei io? etc. 4. Io non sarei così orgoglioso, etc. 5. Io avrei osservato quei negozi, etc. 6. Io sarei stato contento, etc.

(2) *Supply for each verb given in the infinitive the correct form of the conditional, or the conditional perfect, or both, according to sense:* 1. (*partire*) Noi —— volentieri per l'Italia. 2. (*comprare*) Essi —— quest'automobile, ma non hanno danaro. 3. (*comprare*) Noi —— quella casa, ma non avevamo abbastanza danaro. 4. (*mandare*) Secondo lei, suo padre —— una lettera al tuo. 5. (*desiderare*) Io —— un po' di burro. 6. (*ritornare*) Dichiarò che ——, e ritornò. 7. (*preferire*) Egli —— dimenticarla. 8. (*invitare*) Non le —— tu? 9. (*avere*) Seguendo il suo esempio, voi —— torto. 10. (*ritornare*) Dichiarò che ——, e non ritornò. 11. (*arrivare*) Partendo da casa alle otto, noi —— in ritardo. 12. (*firmare*) Son sicuro che mio fratello non —— questa cambiale. 13. (*perdere*) Pensavo che voi vi ——. 14. (*essere*) Da quel che questo signore scrive, Mario e Vittorio —— soli l'estate scorsa.

B. **Raffaello Sanzio**

Raffaello Sanzio nacque a Urbino nel 1483, di venerdì santo. Era ancora nella sua prima giovinezza, quando andò a Perugia per studiarvi la pittura sotto la direzione del celebre pittore Vannucci, chiamato il Perugino. L'alunno diventò ben presto un maestro.

Raffaello andò poi a Firenze per farvi la conoscenza di Leonardo da Vinci e di Michelangelo. In questa città

---

[1] The words used in this and the remaining exercises will be found at the end of the volume.

SELF-PORTRAIT BY RAPHAEL
Galleria Uffizi, Firenze

lavorò con tale ispirazione che, all'età di vent'anni, era già citato tra i grandi artisti del tempo. Fu a Roma però che il suo nome diventò immortale. Presentato alla corte papale, egli vi ricevè tutti gli onori e i riguardi d'un principe. I suoi affreschi, nel Vaticano, rappresentano la vera perfezione dell'arte.

Francesco Primo, re di Francia, cercò ogni mezzo per attirarlo alla sua corte, ma non ci riuscì e dovè contentarsi con l'ordinargli dei quadri. Raffaello dipinse per lui un *San Michele* e una *Sacra Famiglia*.

Le *Vergini* di Raffaello hanno qualche cosa di divino. Il suo capolavoro è la *Trasfigurazione*. Raffaello morì il venerdì santo dell'anno 1520, all'età di trentasette anni.

C. 1. Would you like to go to (in) Italy next summer? 2. I shall sail for Genoa in June with my father and mother. 3. How many months will you spend there? 4. — We shall spend there only two months. 5. I should like to remain the whole summer in that beautiful country, but I must be here in September. 6. I must return to (in) America in time for the opening of the schools. 7. My father thinks also that it would cost too much money to spend three months in Italy. 8. Where would you advise me to (di) go? 9. — I would advise you to (di) visit by all means (a ogni costo) the large and famous cities, such as Rome, Naples, Florence, Milan and Venice. 10. You (Loro) would, however, have great pleasure also in visiting some of the small towns where tourists usually do not go; as, for instance, Urbino. I was there two years ago.

D. 1. Raphael Sanzio was born in Urbino and died in Rome at thirty-seven years of age. 2. I have often heard his [first] name, but I would not have known his surname. 3. He was still young when his first works put him among the great painters of his time; such as (= as they would be), Leonardo da Vinci, Masaccio, Bramante and Buonarroti. 4. Would you have known that Buonarroti is that famous painter, sculptor, architect and poet

generally called Michelangelo? 5. Raphael studied painting under
his father, but soon he went to Florence to (a) perfect himself.
6. The Pope called him to Rome where he worked for years at the
frescoes of the Vatican. 7. At the death of Bramante,[1] Pope Leo X[2]
put him at the head of all the other artists who were working in
Rome. 8. Pope Leo X was a great patron of arts. 9. Without
him, artists would not have found so much encouragement in that
glorious epoch. 10. Raphael would have left us other masterpieces
like his *Transfiguration*, but he died in his youth.

E. *Oral.* 1. Quale città italiana le piacerebbe visitare?
2. Chi nacque a Urbino? 3. In che secolo nacque? 4. Chi
era Raffaello? 5. Qual era il suo cognome? 6. Sa Lei il
nome di qualche altro gran pittore di quel tempo? 7. In
che secolo lavorarono questi pittori? 8. Sa Lei il nome
d'un famoso quadro di Raffaello? 9. In quali città lavorò
Raffaello? 10. Dove sono gli affreschi di questo gran
pittore? 11. Che cosa è il Vaticano? 12. Chi era papa
al tempo di Raffaello? 13. Dove morì Raffaello?
14. Quanti anni aveva quando morì? 15. Qual era il
cognome di Michelangelo? 16. Era Michelangelo solamente pittore? 17. Vi erano altri pittori nella famiglia di
Raffaello? 18. Dov'è il Vaticano? 19. Dov'è Roma?
20. Come chiamiamo Roma di solito?

LESSON XXXV

117. **Comparison.** An adjective may express three degrees of any given quality: the positive (the adjective
itself), the comparative, and the superlative.

The comparative may be of equality or inequality; the
superlative may be relative or absolute.

---

[1] Use no article before *Bramante* and *Pope*.   [2] **Leone Decimo.**

118. The Comparative of Equality

Mario non è così alto come te. *or* **Mario non è alto come te.**	Marius is not so tall as you are.
Ella è tanto ricca quanto Maria *or* **Ella è ricca quanto Maria.**	She is as rich as Mary.
Egli è tanto studioso quanto intelligente.	He is as studious as he is intelligent.

Equality is expressed by the correlative forms **così . . . come,** or **tanto . . . quanto,** which stand for the English *as . . . as* or *so . . . as.*

Note that **così** and **tanto** may be omitted.

119. The Comparative of Inequality

1. **Luigi è più diligente.**	Louis is more diligent.
Arturo è meno diligente.	Arthur is less diligent.

Inequality is expressed by **più,** *more,* or **meno,** *less.*

2. (*a*) **Lo studio è più grande del salotto.**	The study is larger than the parlor.
Egli è più alto di te.	He is taller than you.
Ho meno di venti lire.	I have less than twenty lire.

Than is **di** before nouns, pronouns, or numerals.

(*b*) **Do a te più danaro che a lui.**	I give more money to you than to him.
È più acqua che vino.	It is more water than wine.
Tu sei più invidioso che Paolo.	You are more envious than Paul.

But *than* is rendered by **che:** (1) if the noun or pronoun which forms the second term of the comparison is preceded by a preposition; (2) if the comparison is between two nouns, and is not based on any distinct quality; (3) if by using **di** there is the possibility of **di** being interpreted *of.* Thus, in the third example, if *than* had been rendered by **di,** the sentence might have been taken to mean: *you are more envious of Paul.*

(c) **La sala è più lunga che larga.**	The hall is longer than it is wide.
Ama più dare che ricevere.	He likes to give more than to receive.

Than is always **che** before an adjective, an adverb, an infinitive, or a participle.

(d) **Studia più che non** (*or* **di quel che**) **deve.**	He studies more than he has to.

Than is **che non** or **di quel che** before an inflected verb.

120. Personal Pronouns as Second Terms of a Comparison. From the examples in the preceding section it can be seen that a personal pronoun used as the second term of a comparison is rendered in Italian by its disjunctive form (*see* § 107, 2).

121. The Definite Article before Names of Countries, etc.

1. **l'America** America	**la Francia** France
la Lombardia Lombardy	**la Corsica** Corsica

A name of a continent, country, province, or large island, takes the definite article in Italian.

2. **Il cielo d'Italia.**	Italy's sky *or* The Italian sky.
Siamo in Toscana.	We are in Tuscany.
But: **Le città del Canadà.**	Canada's cities.
La Francia è più grande dell'Italia.	France is larger than Italy.
Siamo nella bella Toscana	We are in beautiful Tuscany.

After the prepositions **di** or **in**, however, no article is used, provided that the name of the continent, country, province,

or large island, is feminine, ends in –a, and is not accompanied
by any qualifying adjective; and provided also, in the case
of di, that preposition and noun are equivalent to an adjective
of nationality, as shown in the first example.

EXERCISE XXXV

A. (1) *Supply the Italian equivalent of* than *in each of
the following sentences:* 1. Egli è più giovane —— sua sorella.
2. Ho più —— cinquanta libri. 3. Fu meno studioso ——
lei. 4. Ell'ama più leggere —— scrivere. 5. Sei più stanco
—— io sono. 6. C'erano più signore qua —— là. 7. Scrivono più lettere a Lei —— a me. 8. Arturo è meno studioso
—— te. 9. Ci sono più signori —— signore. 10. Aveva
meno amici —— noi —— pensavamo. 11. La camera mia
è più grande —— la sua. 12. Codesto libro è più interessante
—— quello. 13. Ell'era più stanca —— ammalata. 14. Olga
è più giovane —— mostra. 15. Avremo più alunne ——
alunni. 16. Il signor Balbi era più vecchio —— sua moglie.
17. Il treno era più in ritardo —— temevo. 18. Ella ha
meno —— diciotto anni.

(2) *Replace the pronouns in parentheses by their correct
Italian equivalents:* 1. Sono più contento di ·(*he*). 2. Egli
era meno calmo di (*I*). 3. Siamo meno orgogliosi di (*you* [1]).
4. Silvia era più elegante di (*she*). 5. Sei più pigro di (*he*).
6. Son più ammalato di (*you* [1]). 7. Essi furono più pronti
di (*we*). 8. Siete più poveri di (*they*). 9. Quello scrittore
è più famoso di (*he*). 10. Egli era meno attivo di (*we*).

(3) *Translate into Italian:* · 1. He was in Piedmont.
2. The sky of Italy is very blue. 3. America is our country.
4. We were in beautiful Liguria. 5. I like the language of
Italy. 6. Naples is in Campania. 7. Rome is in Latium.
8. The Eternal City is the capital of Italy.

[1] Four ways.

B. Geografia dell'Italia

Pochi paesi hanno ricevuto dalla natura confini così precisi e belli come quelli dell'Italia: le Alpi e il mare.

I paesi che confinano con l'Italia sono: la Francia, la Svizzera, l'Austria, e la Iugoslavia.

L'Italia è divisa nelle seguenti diciotto regioni:

I. *Italia Settentrionale:* 1. il Piemonte, 2. la Liguria, 3. la Lombardia, 4. l'Emilia, 5. il Trentino, 6. il Veneto, 7. la Venezia Giulia.

II. *Italia Centrale:* 1. la Toscana, 2. le Marche, 3. l'Umbria, 4. il Lazio, 5. gli Abruzzi.

III. *Italia Meridionale:* 1. la Campania, 2. la Puglia, 3. la Basilicata, 4. la Calabria.

IV. *Italia Insulare:* 1. la Sicilia, 2. la Sardegna.

Importanti gruppi di popolazione italiana abitano territorii non-italiani, quali l'isola di Corsica e la contea di Nizza (oggi tutte e due provincie della Repubblica francese); il Ticino, un cantone della Svizzera, così chiamato dal fiume che lo bagna, e l'isola di Malta, colonia inglese, a sud della Sicilia.

I fiumi principali d'Italia sono il Po, l'Adige, il Tevere, l'Arno e il Piave.

L'Italia è famosa per la straordinaria bellezza dei suoi laghi. Il Lago Maggiore, il Lago di Lugano, e quelli di Como, d'Iseo, e di Garda, sono appiè delle Alpi. Nell' Italia Centrale sono importanti il Lago Trasimeno e quello di Bolsena.

C. 1. Northern Italy has seven regions; Central Italy, five; Southern Italy, four; and Insular Italy, two. 2. Sardinia is larger than Corsica, but smaller than Sicily. 3. In Italy there are more mountains than plains. 4. Lombardy is richer than Tuscany, but a journey through Tuscany is more interesting than a journey through Lombardy. 5. Rome, the Eternal City and Italy's capital, has less than seven hundred thousand inhabitants. 6. Milan has more inhabitants than Rome, but Naples is larger than Rome or Milan. 7. The Po is longer than any (qualsiasi) other river of Italy. 8. It is almost twice as long as the Arno. 9. The Piave, so famous in the history of the Great War, is not so long as The Adige. 10. The Adige passes through the cities of Trento and Verona; the Po, through Turin, Piacenza and Cremona.

D. 1. In Latium there is only one important river, the Tiber; but what river more than this [one] evokes memories of a glorious past? 2. Florence and Pisa are on the Arno. 3. Pisa is now a small city with a famous university. 4. Once, however, Pisa was almost as important as Florence. 5. Many Italian cities are rich in (di) natural beauties, but none is so beautiful as Naples, with its magnificent bay. 6. Naples' beauties are more natural than artistic. 7. Rome, Florence, Milan and Venice are all richer in (di) beautiful churches and glorious monuments than Naples. 8. But in the museum of Naples we find a larger and richer collection of Greek and Roman antiquities than in any (qualsiasi) other museum in (di) the world. 9. There are, in that museum, more statues than paintings. 10. A journey through Italy is more fascinating than we imagine.

E. *Oral.* 1. Quali sono i confini d'Italia? 2. Quali sono i paesi che confinano con l'Italia? 3. In quante regioni è divisa l'Italia? 4. Quali sono le regioni dell'Italia Settentrionale? 5. Quali sono le regioni dell'Italia Centrale? 6. Quali sono le regioni dell'Italia Meridionale? 7. Quali sono le due grandi isole italiane? 8. Quale isola, provincia francese, é abitata da numerosi italiani? 9. In quale isola, colonia inglese, si trovano gruppi italiani? 10. Qual è la capitale d'Italia? 11. Com'è chiamata? 12. Com'è chiamata la regione in cui si trova? 13. Qual è la città italiana che ha più abitanti delle altre? 14. Perchè è così bella, Napoli? 15. Quale fiume è più lungo degli altri fiumi d'Italia? 16. Per quali città passa? 17. Quale fiume evoca gloriose memorie? 18. Quale fiume passa per Firenze? 19. Perchè è famoso il Piave? 20. Quali sono i principali laghi italiani?

LESSON XXXVI

122.   The Present Indicative of Some Irregular Verbs

dire [1] *to say, tell*	*udire to hear*	*venire to come*
dico	ɔdo	vɛngo
dici	ɔdi	viɛni
dice	ɔde	viɛne
diciamo	udiamo	veniamo
dite	udite	venite
dícono	ɔdono	vɛngono

123.   The Past Absolute of Some Irregular Verbs

chiudere	— *chiusi*		rimanere	— *rimasi*
	chiudesti, etc.			rimanesti, etc.
dire	— *dissi*		scendere	— *scesi*
	dicesti, etc.			scendesti, etc.
lɛggere	— *lɛssi*		scrivere	— *scrissi*
	leggesti, etc.			scrivesti, etc.
prɛndere	— *presi*		venire	— *venni*
	prendesti, etc.			venisti, etc.

124.   Idiomatic Present

Aspɛtto da due ore *or*   I have been waiting two hours.
Son due ore che aspɛtto.

È un anno che sono in Italia *or*   I have been in Italy one year
Sono in Italia da un anno.   (*and I am still there,* hence
                                         the present tense).

BUT: Siamo stati un anno in   We have been in Italy one year
Italia.   (*we are not there now,* hence
                                         the present perfect).

To express an act or state that continues from the past into the present, the present tense is used in Italian, while in English the present perfect is used.

[1] **Dire is a contraction of dicere.**

125.   Orthographical Changes of Certain Verbs

1.   peccare to sin: **pecchi, pecchiamo, peccherà,** etc.
      litigare to quarrel: **litighi, litigherà,** etc.

Verbs in –care or –gare insert **h** after the **c** or **g** whenever these letters precede **e** or **i.**

2.   lasciare to leave: **lasci, lasceremo,** etc.
      mangiare to eat: **mangiamo, mangerete,** etc.

Verbs in –ciare or –giare drop the **i** before **e** or **i.**

3.   soffiare to blow: **soffi, soffiamo,** etc.

Other verbs in –iare drop the **i** before another **i.**

4.   mescere to pour: **mesciuto** but **mesco, mescono,** etc.

Verbs in –cere or –gere insert **i** after the **c** or **g** only before the **u** of the past participle.

EXERCISE XXXVI

A. (1) *Continue the following:* 1. Io dico tutto a **mia** madre, tu dici tutto a **tua** madre, etc. 2. Io non odo niente, etc. 3. Io vengo con lei, etc. 4. Io lessi un libro molto interessante, etc. 5. Io scesi dal piano superiore, etc. 6. Io venni a casa di buon'ora, etc.

(2) *Give for each verb in parentheses the correct form of the present indicative:* 1. Voi (*dire*) che Mario sarà qui. 2. Essi (*udire*) che noi veniamo. 3. Arturo non (*venire*) più a scuola. 4. Essi (*dire*) che egli è ammalato. 5. Anch'io l'(*udire*) dire. 6. Non (*venire*) le sue sorelle stasera? 7. Non lo (*sapere*) io, e nessuno qui lo (*sapere*). 8. Noi non (*volere*) aspettare. 9. Chi lo (*potere*) dire? 10. Noi (*dovere*) partire domani mattina.

(3) *Give for each verb in parentheses the correct form of the past absolute:* 1. Io non (*scendere*) dall'automobile. 2. Egli

(*rimanere*) a casa con sua zia. 3. Che cosa (*dire*) essi?
4. Le sue cugine non (*venire*). 5. Tu (*scrivere*) una lettera,
ma io ne (*scrivere*) due. 6. Carlo (*prendere*) due o tre libri. 7. Anch'essi (*leggere*) questo romanzo. 8 Prima egli
(*chiudere*) la porta e poi la finestra. 9. Io (*venire*) ieri sera,
ma non lo trovai. 10. Essi mi (*scrivere*) che erano in Italia.

(4) *Write on the board the Italian translation of the following,
rendering the English you, whenever it occurs, in the* **tu** *form:*
1. We shall begin. 2. You forget. 3. You eat. 4. We
pay. 5. We watch. 6. You advise. 7. You risk. 8. We
shall sacrifice. 9. I shall expel. 10. You study. 11. They
will leave something. 12. They will begin now. 13. We
shall forget. 14. You pay. 15. We shall pay. 16. You
sacrifice everything.

B. **Bonaparte**

Nel principio del secolo scorso l'Italia salutò un liberatore
in Napoleone I, poichè egli sembrava destinato a darle unità
e indipendenza. Ecco come, interpretando le aspirazioni
italiane, cantava allora il poeta Vincenzo Monti:

> Bell'Italia, amate sponde,
>   pur vi torno a riveder!
>   Trema in petto e si confonde
>   l'alma oppressa dal piacer.
> Tua bellezza che di pianti
>   fonte amara ognor ti fu,
>   di stranieri e crudi amanti
>   t'avea posta in servitù.
> Bonaparte al tuo periglio
>   dal mar Libico volò;
>   vide il pianto del tuo ciglio
>   e il suo fulmine impugnò.

Ma Napoleone, italiano di razza, amava la Francia più
dell'Italia. A suo fratello Luigi, che gli proponeva di dare

unità politica all'Italia, egli rispose: « Ciò non farò mai, perchè in tal modo gl'Italiani potrebbero [1] diventare superiori ai Francesi. » Egli mutò molte cose nella penisola, ma ne conservò la divisione in piccoli stati, che era stata causa di tanti mali per gl'Italiani. Uno di questi stati, nella parte settentrionale del paese, ebbe nome di Regno Italico, ma in sostanza fu come una provincia francese.

Napoleone agognava a dominare il mondo, ma la sfortunata campagna di Russia dissipò i suoi sogni ambiziosi e affrettò la sua caduta. Con la disfatta di Waterloo il suo impero crollò, e il trattato di Vienna, nel 1815, restituì le cose d'Europa allo stato di prima.

C. 1. Napoleon was born (**nacque**) at Ajaccio, in the island of Corsica, in 1769. 2. Corsica had always been an Italian island, but in 1768 the Republic of Genoa sold it to France. 3. Napoleon was eleven years old when his family sent him to a military school in France. 4. He was [an] officer of the French army in the years of the Revolution. 5. During the Reign of Terror he took part in (**a**) the siege of Toulon, where he acquired [a] great reputation. 6. Napoleon's sympathies were all for France. 7. He had forgotten his Italian origin. 8. In 1796 he married Josephine Beauharnais. 9. In the same year he left France to (**per**) assume command [2] of the army which the Republic had sent to (**in**) Italy. 10. Some years after he attempted the conquest of Egypt, and acquired new glory.

D. 1. At the beginning of the last century, Napoleon returned to (**in**) Italy. 2. His new army crossed the Alps, occupied Milan, and freed Lombardy from the Austrians, after glorious victories. 3. He came to Italy, greeted as a liberator. 4. Let us not forget that the Italian people considered [3] him as a fellow-patriot. 5. Monti, a great Italian poet, wrote an ode which expressed [4] these feelings. 6. But he loved France more than Italy. 7. He did not follow his brother's advice, and said: " I shall never unite Italy."

---

[1] *could.*
[2] Use the definite article.
[3] Use a singular form.
[4] Use the past descriptive.

8. Italians will never forget these words.   9. We have been studying the Italian language one year, and our professor has spoken to
us more than once about (di) Napoleon.   10. We find his adventurous life very interesting.

E. *Oral.*   1. Dove   nacque   Napoleone   Bonaparte?
2. Dov'è Ajaccio?   3. Che lingua parla il popolo di Corsica?   4. L'isola di Corsica è sempre stata francese?
5. Quale repubblica la vendè alla Francia?   6. Dove
andò Napoleone quando era ragazzo?   7. Chi lo mandò
in Francia?   8. A quale assedio prese egli parte nel 1793?
9. La Repubblica Francese dove lo mandò poi?   10. Quale
altra conquista tentò egli?   11. Quando ritornò in Italia?
12. Come lo salutò il popolo italiano?   13. Chi scrisse
un'ode salutando Napoleone?   14. Napoleone amava molto
l'Italia?   15. Qual paese amava egli?   16. Che cosa proponeva il fratello di Napoleone?   17. Che cosa gli rispose
Napoleone?   18. Che cosa desiderava egli?   17. In quale
anno ebbe luogo la battaglia di Waterloo?   20. Dove morì
Napoleone?

LESSON XXXVII

126.   **The Relative Superlative**

Questo è il più gran teatro della città.	This is the largest theater in the city.
Egli è il più alto.	He is the tallest (*or* taller).
Giovanni è il meno studioso della classe.	John is the least studious in the class.
Egli è l'alunno meno studioso.	He is the least studious pupil.

The relative superlative is formed by placing the definite
article before a comparative of inequality.   If, however, the
superlative follows a noun which already has a definite
article, no other article is required.

Note that there is no distinction between the comparative with the definite article and the superlative relative (see the second example).   Note also that *in* after a superlative is rendered by **di**.

127.   **Reflexive Verbs**

1. **Ci divertiamo.**	We amuse ourselves.
Mostratevi.	Show yourselves.
Si rispettano.	They respect themselves, *or* They respect each other.

A verb the object of which is the same person as its subject is called a reflexive verb.   Any active verb may be made reflexive by the use of the conjunctive pronouns **mi, ti, si, ci,** and **vi** (*see* §§ 97, 98, *and* 100).   As explained in § 97, 4, the plural reflexive pronouns are often used with a reciprocal meaning.

2. Ti sei pentito.	You have repented.
Ci siamo scusati.	We have excused ourselves.

Reflexive verbs are conjugated in the perfect tenses with **essere,** and the past participle agrees with the subject (*see* § 64, 1).

As shown in the first example, certain verbs that are not reflexive in English are so in Italian.

128. Use of the Reflexive Verbs.   The reflexive verbs are used in the following cases:

1. **Si vestì in pochi minuti.**	He dressed himself in a few minutes.
Me ne vergogno.	I feel ashamed of it.

In expressions which in Italian are essentially reflexive in character, whether they are so in English or not.

2. Si toccò il mento.	He touched his chin.
Mi tolsi il cappello.	I took off my hat.

In order to avoid the use of the possessive with parts of the body or clothing.

3. Si parla italiano.	Italian is spoken.
Molte cose si dicono.	Many things are said.

In the third person, singular or plural, translating an English passive verb with agent unexpressed.

4. Si fa così.	One does so, we do so, they do so, etc.
Si deve lavorare.	One must work, people must work, etc.
Si è felici.	One is happy.
Si è stati felici.	One has been happy.

In the third person singular, to render the impersonal *one, we, they, people,* etc. As shown in the third example, the verb **essere,** although used in the singular, takes a following adjective (and the past participle, if the tense is a perfect) in the plural. Other verbs, such as **restare, rimanere, diventare, divenire,** etc. often follow the same construction.

EXERCISE XXXVII

A. (1) *Translate into Italian:* 1. This is the most comfortable room. 2. The least heavy suitcase was that of Miss Perrelli. 3. That was our most difficult lesson. 4. The nearest house was empty. 5. The ruby is the more precious of these two stones. 6. Charles is the most diligent pupil in the class. 7. They are the richest men in this city. 8. She is the younger of the two sisters.

(2) *Supply the reflexive pronoun and the present perfect of the verb given in the infinitive, using the proper form of the past participle:* 1. (*aiutare*) Noi ... 2. (*sacrificare*) Ella ... 3. (*mostrare*) Io ... 4. (*guarire*) Esse ... 5. (*preparare*)

Tu . . . 6. (*vendere*) Essi . . . 7. (*occupare*) Voi . . . 8. (*rifiu-*
tare) Egli . . . 9. (*incontrare*) Le sorelle . . . 10. (*divertire*)
Ella . . .

(3) *Translate into Italian:* 1. French was spoken. 2. We
used to respect each other. 3. I am washing my hands.
4. The gloves were found. 5. One remains young. 6. People
were afraid. 7. People were very glad. 8. One answers
so. 9. The most beautiful things are preferred. 10. One
studies willingly. 11. People are proud. 12. We had a
good time. 13. Many things were asked. 14. One becomes rich.

B.   La Restaurazione

Dopo il crollo dell'impero napoleonico, nel 1815, i rappre-
sentanti delle potenze europee si adunarono a congresso, a
Vienna, e con diversi trattati credettero assicurare al continente una pace duratura.   Ma solamente i più assoluti
interessi dinastici furono tenuti in conto, e non si rispettò nè
storia, nè tradizioni, nè i più sacri diritti dei popoli.   Quello
che importava era di cancellare ogni ricordo della rivoluzione
e di Napoleone, di soffocare quelle idee di libertà che avevan
messo radice dovunque, e di rammentare ai popoli stessi
che essi non erano che sudditi dei loro principi, servi dei
loro padroni.

Specialmente l'Italia, che il principe di Metternich,
ministro austriaco, aveva chiamata « un'espressione geografica, » fu vittima delle decisioni di questo congresso.
Essa fu ancora una volta sminuzzata in staterelli, a capo
dei quali si misero i principi che Napoleone aveva spodestati.
La Lombardia, il Veneto, il Trentino e la Venezia Giulia
furono annessi all'Austria; il Piemonte, la Liguria e la
Sardegna formarono il regno di Sardegna; si ricostituirono
i ducati di Parma, di Modena, e di Lucca; la Toscana fu
creata granducato sotto Ferdinando III di Lorena-Austria;

Photo Alinari

Milan Cathedral.

e il resto dell'Italia fu diviso in Stati della Chiesa, **governati dal Papa**, e Regno delle Due Sicilie, con Napoli per capitale, abbandonato alla tirannia dei Borboni.

C. 1. After Napoleon's downfall, a great international convention was called at Vienna. 2. This took place in the year 1815. 3. Europe's statesmen said that they wished to assure a lasting peace. 4. But only the princes' interests were respected. 5. They did not care for (**di**) the interests of the people. 6. They had forgotten the lessons of recent history. 7. Liberty was stifled. 8. Prince Metternich was at the head of the congress. 9. He was Austria's prime minister, and had called Italy "a geographical expression." 10. Fortunately today one laughs at (**di**) his stupidity, for Italy is again a united nation.

D. 1. What is Austria today but (**se non**) one of the smallest states in Europe? 2. History avenges itself. 3. The richest regions in Italy were abandoned to Austria. 4. Venice, the Queen of the Adriatic, and one of the most glorious cities in the world, had lost its independence. 5. In Tuscany people had as [a] sovereign Ferdinand III.[1] 6. He was a relative of Austria's emperor. 7. Rome and Central Italy passed under the absolute rule of the Popes. 8. But the most perfidious government in Italy was that of Naples, where the Bourbons occupied the throne. 9. Gladstone called this government "the negation of God." 10. Italians have not forgotten the martyrdom of their fathers.

E. *Oral.* 1. Che ebbe luogo nel 1815? 2. Dove si adunò il congresso? 3. Che cosa si credette d'assicurare all'Europa con questo congresso? 4. Chi ne fu il capo? 5. Come aveva egli chiamato l'Italia? 6. Quali interessi furono rispettati al Congresso di Vienna? 7. A qual governo si abbandonò la Lombardia? 8. Quali altre regioni furono abbandonate all'Austria? 9. Chi si creò granduca di Toscana? 10. Quali altri ducati si crearono nell'Italia Settentrionale? 11. Di quali regioni si formò il regno di Sardegna? 12. Dove governava il Papa? 13. Su

---

[1] **Ferdinando Terzo.**

quali regioni governava? 14. L'Italia Meridionale e la Sicilia da chi erano tirannizzate? 15. Come chiamò Gladstone il governo dei Borboni? 16. Qual era la capitale dei Borboni? 17. Quale nazione doveron gl'Italiani considerare come loro nemica? 18. Che cosa è l'Austria oggi?

LESSON XXXVIII

129. The Absolute Superlative

1.

una gentil*i*ssima signora	a very kind lady
un amico molto devoto	a most devoted friend
un mare calmo calmo	a very calm sea

The absolute superlative is formed in one of the following ways:

(*a*) By adding –*issimo* to the adjective after its last vowel has been dropped. Note, however, that some adjectives, in adding this suffix, undergo an orthographic change: ricco, ricch*i*ssimo.

(*b*) By placing before the adjective some qualifying adverb, such as molto, *very*, assai, *quite*, immensamente, *immensely*, estremamente, *extremely*, etc.

(*c*) By repeating the adjective, a rare usage.

2.

acre	sour	ac*ε*rrimo
c*ε*lebre	celebrated	celeb*ε*rrimo
*i*ntegro	righteous	integ*ε*rrimo
m*i*sero	wretched	mis*ε*rrimo
s*a*lubre	healthful	salub*ε*rrimo

The adjectives listed above have an absolute superlative in –*ε*rrimo.

130. Comparison of Adverbs

The comparison of adverbs is made exactly like that of adjectives. The suffix –mente is added to a superlative in –issimo (after the final o has been changed into an **a**) to form the absolute superlative of an adverb: **ricchissima-mente.**

131. Irregular Comparison. The following adjectives and adverbs are compared irregularly:

Positive		Comparative	Rel. Superlative	Abs. Superlative
buono	good	migliore	il migliore	ottimo
bɛne	well	mɛglio	il mɛglio	ottimamente
cattivo	bad	peggiore	il peggiore	pɛssimo
male	badly	pɛggio	il pɛggio	pessimamente
alto	high	superiore	il superiore	suprɛmo
basso	low	inferiore	l'inferiore	infimo
grande	big	maggiore	il maggiore	massimo
piccolo	little	minore	il minore	minimo
molto	much	più	il più	moltissimo
poco	little	meno	il meno	pochissimo

1. While the adverbs **bɛne, male, molto** and **poco** have only the irregular comparative, the adjectives **buɔno, cattivo, alto, basso, grande** and **piccolo** are compared also regularly.

Maggiore and **minore** usually mean *older* and *younger*. **Superiore** and **inferiore** are generally used in a figurative sense. All the above-listed adjectives have also a regular absolute superlative.

EXERCISE XXXVIII

A. (1) *Give three different absolute superlatives for each of the following adjectives and adverbs:* povero, stanco, acre, delizioso, calmo, misero, elegantemente, giusto, veramente, presto, esatto, vecchio, duramente, salubre, rapidamente.

(2) *Use them in sentences.*

(3) *What is the difference between* **migliore** *and* **meglio**? *Is this clear from the English equivalent? How about* **peggiore** *and* **peggio**?

(4) *Write on the board the comparative and the absolute superlative of:* buono, bene; piccolo, poco; facile, molto; cattivo, male; alto, basso; grande, giovane.

(5) *Use each form in sentences.*

(6) *Continue the following:* 1. Io mi sarò lavato, etc. 2. Io m'ero guardato nello specchio, etc. 3. Quand'io mi fui preparato, etc. 4. Non mi sono io guarito? etc. 5. Io m'ero rifiutato, etc. 6. Io mi sarò trovato, etc. 7. Appena io mi fui apparecchiato, etc. 8. Io mi sono mostrato, etc.

B.   I Carbonari

Le idee liberali avevano fatto grandi progressi in Italia, e il malcontento causato dal Congresso di Vienna fu generale in tutta la penisola. I patriotti, aspirando all'unità e indipendenza della Patria, si unirono in società segrete per lottare contro i governi della reazione e preparare l'avvento d'una grande e libera Italia.

Tra le società segrete formate in quei tempi, la più estesa fu quella detta dei Carbonari, parola simbolica scelta per denotare quei patriotti che dovevano preparare l'esca per il grande incendio che presto doveva scoppiare. Un linguaggio convenzionale era stato stabilito per eludere la vigilanza della polizia, sospettosa quanto mai, che colpiva con estrema ferocia ogni persona sospetta.

In Napoli, ove più fiero che altrove era il despotismo sotto Ferdinando Primo di Borbone, i Carbonari ebbero la loro sede principale. Malgrado la brutale persecuzione della polizia, la loro organizzazione si estendeva sempre più e vi partecipavano nobili e plebe, e specialmente i soldati, memori delle liberali tradizioni dei governi francesi.

Principale organizzatore e capo della carboneria napoletana era Guglielmo Pepe, il quale, avendo militato sotto Giuseppe Napoleone e Gioacchino Murat, aveva ottenuto il grado di generale.

L'UNIFICAZIONE DELL'ITALIA

Following the Treaty of Vienna (1815) and up to the first victorious war of independence, Italy was divided into many petty states. Lombardy, Venetia, Trentino, and Julian Venetia were ruled by Austria. Piedmont, Liguria, Sardinia, Nice, and Savoy formed a kingdom under the dynasty of Savoy. Parma, Modena, and Lucca were independent duchies; south of them there was the Grand Duchy of Tuscany, while Central Italy formed the States of the Church, and Southern Italy was ruled by the Bourbons. The dates shown in the map indicate the years in which these various regions were consolidated. Savoy and Nice were ceded to France in 1860.

C. 1. The Congress of Vienna had caused the greatest dissatisfaction all over (in tutta) the peninsula. 2. Italians wanted to be free and united. 3. Their governments were very bad, and were all under the influence of Austria. 4. The worst of them was that of Naples. 5. People suffered the worst abuses on the part (da parte) of the police. 6. The provinces of Southern Italy were in a very wretched condition. 7. For these reasons, and because they wished to (di) see their fatherland redeemed from the foreign yoke, Italians organized themselves into secret societies. 8. The most famous of these societies was that of the Carbonari. 9. To it belonged the best citizens and the truest patriots. 10. They thought more of (a) their country than of (a) themselves.

D. 1. What is worse than despotism? 2. It is better to risk everything than to live a life of slaves. 3. The despotism under which Italians suffered was still worse because it was the despotism of a foreign power. 4. Italians suffered much to (per) gain their liberty. 5. Many patriots sacrificed their lives [1] on the scaffold. 6. But their martyrdom was not in vain. 7. It helped to (a) spread revolutionary ideas, and hastened the triumph of a very noble cause. 8. The Carbonari were well organized in every part of Italy, but they were especially very powerful in (a) Naples. 9. Their head was Guglielmo Pepe. 10. He was one of the best patriots and a very good general.

E. *Oral.* 1. Quali idee avevano fatto progressi in Italia? 2. Furono contenti gl'Italiani delle decisioni del Congresso di Vienna? 3. Perchè non ne furono contenti? 4. Che cosa desideravano i patriotti italiani? 5. Che cosa organizzarono allora? 6. Perchè erano segrete le loro società? 7. Qual era la più estesa di queste società? 8. Perchè si chiamava la società dei Carbonari? 9. Quale potenza straniera dominava in Italia? 10. Dominava in tutta l'Italia? 11. In quale parte della penisola era più fiero che altrove il despotismo? 12. Chi era il re di Napoli? 13. Era sospettosa la polizia? 14. Solamente i nobili erano

---

[1] Translate, *the life.* The singular used distributively.

Carbonari? 15. Chi era il capo della carboneria napoletana? 16. Considerava egli Napoli o tutta l'Italia come sua
patria? 17. Qual era la professione di Guglielmo Pepe?
18. Sotto chi aveva egli militato?

LESSON XXXIX

132.   Ordinal Numerals

1.

1st	primo	13th	tredicesimo	
2d	secondo	14th	quattordicesimo	
3d	terzo	15th	quindicesimo	
4th	quarto	20th	ventesimo	
5th	quinto	21st	ventunesimo	
6th	sesto	22d	ventiduesimo	
7th	settimo	30th	trentesimo	
8th	ottavo	101st	centesimo primo	
9th	nono	102d	centesimo secondo	
10th	decimo	111th	centundicesimo	
11th	undicesimo	1000th	millesimo	
12th	dodicesimo	2000th	duemillesimo	

Except for the first ten numbers, ordinal numerals are
formed by dropping the last vowel of the corresponding
cardinal numeral and adding –esimo. But the last vowel of
23, 33, etc., being a stressed vowel, is kept: ventitreesimo.

2. From 11th on, also the following forms are used: 11th,
decimo primo; 12th, decimo secondo; 13th, decimo terzo;
85th, ottantesimo quinto, etc.

133.   Use of the Ordinal Numerals

1.   la dodicesima stanza   the twelfth stanza

Ordinal numerals are adjectives, and agree as such.

2.   il secolo quinto   the fifth century
il secolo decimo quarto ⎫
il trecento   ⎬   the fourteenth century

The number of a century is expressed by ordinals. Beginning, however, from the thirteenth century, it is more customary to use the following expressions:

il duecento	the 13th century	il seicento	the 17th century
il trecento	the 14th century	il settecento	the 18th century
il quattrocento	the 15th century	l'ottocento	the 19th century
il cinquecento	the 16th century	il novecento	the 20th century

3. Leone decimo   Leo the Tenth
   Luigi decimoquarto   Louis XIV
   Canto sesto   Canto VI
   Capitolo quinto   Chapter five

Ordinal numerals are used, without article, after names of rulers and the words **canto, capitolo, volume,** etc.

4. **Ne ho due terzi.**   I have two thirds of it.

They are also used to express fractions. *Half* is **la metà;** the adjective *half* is **mezzo.**

5. See § 77 for numerals in dates.

134.   Passive Voice

   Essi son consigliati da me.   They are advised by me.

The passive voice is formed by means of the auxiliary **essere** and the past participle of the verb conjugated, which participle agrees in gender and number with the subject. This voice is less frequently used in Italian than in English, for the reason that, when no agent is expressed, the reflexive is preferred (*see* § 128, 3).

135. Use of the Auxiliary *essere*. As has been seen, the auxiliary **essere** is used in forming the perfect tenses of **essere,** those of the reflexive or reciprocal verbs (*see* § 127, 2), and in conjugating the passive voice. ·It ·is used also:
(a) with impersonal verbs, such as **piovere,** *to rain,* **nevicare,**

to snow, etc.; (*b*) with **piacere,** *to please,* **parere** and **sembrare,** *to seem;* (*c*) with some intransitive verbs denoting motion, rest, or change of condition. Such, among others, are:

andare	to go	**morire**	to die	**salire**	to go up
arrivare	to arrive	**nascere**	to be born	**scendere**	to go down
cadere	to fall	**partire**	to depart	**stare**	to stay
correre	to run	**restare**	to remain	**uscire**	to go out
entrare	to enter	**ritornare**	to return	**venire**	to come
giungere	to arrive				

EXERCISE XXXIX

A. (1) *Continue the following:* 1. Io sono arrivàto a casa, etc. 2. Io sono stato aiutato da lui, etc. 3. Non sono io venuto di buon'ora? etc. 4. Io non sono stato riconosciuto, etc. 5. Quand'io fui entrato nella chiesa, etc. 6. Io ero restato a casa, etc.

(2) *Read aloud in Italian:* 4th, 6th, 9th, 5th, 3d, 7th, 1st, 8th, 2d, 10th, 14th, 20th, 48th, 97th, 100th, 105th, 106th, 107th, 108th, 109th, 145th, 200th, 290th, 1000th.

(3) *Translate into Italian in two different ways:* The nineteenth century, the fourteenth century, the seventeenth century, the sixteenth century, the thirteenth century.

(4) *Supply the passive form of the past absolute of the verb given in the infinitive:* 1. (*ricevere*) Noi non —— da lui. 2. (*vedere*) Ella non —— da nessuno. 3. (*preferire*) Quel libro —— dagli studenti. 4. (*sorvegliare*) La cuoca —— da Silvia. 5. (*identificare*) I miei amici —— da me alla banca. 6. (*consegnare*) Il danaro mi —— dall'impiegato. 7. (*salutare*) Quelle signorine —— da noi. 8. (*perdere*) La lettera —— dal ragazzo. 9. (*capire*) Quelle parole non —— da tutti 10. (*vendere*) I mobili —— da noi.

B. **Tentativi di Rivoluzione**

Ispirato dal successo della rivoluzione spagnola del 1820, il popolo napoletano, guidato dai Carbonari, si ribellò nello

Photo R. P. L. Ledésert

BOLOGNA STREET SCENE

o

stesso anno, e Ferdinando I di Borbone, spaventato nel vedere l'esercito parteggiare per i rivoltosi, si affrettò a concedere l'invocata costituzione e a giurarvi fede. Ma poco dopo, col pretesto di perorar la causa della libertà del suo popolo davanti ai sovrani della Santa Alleanza, si rifugiò in Austria. Ne ritornò con un esercito di cinquantamila austriaci e, spergiuro, abolì la costituzione e colpì i capi del movimento liberale con la prigionia, l'esilio e la forca.

Ma era appena abortita questa rivoluzione, quando un'altra ne scoppiò nel Piemonte. Ivi i rivoluzionari adottarono la bandiera tricolore, verde, bianca e rossa, e non solamente domandarono una costituzione, ma anche guerra contro l'Austria. Temendo una guerra civile e volendo evitare al suo paese l'intervento straniero, il re, Vittorio Emanuele I, abdicò in favore di suo fratello, Carlo Felice. Questi, ottenendo l'aiuto dell'esercito austriaco, riuscì a domare la rivolta e a ripristinare il governo assoluto.

Nel 1830 altre insurrezioni ebbero luogo a Modena, a Parma e negli Stati Papali, e parimente furono domate dai soldati austriaci. E intanto, in Lombardia e nel Veneto, la polizia imperiale creava il terrore, arrestando e chiudendo nelle più orribili prigioni ogni buon patriotta. La fortezza dello Spielberg, in Moravia, ingoiò centinaia di vittime, tra cui il Conte Confalonieri, capo dei Carbonari di Lombardia, e i letterati Pietro Maroncelli e Silvio Pellico. Quest'ultimo ci ha lasciato, nel suo libro *Le mie prigioni*, una commovente descrizione dei suoi tormenti.

C. 1. The government of nearly every European country, at the beginning of the nineteenth century, was monarchical. 2. In 1830 the emperor of Austria was Francis the First. 3. In the same year Pope [1] Pius the Eighth died, and was succeeded by Gregory the Sixteenth. 4. More than half of Italy was at that time under the direct or indirect rule of the emperor of Austria. 5. The first

---

[1] Use no article before the word.

struggle for liberty took place in (a) Naples.   6. New ideas had
entered into the minds [1] of all Italians, from the Alps to Sicily.
7. A new epoch had arrived.   8. Italians refused to (di) be governed
by foreigners.   9. They wanted the end of absolute monarchy.
10. Above all, they wished to (di) be united.

D.   1. A democratic constitution was granted by the sovereign.
2. It was based on that constitution which the king of Spain,
Ferdinand the Seventh, had granted the same year.   3. But the
king of Naples betrayed his people.   4. He had gone to (in) Austria
under a pretext and had returned at the head of an Austrian army.
5. Many Neapolitan patriots suffered then prison and exile.
6. Some lost their lives [2] on the scaffold.   7. The second attempt
took place in 1821 in Piedmont.   8. Nothing was attempted in
Lombardy and Venetia because the Austrian police [3] had created
a reign of terror in those provinces.   9. But the stupid cruelty of
Austria was revealed in all its horror by Silvio Pellico when he
published *Le mie prigioni*.   10. He won for Italy the sympathy of
the whole civilized world.   11. Italy, which had lost its independence in the sixteenth century, had been [the] prey of Spaniards,
French, and Germans in the seventeenth and eighteenth centuries.
12. Now she was ready to (a) become again a free country.

E.   *Oral.*   1. Quale rivoluzione ispirò i Carbonari?   2. In
che anno ebbe luogo il primo tentativo di rivoluzione in
Italia?   3. Dove ebbe luogo?   4. Chi era re di Napoli
allora?   5. Chi era il capo della carboneria napoletana?
6. Fu fedele al suo popolo e al suo giuramento il re di Napoli?   7. Dove andò?   8. Con chi ritornò a Napoli?
9. Come finirono i capi del movimento liberale?   10. Dove
scoppiò la seconda rivoluzione?   11. Che bandiera adottarono i patriotti piemontesi?   12. Che desideravano dal
loro re?   13. Chi era re del Piemonte nel 1821?   14. A chi
lasciò egli il trono?   15. Come finì questa seconda rivoluzione?   16. In quali altri stati ebbero luogo insurrezioni?
17. Perchè il popolo di Lombardia restò calmo?   18. Chi

---

[1] Use the singular.   [2] What number?   [3] A singular noun.

era il capo dei Carbonari di Lombardia? 19. Quali letterati furono mandati dall'Austria in prigione? 20. Che libro pubblicò Silvio Pellico appena gli fu ridata la libertà?

LESSON XL

136.   Present Subjunctive of Model Verbs

I buy, etc.	*I sell, etc*	*I finish, etc.*	*I depart, etc*
compr i	vend a	fin isc a	part a
compr i	vend a	fin isc a	part a
compr i	vend a	fin isc a	part a
compr iamo	vend iamo	fin iamo	part iamo
compr iate	vend iate	fin iate	part iate
compr ino	vend ano	fin isc ano	part ano

Note that the three persons of the singular in this tense are identical with each other in all Italian verbs. Note also that the larger number of the verbs of the third conjugation add –isc to their stem in the singular forms and in the 3d person plural (*see* § 30).

137.   Present Subjunctive of *essere* and *avere*

I (may) be, etc.	*I (may) have, etc.*
sia	abbia
sia	abbia
sia	abbia
siamo	abbiamo
siate	abbiate
siano	abbiano

138.   Present Perfect Subjunctive

I bought, or (may) have bought, etc.	*I sold, or (may) have sold, etc.*	*I finished, or (may) have finished, etc.*
abbia comprato, etc.	abbia venduto, etc.	abbia finito, etc.

I was, or (may) have been, etc.	*I had, or (may) have had, etc.*
sia stato, –a, etc.	abbia avuto, etc.

139. The Subjunctive in Noun Clauses [1]

Desidero che tu parli con lui.	I wish you to talk with him.
Eviti ch'essi la vedano.	Avoid their seeing you.
Egli ordina che tu dica tutto.	He orders you to say everything.
È meglio che Lei resti.	It is better for you to stay.
Son contento ch'essa sia qui.	I am glad she is here.
Non so se questo sia vero.	I don't know whether this is true.
Credo che siano arrivati.	I think (= presume) they have arrived.
But: Credo che arriveranno.	I think they will arrive.

1. The subjunctive is used after verbs expressing: (a) desire, will, preference; (b) command, prohibition; (c) expression of opinion; (d) emotion (joy, sorrow, wonder, fear, anger, shame, etc.); (e) doubt, ignorance; (f) believing, thinking, hoping, suspecting, — provided that doubt is implied and that the dependent clause has no future idea, in which case the future must be used, as shown in the last example.

2. In all the cases just mentioned the subjunctive is used only if the main clause and the dependent clause have *different subjects*.

3. The examples above show that the infinitive, the present participle, or a tense of the indicative, may be found in English where the Italian syntax requires the subjunctive.

140. The Infinitive in Noun Clauses

Desidero di partire.	I wish to leave.
Son contento d'esser venuto.	I am glad I came.

---

[1] A clause that is the subject or the object of a verb is called a noun clause.

If the principal and the dependent verbs of a sentence have the same subjects, the infinitive must be used instead of the subjunctive.

A. (1) *Continue the following:* 1. Il professore vuole che io parli italiano, il professore vuole che **tu** . . ., etc. 2. Ella teme che io non segua il suo consiglio, etc. 3. I miei amici sperano che io non parta, etc. 4. È meglio che io spieghi questa regola, etc. 5. Carlo non sa se io abbia rifiutato, etc. 6. Egli è contento che io sia partito, etc.

(2) *Supply first the present subjunctive and then the present perfect subjunctive of the verb given in the infinitive:* 1. (*pagare*) Io temo ch'egli non ——. 2. (*restare*) Son contento che mia sorella —— a casa. 3. (*perdere*) Egli teme che io —— il suo libro. 4. (*vedere*) Son contento che essi —— ogni cosa. 5. (*arrivare*) Desidero che essi —— a tempo. 6. (*essere*) Temo ch'essi —— stanchi. 7. (*entrare*) Preferisco che voi —— con me. 8. (*essere*) Non crediamo che tu —— diligente. 9. (*avere*) Egli teme che Olga —— paura. 10. (*dormire*) Preferisco che i ragazzi ——. 11. (*partire*) Mi dispiace[1] che le mie cugine ——. 12. (*invitare*) Son contento che tu lo ——. 13. (*entrare*) Temo che essi —— in quella casa. 14. (*imparare*) Mi dispiace che tu —— queste cose.

(3) *Translate into Italian:* 1. I don't believe he has worked. 2. She wishes him to love his country. 3. I avoid seeing them. 4. Does he avoid my seeing him? 5. You are glad that it is too late. 6. I think he will write. 7. She doubts that I have been home. 8. Do you think they have returned? 9. He is glad to return to school. 10. He fears they have arrived. 11. We think they will not return. 12. I want to forget.

---

[1] *I am sorry.*

A TYPICAL ITALIAN STREET, BOLOGNA

B.   Mazzini e la Giovane Italia

I patriotti italiani non si lasciarono avvilire dagl'insuccessi incontrati, ma si prepararono più energicamente che mai a nuove lotte.

I Carbonari avevan fatto cosa eroica tenendo vivo lo spirito rivoluzionario, ma la loro propaganda non aveva avuto molto effetto sulla massa del popolo, e le insurrezioni da loro provocate erano state locali. Col 1830 le cose cambiarono, e un nuovo movimento fu principiato da giovani che, per serietà d'intenti, ardente entusiasmo e spirito di sacrifizio, destarono l'ammirazione di tutto il mondo civile.

Primo tra questi giovani, e loro guida e maestro, fu Giuseppe Mazzini (1805–72), il profeta dell'unità d'Italia. Uomo di grande cultura, profondo intelletto e nobilissimo animo, egli si dedicò tutto alla redenzione della sua patria, affrontando prima il carcere e poi un lunghissimo esilio.

Nel 1831 egli fondò una nuova società chiamata *La Giovane Italia*, con lo scopo di liberare il paese dal dominio straniero e stabilire un governo centrale repubblicano a base democratica. A questa società aderì presto la migliore gioventù italiana, ed essa contò, qualche anno dopo la sua fondazione, ben sessantamila membri, tanti e tanti dei quali sacrificarono la vita per il loro'ideale.

Mazzini non fu un uomo di stato; nel suo quasi ascetico idealismo, egli mancava di senso pratico; ma egli certamente contribuì più di ogni altro italiano a creare quell'entusiasmo patriottico che fu base essenziale al successo dei grandi progetti del vero fondatore dell'unità italiana, Camillo Benso, conte di Cavour.

C. 1. I wish you to have a good idea of Mazzini's times. 2. When he founded Young Italy, the peninsula was [the] prey of despotism. 3. It was under the hated rule of Austria. 4. At his death it was a united and independent nation. 5. I advise you[1] to (**di**) study the history of the Risorgimento. 6. Italians have thus called that period of their history which goes from the foundation of Young Italy to the taking (**presa**) of Rome. 7. The influence of Mazzini on Italian youth is undeniable. 8. He inspired his generation with his noble ideas and his generous spirit of sacrifice. 9. We feel sorry (= it displeases us) that so many young patriots sacrificed their lives.[2] 10. But the salvation of their country demanded it.

D. 1. Mazzini suffered prison and exile. 2. He also risked his (= the) life many times. 3. Italians loved their country above everything. 4. I hope that it is so even today. 5. In reading Mazzini's life we doubt that his plans were always wise. 6. He was an idealist, not a statesman. 7. But who doubts that he was a deep thinker, and that he had a very generous soul? 8. I hope that all young Italians of today learn what Mazzini taught in his books. 9. In them we read that we must love our family, our country and all humanity. 10. His motto was " God and [the] People." 11. " Place (**voi** *form*) the youth of the nation at the head of the insurgent masses," he declared. 12. " You (**voi**) do not know what magic influence the voice of youth has on the crowds."

E. *Oral.* 1. Si lasciarono avvilire i patriotti italiani dagl'insuccessi incontrati? 2. Qual è il merito dei Carbonari? 3. Erano state generali le insurrezioni provocate da loro? 4. Chi fu Giuseppe Mazzini? 5. Che cultura, che intelletto, che anima aveva egli? 6. A che cosa dedicò egli la sua vita? 7. Che cosa soffrì egli per la sua patria? 8. Che cosa fondò nel 1831? 9. Qual era lo scopo della Giovane Italia? 10. Desiderava Mazzini di fondare un governo monarchico? 11. Insegnava Mazzini solamente l'amor di patria? 12. Quanti membri contava la Giovane Italia qualche anno dopo la sua fondazione? 13. Fu Mazzini un uomo di stato? 14. Aveva egli molto senso pratico? 15. Come contribuì egli al trionfo della causa italiana? 16. Chi fu il vero fondatore dell'unità italiana?

---

[1] Indirect object   [2] Number?

17. Come si chiama il periodo di storia italiana che include la lotta per l'indipendenza? 18. Con quale anno comincia questo periodo? 19. Con quale evento finisce? 20. Qual era il motto di Mazzini?

LESSON XLI

141.   Impersonal Verbs

Mi sembra che sia lui.	It seems to me that it is he.
Bisogna che Lei lo veda.	It is necessary for you to see him.
Bisogna vederlo.	It is necessary to see him.

1. A verb without a definite subject is called impersonal. Impersonal verbs are used only in the third person singular. Note that the pronoun *it*, which precedes an impersonal verb in English, is never translated in Italian.

2. After impersonal expressions of possibility, necessity, desire, emotion or doubt, the subjunctive is used if the dependent clause has a personal subject. If there is no personal subject, the infinitive is used in the dependent clause, as shown in the third example.

Many impersonal expressions are used to express natural phenomena. The most important of them are:

Piove.	It is raining.
Nevica.	It is snowing.
Tira vento.	The wind blows.
Tuona.	It thunders.
Lampeggia.	It lightens.
Che tempo fa?	What kind of weather is it?
Fa bel tempo.	It is fine weather.
Fa cattivo tempo.	It is bad weather.
Fa caldo.	It is warm.
Fa molto caldo.	It is hot.
Fa freddo.	It is cold.
Fa fresco.	It is cool.

142.   Demonstrative Pronouns

1. Questo libro è migliore di   This book is better than that
   quello.   one.

Demonstrative adjectives (*see* § 88) are used also as pronouns.   **Quello** often renders the English *the one, that one.*

2. Ciò non è giusto.   This (*or* that) is not right.

The pronoun **ciò** is often used instead of **questo** or **quello.**

3. Questi merita lode.   This man deserves praise.
   Il consiglio di costui è cat- This fellow's advice is bad.
   tivo.

There are certain forms of demonstrative pronouns in Italian that are used exclusively with reference to persons. They are shown in the following table:

SINGULAR		PLURAL
Masc.	*Fem.*	*Masc. and Fem.*
questi ⎱ this man costui ⎰	costei this woman	costoro ⎰ these men ⎱ these women
quegli ⎱ that man colui ⎰	colei that woman	coloro ⎰ those men ⎱ those women

Questi and **quegli** are used only as subject pronouns. **Costui, costei** and **costoro** generally convey an idea of contempt.

4. Mazzini e Garibaldi erano   Mazzini and Garibaldi were
   nati in Liguria; questi   born in Liguria; the former
   a Nizza, e quegli a Ge-   in Genoa, and the latter in
   nova.   Nice.
   Anna e Luisa suonano mol-   Anna and Louise play very
   to bene; questa il violino,   well; the former the piano,
   e quella il pianoforte.   and the latter the violin.

The English *former* and *latter* are rendered by **quegli** and **questi** respectively when referring to men; otherwise, by **quello** and **questo,** which are inflected according to the meaning. Note that the idiom, as given in the example above, is literally *the latter . . . the former.*

EXERCISE XLI

A. (1) *Supply first the present subjunctive and then the present perfect subjunctive of the verb given in the infinitive:* 1. (*imparare*) Bisogna ch'egli —— i verbi. 2. (*preferire*) Mi sembra che tu —— gli svaghi allo studio. 3. (*ritornare*) È possibile che i nostri amici —— col treno diretto. 4. (*riconoscere*) Bisogna che voi le ——. 5. (*finire*) È difficile ch'ella —— questo lavoro in così pochi giorni. 6. (*essere*) Le sembra che questi studenti —— abbastanza diligenti? 7. (*osservare*) Mi dispiace che voi non —— ogni cosa. 8. (*ricevere*) Bisogna ch'egli —— quella lettera. 9. (*essere*) Non è possibile ch'ella —— a casa. 10. (*partire*) Bisogna che queste signorine ——. 11. (*avere*) Mi sembra che Carlo —— torto. 12. (*invitare*) È probabile che Anna le ——.

(2) *Translate into Italian:* 1. It was snowing. 2. It will rain. 3. It is hot. 4. It thundered this morning. 5. The wind was blowing. 6. It will lighten. 7. It is bad weather. 8. It is cool. 9. Probably it is snowing. 10. It had rained.

(3) *Substitute for each name an appropriate demonstrative pronoun:* 1. Ho parlato con Vittorio. 2. Anna desidera di venire con noi. 3. Le parole di Carlo e d'Arturo furono ascoltate da tutti. 4. Non voglio che Alberto sia in questa stanza con te; la sua compagnia non è buona. 5. Evita d'andare con Olga.

B.   **Il Quarantotto**

Nel 1848 insurrezioni scoppiarono da un capo all'altro della penisola, e al principio la fortuna favorì la causa dei

THE MATTERHORN

patriotti italiani poichè in molti stati i principi si affrettarono ad accordare costituzioni. Carlo Alberto, re d'idee liberali, che era salito al trono del Piemonte nel 1831, fu uno di questi.

Milano, principale città di Lombardia, si ribellò contro l'Austria e in cinque memorande giornate d'eroica lotta ne scacciò le truppe, dichiarando poi d'unirsi, con tutta la regione, al Piemonte. Anche Venezia si sollevò contro lo straniero e, sotto la guida di Daniele Manin, si ricostituì a repubblica. Firenze seguì l'esempio di Venezia. A Napoli, re Ferdinando II fu costretto, come suo padre lo era già stato, ad accordare una costituzione. Un'altra sommossa ebbe luogo a Roma; il Papa, Pio IX, fu spodestato e la città fu organizzata a Repubblica Romana, con Mazzini e Garibaldi alla testa.

Nuovo impeto ricevè il movimento nazionale quando Carlo Alberto dichiarò guerra all'Austria per liberare l'Italia dall'odiato nemico. « L'Italia farà da sè, » affermò egli con orgoglio, e il governo austriaco, impedito da un' insurrezione che era scoppiata a Vienna, non sembrava poter disporre di molti soldati per combattere gl'Italiani. Il momento era propizio alla causa della libertà, o almeno così sembrava.

C. 1. It is well for Italians to remember that all the Italian rulers, except those of the House of Savoy, were an obstacle to their unity. 2. In eighteen hundred forty-six Rome had a new pope, Pius the Ninth. 3. For some time he was very popular in Italy, for his ideas seemed liberal. 4. He granted an amnesty to those who were guilty of political offences. 5. He entrusted the administration of the Papal States to an able and enlightened minister, Rossi. 6. Having shown himself hostile to Austrian influences, he aroused many hopes for Italian unity. 7. " They think," he once declared, " that I am a Napoleon, and I am only a poor parish priest." 8. The movement for Italian unity became powerful. 9. When the revolution burst out, Rome was at the head of it.

10. In eighteen hundred and forty-eight all Italy, from the Alps to Sicily, longed for independence and unity.

D. 1. The efforts of the Italians were not co-ordinated. 2. Lombardy and Venetia wished to be free from Austria; the former by uniting itself to Piedmont, the latter by restoring the old republican government. 3. You must [1] not forget that Venice had been a glorious republic for many, many centuries. 4. In the same year Florence adopted a republican government. 5. After the revolution another republic was established in the Eternal City. 6. Mazzini and Garibaldi were at the head of it. 7. Both served the Roman Republic; the former with his (= the) mind, the latter with his (= the) sword. 8. Southern Italy, having forced Ferdinand the Second to (a) grant a constitution, was organizing itself under a new government. 9. All this is very interesting, but you must [1] use a map in order to understand well what was happening. 10. It seems to me that, with the aid of the map which is in this book, it is easier to follow these events.

E. *Oral.* 1. Chi era re del Piemonte nel 1848? 2. Che idee aveva egli? 3. Che cosa accordò egli al suo popolo? 4. Qual è la città principale della Lombardia? 5. Che cosa ebbe luogo a Milano nel quarantotto? 6. Quanti giorni durò la lotta in Milano contro le truppe austriache? 7. Qual governo desiderava il popolo di Lombardia? 8. Chi era a capo del popolo a Venezia? 9. Quali eventi ebbero luogo a Venezia? 10. Firenze e Roma che specie di governo organizzarono? 11. Quali erano i capi della Repubblica Romana? 12. Quale dei due era alla testa dei soldati romani? 13. Chi dichiarò guerra all'Austria? 14. Con quale scopo? 15. Qual era il motto di Carlo Alberto? 16. Perchè il momento sembrava propizio alla causa italiana? 17. Erano gli sforzi degl'Italiani ben coordinati? 18. Perchè non lo erano? 19. Chi era re di Napoli nel quarantotto? 20. Di chi era figlio?

---

[1] Translate in two ways, using the verbs **bisognare** and **dovere**.

LESSON XLII

143. Past Subjunctive of Model Verbs

I bought, or *might buy, etc.*	*I sold,* or *might sell, etc.*	*I finished,* or *might finish, etc.*
compr assi	vend essi	fin issi
compr assi	vend essi	fin issi
compr asse	vend esse	fin isse
compr assimo	vend essimo	fin issimo
compr aste	vend este	fin iste
compr assero	vend essero	fin issero

Note that –ss– appears in all forms of this tense except the second plural, that the second person plural is identical with the second person plural of the past absolute, and that, except for the characteristic vowel, the endings are the same for all three conjugations.

144. Past Subjunctive of *essere* and *avere*

I was, or *might be, etc.*	*I had,* or *might have, etc.*
fossi	avessi
fossi	avessi
fosse	avesse
fossimo	avessimo
foste	aveste
fossero	avessero

145. Past Perfect Subjunctive

I had bought, or *might have bought, etc.*	*I had sold,* or *might have sold, etc.*	*I had finished,* or *might have finished, etc.*
avessi comprato, etc.	avessi venduto, etc.	avessi **finito,** etc.

I had been, or *might have been, etc.*	*I had had,* or *might have had, etc.*
fossi stato, –a, etc.	avessi avuto, etc.

146. Sequence of Tenses

1. **Desidero che tu parli.**   I wish you to talk.
   Digli che scriva.   Tell him to write.
   Non sospetterà ch'io sia   He will not suspect that I have
      uscito.   gone out.

A principal verb in the present, imperative, or future, is followed by the present or present perfect subjunctive.

2. **Mi pregò che la salutassi.**   He begged me to greet her.
   Vorrebbe che tu venissi.   He would wish you to come.

A principal verb in a past tense or in the conditional (*see* §§ 112, 113, 114) is followed by the past or past perfect subjunctive.

3. **Ha detto che tu vada a**   He said you should go home.
      casa.
   Ha voluto che io rimanessi.   He wanted me to remain.

A principal verb in the present perfect is followed by the present or the past subjunctive as the sense may require. In the first example given above the subjunctive expresses an uncompleted event; in the second, a completed one.

EXERCISE XLII

A. (1) *Continue the following:* 1. Carlo voleva che io ascoltassi, Carlo voleva che **tu . . .**, etc. 2. Bisognava che io venissi, etc. 3. Non era vero che io fossi stanco, etc. 4. Preferì che io telefonassi, etc. 5. Elena dubitava che io avessi avuto ragione, etc. 6. Egli desiderava che io vendessi dei biglietti, etc.

(2) *Supply first the past subjunctive and then the past perfect subjunctive of the verb given in the infinitive:* 1. (*trattare*) Egli temè che suo fratello —— quell'affare. 2. (*partire*) Fui contento ch'essi ——. 3. (*perdere*) Temei che voi lo ——. 4. (*seguire*) Mi dispiaceva che tu —— l'esempio di quel ragazzo.

P

5. (*rispondere*) Tememmo che Anna gli ——.   6. (*uscire*) Era possibile che noi —— prima di voi.   7. (*prestare*) Mi sembrò che Arturo —— a Carlo cento lire.   8. (*invitare*) Non era possibile che noi le ——.   9. (*riconoscere*) Bisognava ch'ella mi ——.   10. (*essere*) Mi sembrava che voi —— in Italia.   11. (*ripetere*) Non era possibile che io —— quel lavoro.   12. (*venire*) Temevo ch'esse —— in ritardo.   13. (*viaggiare*) Tuo padre voleva che tu ——.   14. (*prepararsi*) Mi dispiaceva che voi non ——.   15. (*essere*) Volevano che noi —— con loro.   16. (*pagare*) Fui contento che essi mi —— subito.

B.   **Il Quarantanove**

Le speranze degl'Italiani furono crudelmente deluse, poichè il loro comune nemico non era così debole com'essi avevano pensato. Oltre a ciò, essi non erano uniti, e questa loro discordia facilitò la vittoria dell'Austria, che potè batterli separatamente.

All'audace sfida del Piemonte non fu dato appoggio dagli altri stati. Numerosi volontari andarono a combattere sotto le bandiere di Carlo Alberto, ma l'esercito piemontese era molto inferiore di forze a quello che l'Austria aveva mandato in Italia, e fu battuto a Custozza nel 1848 e a Novara nel 1849. Carlo Alberto, che invano aveva cercato la morte sul campo di battaglia, abdicò in favore di suo figlio, Vittorio Emanuele II, e andò in volontario esilio.

L'Austria offrì vantaggiose condizioni di pace al nuovo re, ma domandò che la costituzione data da Carlo Alberto fosse abolita e la monarchia assoluta restaurata nel Piemonte. Tali condizioni furono però recisamente rifiutate da Vittorio Emanuele con queste parole: « Quel che mio padre ha giurato, è sacro per me. Se io devo soccombere, voglio soccombere senza onta. La mia stirpe conosce la via dell'esilio, non quella del disonore. »

Un'onda di reazione passò per l'Italia. I governi rivoluzionari, che erano stati stabiliti qua e là per la penisola,
furono abbattuti a uno a uno dopo eroiche lotte, e migliaia
di patriotti furono mandati al patibolo o torturati in orridi
carceri. La Repubblica Romana fu rovesciata da un
esercito francese mandato da Luigi Napoleone, e Pio Nono
ritornò a Roma.

La causa dell'indipendenza pareva perduta, ma un raggio
di conforto restava agl'Italiani, poichè il Piemonte, materialmente sconfitto, era uscito dalla lotta moralmente vittorioso. Tutte le speranze dei patriotti furono fondate da allora
sul giovane re, Vittorio Emanuele II, il quale, per la sua
fedeltà allo statuto, ricevè il nome di *Re galantuomo.*

C. 1. Italians had thought that the Austrians were not so strong
as they proved to (di) be. 2. Their hopes were vain, for they were
too weak to (per) beat their enemy. 3. They had thought that
the moment was opportune. 4. A revolution had burst out in (a)
Vienna, and the Austrian monarchy was in danger. 5. No help,
however, was given to Charles Albert by the other Italian states.
6. It was necessary that the Italian patriots be united, but on the
contrary each state had different aims. 7. Some Italians wanted
their country to be organized under a republican government.
8. Others wanted all Italy to be under the rule of the House of
Savoy. 9. The army of Charles Albert was beaten twice, at
Custozza and at Novara. 10. Piedmont had to [1] abandon the
struggle and conclude a peace with Austria.

D. 1. Charles Albert went into voluntary exile and died soon
after of [a] broken heart. 2. Victor Emmanuel II, the Honest
King, received the crown on the battlefield. 3. He believed that
his father's oath was sacred to (per) him. 4 Austria wished him to
repeal the constitution, but he refused with proud words. 5. That
constitution was destined to (a) become the constitution of all Italy.
6. The reaction was violent everywhere in Italy, and particularly

---

[1] Translate in two ways, using the verbs **bisognare** and **dovere**.

in Southern Italy. 7. Ferdinand II ordered many cities to be bombarded because they had revolted against him. 8. For this he was called King Bomba. 9. The results of these struggles were most discouraging to (**per**) those who had consecrated their lives to the liberation of Italy. 10. Thenceforth, Italian hopes were centered on the House of Savoy.

E. *Oral.* 1. Perchè avevano sperato gl'Italiani che l'ora della liberazione fosse arrivata? 2. Era debole l'Austria? 3. Perchè la discordia regnava tra i patriotti? 4. Carlo Alberto ricevè aiuti dagli altri stati della penisola? 5. Quale esercito fu battuto? 6. Dove? 7. In che anno Carlo Alberto abdicò? 8. Come si chiamava il nuovo re? 9. Che cosa desiderava l'Austria dal nuovo re? 10. Accettò Vittorio Emanuele le condizioni dell'Austria? 11. Perchè non le accettò? 12. Dove andò Carlo Alberto dopo la battaglia di Novara? 13. Quando morí? 14. Chi combattè contro la Repubblica Romana? 15. Chi rientrò in Roma, dopo che il governo repubblicano fu rovesciato? 16. Avevano un raggio di conforto gl'Italiani? E perchè? 17. Su chi erano fondate le loro speranze? 18. Come fu chiamato da allora in poi Vittorio Emanuele II? 19. Come fu chiamato Ferdinando II di Napoli? 20. Perchè fu chiamato così?

LESSON XLIII

Review

A. *Continue the following:* 1. Io non dico niente, etc. 2. Che cosa le diss'io? etc. 3. Io gli spiego questa regola, etc. 4. Bisogna che io finisca questo lavoro, etc. 5. Io scesi subito dal treno, etc. 6. Sembrava che io dovessi rimaner qua, etc. 7. Io non lessi quel brano di prosa, etc. 8. Volevano che io partissi subito, etc. 9. Bisogna che io porti questa valigia da me stesso, etc.

B. *Review Questions:* 1. How many degrees of a given quality may an adjective express? 2. How many kinds of comparatives are there, and what are they called? 3. How is a comparative of equality formed? Give two examples. 4. How is a comparative of inequality formed? Give two examples. 5. What rules are to be followed in rendering the English *than?* 6. Does the definite article always precede the name of a country? 7. Explain the idiomatic present and give an example. 8. What orthographical changes do certain Italian verbs undergo in their conjugation? 9. What is a relative superlative and how is it formed in Italian? Give two examples. 10. What is a reflexive verb? Give an example. 11. How do you ordinarily render in Italian an English passive verb with agent unexpressed? Give an example. 12. How are the impersonal *one, we, people,* etc., to be translated in Italian? 13. Tell what an absolute superlative is, and in how many ways it can be rendered. 14. Give the comparative and the absolute superlative of **buono, bene, grande, piccolo, cattivo, male** and **molto.** 15. Give the ordinal numerals from 1st to 15th. 16. In what cases is the verb **essere** used as an auxiliary? 17. Mention five intransitive verbs of motion which take the auxiliary **essere.** 18. How many tenses has the indicative mood, and what are they called? 19. How many tenses has the subjunctive mood, and what are they called? 20. What is a noun clause, and when does a noun clause take the subjunctive? 21. Explain the sequence of tenses. 22. Give the demonstrative pronouns which are used exclusively with reference to persons.

C. *Supply the Italian equivalents of* than *in each of the following, sentences:* 1. Caserta è più vicina a Napoli —— a Roma. 2. Egli era meno povero —— me. 3. Anna ha meno —— ventidue anni. 4. Carlo è più intelligente —— studioso. 5. La cosa è meno facile —— si pensa. 6. Mi piace più remare —— pescare. 7. Paghiamo più —— riscuotiamo. 8. Genova è una città più commerciale —— artistica. 9. Olga è stata più esatta —— Silvia. 10. Essi sono più impazienti —— noi.

D. *Supply the correct form of the conditional of the verb given in the infinitive:* 1. (*parlare*) Noi ——, ma non possiamo. 2. (*essere*)

Voi —— con loro durante l'estate. 3. (*preferire*) Egli —— restare a casa. 4. (*invitare*) Chi li ——? 5. (*essere*) Da quel che Carlo dice, essi —— ricchi. 6. (*passare*) Scrisse che —— per Roma. 7. (*vendere*) Io —— volentieri la mia automobile. 8. (*pulire*) Chi —— la casa? 9. (*desiderare*) Le ragazze —— d'uscire. 10. (*mandare*) Me lo —— tu?

E. *Supply the correct form of the present indicative of the verb given in the infinitive:* 1. (*fare*) Voi —— male, amico mio. 2. (*dire*) —— tu ch'io ho torto? 3. (*dare*) Essi —— un esempio di vera virtù. 4. (*udire*) Non —— esse quel che diciamo? 5. (*venire*) Io —— qua tre volte al giorno. 6. (*sapere*) Noi —— che voi siete esatti. 7. (*andare*) Quando —— essi al lavoro? 8. (*volere*) Noi —— partire il primo del mese. 9. (*potere*) Essi —— far quel che vogliono. 10. (*dovere*) Anche noi —— far caso di queste cose.

F. *Supply the correct form of the past absolute of the verb given in the infinitive:* 1. (*venire*) Quelle ragazze non ——. 2. (*scendere*) Anch'io —— dalla vettura. 3. (*leggere*) Egli —— la lettera e poi me la consegnò. 4. (*conoscere*) Io —— quella signora a Venezia. 5. (*vedere*) Chi —— essi? 6. (*volere*) Essi non —— venir con noi. 7. (*sapere*) Egli —— che non avevano accettato l'invito. 8. (*mettere*) Chi —— la lettera alla posta? 9. (*rispondere*) Le mie cugine non ——. 10. (*vedere*) Geltrude non —— che avevo pagato.

G. *Supply the reflexive pronoun and the present perfect of the verb given in the infinitive, using the proper form of the past participle:* 1. (*divertire*) Voi . . . 2. (*spiegare*) Ella . . . 3. (*chiamare*) Noi . . . 4. (*telefonare*) Anna e Maria . . . 5. (*mostrare*) Tu . . . molto diligente. 6. (*rifiutare*) Lei . . . d'aiutarmi. 7. (*capire*) Amico caro, noi . . . 8. (*sacrificare*) Essi . . . per la Patria. 9. (*preparare*) Queste alunne . . . bene per la lezione d'oggi. 10. (*guardare*) Ella . . . nello specchio.

H. *Give the relative superlative and two different absolute superlatives for each of the following adjectives or adverbs:* buono, integro, lentamente, orgoglioso, bene, alto, piccolo, elegante, celebre, grande, facilmente, poco, basso, molto, comodamente.

I. *Supply the proper form of the correct subjunctive tense:* 1. (*dimenticare*) Bisognò ch'egli le ——. 2. (*essere*) Non è vero che io —— al teatro ieri sera. 3. (*partire*) Tememmo che Geltrude e Anna ——. 4. (*esser pagato*) Preferirò che essi —— da te. 5. (*esser sorvegliato*) Si diceva che quegli uomini —— dalla polizia. 6. (*parlare*) È bene che tu ——. 7. (*vedere*) Bisogna che io la ——. 8. (*riconoscere*) Non era possibile che noi li ——. 9. (*imparare*) Temei che Olga non —— a parlare italiano. 10. (*visitare*) Gli dispiace che tu non lo ——. 11. (*incontrare*) Fummo contenti che voi ci ——. 12. (*domandare*) Preferimmo che tu glielo ——. 13. (*avere*) Non credo che mia cugina —— quel libro. 14. (*ritornare*) Temo che le ragazze non —— ancora. 15. (*telefonare*) Bisognava che noi gli —— subito. 16. (*lasciare*) Bisognerà che voi —— questi amici. 17. (*identificare*) Mi sembrava che tu li —— alla banca. 18. (*firmare*) Non era probabile che il mio amico —— quella cambiale. 19. (*partire*) Le sembrava possibile che essi —— senza salutarci? 20. (*ripetere*) Non bisogna ch'essi glielo —— due volte.

J. *Supply the proper tense forms (present, present perfect, past absolute, or future) in each of the following sentences:* 1. (*essere*) Noi —— in questa stazione da più d'un'ora ed egli non è ancora arrivato. 2. (*arrivare*) Quand'egli ——, sarò contento. 3. (*essere*) Stamani non —— alla scuola perchè il professore è ammalato. 4. (*studiare*) Egli —— la lingua italiana da quasi due anni. 5. (*imparare*) Se Carlo ——, lo loderò. 6. (*scrivere*) Ieri mattina io —— una lettera a mia madre. 7. (*spiegare*) Quando il professore mi —— quella regola, la capii. 8. (*aspettare*) Essi —— da alcuni giorni, ma l'amico non arrivava. 9. (*trattare*) Se tu —— quell'affare per me, non perderò tempo. 10. (*avere*) Se voi —— bisogno di qualche cosa, potevate domandarmelo.

K. *For each of the following verbs give the required form of all the simple and compound tenses of the indicative, the subjunctive, and the conditional moods:*

passeggiare — 1st person plural	essere — 3d person plural
temere — 2d person singular	conoscere — 3d person singular
partire — 2d person plural	udire — 1st person singular

LESSON XLIV

147 The Subjunctive in Adjectival Clauses [1]

The subjunctive is used in adjectival clauses (introduced by a relative pronoun) in the following cases:

1. **È il migliore alunno che ci sia in questa classe.**   He is the best pupil there is in this class.
   È il solo libro ch'io abbia.   It is the only book I have.

After a relative superlative, or the word *only*.

2. **'Chiunque sia, lo lasci entrare.**   Whoever he is, let him enter.
   Checchè io dica, avrò torto.   Whatever I say, I shall be wrong.

After indefinites meaning *whoever, whatever, however.*

3. **Non c'è nessuno che parli italiano.**   There is no one who speaks Italian.

After negative expressions.

4. **Cerco un ragazzo che sappia suonare il violino.**   I am looking for a boy (= *any boy*) who can play the violin.
   BUT: **Cerco il ragazzo che sa suonare il violino.**   I am looking for the boy (= *a definite boy*) who can play the violin.

If the relative pronoun has an indefinite antecedent.

148. Use of the Infinitive

1. **Il viaggiare è istruttivo.**   Traveling is instructive.
   Amo il cavalcare.   I like horseback riding.
   Questo è vero soffrire.   This is real suffering.

An infinitive may be used as a verbal noun (subject, object, or predicate noun), in place of the English present

---

[1] A clause that modifies a noun or pronoun is called an adjectival clause.

participle (gerund). When used as a subject or a direct object, it normally takes the definite article.

2. **Continuò senza esitare.**	He continued without hesitating.
Dal dire al fare, c'è di mezzo il mare.	Between the saying and the doing lies the depth of the sea.

The infinitive is generally used in Italian after a preposition where the English requires a present participle.[1] In this case also the definite article usually precedes the infinitive, except when the infinitive follows **di**, *of*, **invece di**, *instead of*, **prima di**, *before*, **dopo di**, *after*, or **senza**, *without*.

EXERCISE XLIV

A. (1) *Supply the proper form of the verb given in the infinitive:* 1. (*guardare*) Non c'era nessuno che ci ——. 2. (*pagare*) Checchè egli ——, non sarà abbastanza. 3. (*essere*) Trovate un uomo che —— veramente felice. 4. (*conoscere*) È la sola signora ch'io ——. 5. (*essere*) Egli è un uomo che —— veramente felice. 6. (*arrivare*) Chiunque ——, io non ricevo oggi. 7. (*visitare*) Firenze era la sola città di Toscana ch'essi ——. 8. (*essere*) Mi dia un romanzo che —— interessante. 9. (*avere*) Questi erano i più bei fiori ch'egli ——. 10. (*comprare*) Sto scrivendo al signore che —— la mia casa. 11. (*domandare*) Checchè essi ——, non rispondete loro. 12. (*potere*) Era il migliore amico che si —— trovare. 13. (*menare*) Mostratemi la via che —— alla posta. 14. (*menare*) Mostratemi una via che —— a Piazza Garibaldi. 15. (*scrivere*) Chiunque ci ——, non risponderemo.

(2) *Translate into Italian:* 1. Studying was an amusement for her. 2. We prefer reading to writing. 3. You

---

[1] But see § 103, 3 for the Italian equivalent of the English present participle preceded by the prepositions *by*, *in*, *on*, and *through*.

cannot travel without carrying a valise. 4. Telephoning is useless now, for he is not at home. 5. Between fishing and rowing, I prefer rowing. 6. By listening to him, you will learn many things. 7. He departed after having spoken to us. 8. I do not like being alone. 9. As for (**circa**) catching any fish (*pl.*), it was a different matter (**un altro paio di maniche**). 10. It is studying that he does not like. 11. Instead of working, he was amusing himself. 12. She began by (**con**) recognizing that she had been wrong.

B.   Vittorio Emanuele e Cavour

Fortunatamente per l'Italia, il Piemonte aveva in Vittorio Emanuele II un re d'integerrima fede e ardente patriottismo. Egli era in armonia col suo popolo, e col suo popolo bramava di veder tutta l'Italia unita e indipendente.

Non era salito al trono che da qualche anno, quando chiamò al governo Camillo Benso, conte di Cavour (1810–61), il quale ben presto si rivelò uno dei più grandi uomini di stato dell'epoca. A lui principalmente gl'Italiani devono la loro liberazione.

Nato a Torino di distinta famiglia piemontese, Cavour aveva viaggiato in Europa, e specialmente in Francia e in Inghilterra, venendo a contatto coi capi dei partiti liberali di quei paesi. Arrivato al potere, fu sua prima cura quella di migliorare le condizioni economiche del Piemonte, costruendo ferrovie, favorendo le industrie e il' commercio, e migliorando le scuole.

L'insuccesso della campagna del quarantotto aveva dimostrato che altre vie bisognava seguire per realizzare il sogno dei patriotti italiani. Cavour aveva poca fede nelle sommosse e considerava Mazzini un fanatico che per la sua mancanza di moderazione e di senso pratico poteva rovinare ogni progetto. L'idea geniale di Cavour fu d'interessare la Francia alla causa italiana, offrendo per un possibile aiuto

Nizza e la Savoia, e in base a tale eventuale compenso si venne a un'alleanza tra il governo di Napoleone III e quello di Vittorio Emanuele II.

C. 1. Among the Italian princes, Victor Emmanuel II was the only [one] whom the nation could respect and love. 2. He was an ardent patriot and desired more than anything else (**ogni altra cosa**) the independence of his country. 3. His wife was an Austrian princess, but this did not prevent (**trattenne**) him from desiring war [1] with (**contro**) Austria. 4. He intended to follow his father's example. 5. He could not realize his dream without risking his (= the) throne. 6. Whatever one may think, he needed courage and perseverance,[2] in his difficult task. 7. There was no one who could serve his cause better than Cavour. 8. Garibaldi was not yet very famous. 9. On Mazzini one could not count, for Mazzini was an intransigent republican. 10. Besides, neither Garibaldi nor Mazzini was a statesman, and what Italy now needed was the leadership of a statesman of genius.

D. 1. Cavour was one of the greatest men Italy ever had. 2. He was born in Turin of [a] noble family. 3. He liked traveling and visited many foreign countries. 4. In France and England he came in contact with many important men. 5. When the king entrusted the government to him, Cavour showed what he was worth. 6. Building railroads, protecting industry and commerce, and improving the schools, were his first tasks. 7. Eager to (**di**) accomplish the unity of Italy, he was looking for a plan which would facilitate it, and he found it. 8. Italians had understood that other methods than (**che**) those of 1848 must be followed. 9. Cavour prepared and brought about the alliance with France. 10. France was the only country which could help Italy in a war against Austria.

E. *Oral.* 1. Perchè gl'Italiani speravano in Vittorio Emanuele II ? 2. Che cosa bramava egli ? 3. Era italiana sua moglie ? 4. Lo trattenne ciò dall'attuare i suoi progetti ?

---

[1] Use the definite article.   [2] Use no article.

5. Chi chiamò egli al governo? 6. Perchè non chiamò Mazzini al governo? 7. Dov'era nato Cavour? 8. A che famiglia apparteneva egli? 9. Dove aveva viaggiato Cavour? 10. Con chi era venuto a contatto viaggiando in Francia e in Inghilterra? 11. Qual fu la sua prima cura, appena arrivato al potere? 12. Aveva egli molta fede nei metodi di Mazzini? 13. Chi credeva egli che Mazzini fosse? 14. Qual fu l'idea geniale di Cavour? 15. Che cosa voleva egli dalla Francia? 16. Che offrì egli alla Francia? 17. Chi era alla testa del governo francese allora? 18. Che cosa procurò Cavour per il Piemonte? 19. Che cosa rischiò Vittorio Emanuele? 20. Qual era il suo sogno?

LESSON XLV

149.   The Subjunctive in Adverbial Clauses [1]

Gli parlai prima ch'egli uscisse.	I spoke to him before he went out.
Lo mostrò perchè io lo comprassi.	He showed it in order that I might buy it.
Aspetterò purchè egli ritorni presto.	I shall wait provided he returns soon.
Benchè fosse ricco, non era generoso.	Although he was rich, he was not generous.
Uscì senza che lo vedessero.	He went out without their seeing him.

The subjunctive is used in adverbial clauses introduced by certain conjunctions, the most important of which are:

TIME: **prima che** or **avanti che,** *before;* **finchè,** *until* (referring to the future);

PURPOSE: **perchè** or **affinchè,** *in order that;*

CONDITION: **purchè,** *provided that;* **a meno che . . . non,** *unless;*

---

[1] A clause that modifies a verb is called an adverbial clause.

CONCESSION: **benchè** or **quantunque** or **sebbene**, *although;*
             dato che, *granted that;* **se mai,** *in case;*
NEGATION: **senza che,** *without.*

150.   The Subjunctive in Independent Clauses

1. **Che Dio lo aiuti !**   May God help him !

The subjunctive is used to express a wish or imprecation.

2. **Firmi questa ricevuta.**   Sign (*or* let him sign) that re-
                                     ceipt.

   Lo finiscano.   Finish (*or* let them finish) it.

It is used also, in its present tense, to supply the 3d person singular and the 3d person plural of the imperative (*see* § 91).

The idea expressed may be a direct imperative in formal address (**Lei** or **Loro** forms), or an indirect imperative translating such English phrases as *let him sign,* — the *let* having the force of a command.

151.   Idiomatic Uses of *da*

1. **Vado dal signor De Viti.**   I am going to Mr. De Viti's.
   Ritornò da sua madre.   He returned to his mother.
   Vanno da lui ogni giorno.   They go every day to his house.
BUT: **Vado a casa mia.**   I am going to my house. (**Vado
                                     da me** would mean *I am go-
                                     ing by myself.*)

The preposition **da** is frequently used with the meaning of *at* or *to the house* (*shop, office, place,* etc.) *of,* when followed by a proper name or a noun referring to a person. This use is current also with **da** preceding a disjunctive personal pronoun (third example), provided that the subject and the pronoun which is the object of **da** refer to different persons, for otherwise the meaning would be *by myself, by yourself,* etc.

2. **Era il ragazzo dai capelli**   It was the boy with curly hair.
   ricci.

Da is used in describing a personal, characteristic quality.

3. **Parlò da uomo d'onore.**   He spoke as a man of honor.

Da is also used as the equivalent of the English *as, like,*
when they stand for such phrases as *in the manner of, in the
character of.* Note that in this case the indefinite article is
omitted in Italian.

EXERCISE XLV

A. (1) *Supply the missing conjunctions according to sense:*
1. Partirono —— egli uscisse. 2. Lo so, —— tu me lo
ripeta. 3. Glielo dico —— Lei lo impari. 4. Usciremo, ——
piova. 5. Lavorerò, —— sia stanco. 6. Entrò nella sala
—— noi lo vedessimo. 7. Chiamai il mio amico —— egli
m'identificasse. 8. Uscirò, —— voi m'accompagniate.
9. —— egli scriva, arriverà la lettera a tempo? 10. Non
studiò, —— glielo avessi ordinato.

(2) *Supply the proper form of the verb given in the infinitive:*
1. (*vedere*) Uscii dal salotto senza ch'essi mi ——. 2. (*lavorare*) Ti lasciamo solo affinchè tu ——. 3. (*ritornare*) Andate
a passeggiare purchè —— presto. 4. (*venire*) Egli scrisse
quella lettera prima che noi ——. 5. (*prestare*) Non posso
partire a meno che Lei non mi —— del danaro. 6. (*guarire*)
Il medico le dà queste medicine affinchè Lei ——. 7. (*imparare*) Dato ch'egli ——, potremo occuparlo? 8. (*vedere*)
Le dico queste cose perchè Lei —— ch'egli aveva torto.
9. (*potere*) Egli è uscito prima ch'io —— mostrargli questa
cartolina. 10. (*parlare*) Lo capii senza ch'egli mi ——.

(3) *Translate into Italian, rendering the direct address both
in the* **Lei** *and* **Loro** *forms, whenever it occurs:* 1. Depart.
2. Let them sacrifice themselves. 3. Endorse. 4. Let her
dictate. 5. May God advise him! 6. Put it here. 7. Let
him work. 8. Come down. 9. Let them follow my example. 10. Be glad. 11. Have courage. 12. Open the
windows.

(4) *Translate into Italian, using* **a** *or* **da** *in each sentence:*

1. I shall return to Mrs. Coppola's house. 2. I was in Venice a month ago. 3. He was leading him to the cashier's office. 4. He answered as an intelligent person. 5. You will sleep at my house. 6. We shall not be in Rome during the summer. 7. I returned to their office. 8. She spoke to the gentleman with the gray hat. 9. I went to her house. 10. Here are the black-shirt (= with the black shirt) patriots.

B.   **Guerra del 1859**

I tempi sembravano finalmente maturi, nel 1859, quando Vittorio Emanuele, in un discorso al parlamento piemontese, pronunziò le storiche parole: « Noi non possiamo rimanere insensibili al grido di dolore che verso di noi si leva da tante parti d'Italia. »

L'Austria, sospettosa quanto mai, mandò un ultimatum al Piemonte, in cui esigeva che l'esercito piemontese fosse disarmato entro tre giorni e che dal Piemonte fossero espulsi tutti quei patriotti italiani che ivi s'erano rifugiati. Era precisamente quel che Cavour desiderava. Egli rispose all'Austria con un dignitoso rifiuto, e l'Austria dichiarò guerra.

Da ogni regione della penisola migliaia di volontari vennero a offrirsi per la difesa della Patria, e a Garibaldi fu dato il comando di queste truppe, che presero il nome di *Cacciatori delle Alpi*. Intanto, mentre l'esercito piemontese difendeva eroicamente il Ticino, Napoleone III passava in Italia alla testa di centomila uomini per lottare contro il comune nemico.

Le battaglie di Montebello, Palestro e Magenta si seguirono a breve distanza di tempo sempre con la vittoria dalla parte degli alleati, e Vittorio Emanuele e Napoleone entrarono trionfanti in Milano. Poco dopo due altre vittorie, quelle di Solferino e di San Martino, completarono la liberazione della Lombardia. Ma a questo punto Napoleone offrì pace all'Austria, e il Piemonte dovè seguirne l'esempio, malgrado la violenta opposizione di Cavour. L'Austria restava padrona del Veneto, ma dichiarava di disinteressarsi da quel momento in poi dei problemi d'Italia.

C. 1. Victor Emmanuel spoke to the Piedmontese parliament as a man of heart. 2. His speech had an echo of sympathy in all Europe. 3. Before he pronounced those words, nobody had dared to criticize Austria so openly from a throne. 4. The parliament was assembled in Turin, in the spring of 1859. 5. Remember this date! 6. Austria's ambassador went to Cavour and handed him an ultimatum. 7. In it war was threatened, unless Piedmont disarmed within three days. 8. It was also demanded that the government of Victor Emmanuel should expel all Italian exiles who were living in the kingdom. 9. England wanted a conference to be assembled in order that the imminent war could be avoided. 10. Austria refused this proposal, just (**proprio**) as Cavour had hoped.

D. 1. Although it was a very bloody war, it lasted only about two months. 2. " May God save Italy and our children ! " — every Italian mother was praying. 3. Thousands of volunteers were coming from every part of Italy in order that the Fatherland might be saved. 4. To Garibaldi was entrusted the command of this splendid youth. 5. Although he was [a] republican, Garibaldi did not hesitate to (a) fight under the flag of the Honest King. 6. His men with the red shirts fought as heroes. 7. The Austrians were beaten in several battles. 8. Before they could prevent it, the allied troops entered into Milan with Victor Emmanuel and Napoleon III at their [1] head (**testa**). 9. The joy which the population showed in Milan cannot be described. 10. But the emperor of the French hastened peace, and only Lombardy was freed from the Austrian yoke.

E. *Oral.* 1. Per che cosa erano maturi i tempi nel 1859 ? 2. In quale città era adunato il parlamento piemontese in

---

[1] Replace the possessive with the definite article.

quell'anno? 3. Che cosa pronunziò Vittorio Emanuele?
4. Da dove veniva il grido di dolore? 5. Che cosa mandò
l'Austria al Piemonte? 6. Che cosa si domandava in
quell'ultimatum? 7. Che cosa si minacciava? 8. Come
rispose Cavour a queste domande? 9. Chi fu a dichiarar
guerra? 10. Fu Cavour contento di questo? 11. Chi
venne a difendere la Patria? 12. A chi ne fu affidato il
comando? 13. Che idee aveva Garibaldi? 14. Perchè
andò a combattere nell'esercito piemontese? 15. Com'erano
chiamati i suoi soldati? 16. Chi era l'alleato di Vittorio
Emanuele II? 17. Quali battaglie ebbero luogo in quella
guerra? 18. Chi ebbe la vittoria? 19. Dove entrarono le
truppe alleate? 20. Quale regione fu liberata dal giogo
dell'Austria? 21. Perchè il Veneto non fu liberato? 22. Fu
contento Cavour di quella pace?

LESSON XLVI

152.   **Conditional Clauses**

1. **Se avessi quel libro, stu-**   If I had that book, I should
   dierei.   study.
   (This implies: **Non ho quel libro.**)

   Se domani avessi del da-   If I should have money tomor-
   naro, comprerei quell'au-   row, I should buy that auto-
   tomobile.   mobile.
   (This implies: **È dubbio** (*doubtful*) **ch'io abbia del danaro
   domani.**)

The past subjunctive is used in a conditional clause (or *if-*
clause) to imply that the statement is either contrary to fact
in the present or doubtful in the future. In the conclusional
clause of such a sentence the conditional is used.

2. **Se avessi avuto quel libro,**   If I had had that book, I should
   avrei studiato.   have studied.
   (This implies: **Non avevo quel libro.**)

Q

When the conditional clause refers to past time **the** past perfect subjunctive is used, and the conclusion is rendered in the conditional perfect.

153. The Irregular Verb *porre, to put*

Infinitive and Participles

porre ponɛndo posto

Indicative

Present	Past Descriptive	Past Absolute	Future
pongo	*ponevo*	posi	porrɔ́
poni	*ponevi*	*ponesti*	porrai
pone	*poneva*	pose	porrà
poniamo	*ponevamo*	*ponemmo*	porremo
ponete	*ponevate*	*poneste*	porrete
pongono	*ponevano*	posero	porranno

Subjunctive		Conditional	Imperative
Present	Past		
ponga	*ponessi*	porrei	
ponga	*ponessi*	porresti	poni
ponga	*ponesse*	porrɛbbe	
poniamo	*ponessimo*	porremmo	poniamo
poniate	*poneste*	porreste	ponete
pongano	*ponessero*	porrɛbbero	

154. Formation of Irregular Verbs. Certain parts of all irregular verbs (except ɛssere) are regular, as a rule : the present participle, the past descriptive, the past subjunctive, the second person plural of the present indicative, and the second person·singular and first and second persons plural of the past absolute. These forms are printed above in boldface italics.

As for the irregular forms, the following rules should be noted:

1.	porre (for ponere)	condurre (for conducere)
	ponɛndo	conducɛndo
	ponete	conducete

Several verbs of the second conjugation have a contracted infinitive. In all such verbs the regular stem appears in the present participle.

2.	pongo	ponga
	pongono	pongano

From the first person singular of the present indicative are formed: (a) The third person plural of that tense; (b) The whole present subjunctive, except the first and second persons plural: these can be made from the first person plural of the present indicative.

3.	poni	poni
	poniamo	poniamo
	ponete	ponete

The three forms of the imperative are precisely like the corresponding forms of the present indicative, except that in the first conjugation the 2nd person singular ends in –i in the indicative, –a in the imperative.

4.	porrɔ	andrɔ
	porrɛi	andrɛi

The only irregularity in the future and conditional is that they are contracted in many verbs even when the infinitive is not contracted. The commonest type of contraction is shown in the verb **andare**; it consists of the dropping of the e which precedes the r of the infinitive used as a stem.

5.	posi
	pose
	posero

From the first person singular of the past absolute are formed the third singular and plural of that tense (see § 108).

NOTE. — The verbs **essere, avere, andare, dare, fare, stare, dire,** **sapere** and **volere** are exceptions to the rules given above.

155. Study the inflection of **dovere, potere, rimanere, vedere** and **volere** (*see* § 169, 113, 205, 260, 370, 374.)

EXERCISE XLVI

A. (1) *Supply the proper form (two when possible, see* § 152, 1, 2) *of each verb given in the infinitive:* 1. Se questo ragazzo (*studiare*) —, suo padre e sua madre (*essere*) — contenti. 2. Se voi (*essere*) — in Italia, quali città (*visitare*) —? 3. Se io (*avere*) — danaro, (*potere*) — andare in Italia l'estate ventura. 4. Se essi (*avere*) — un'automobile, non (*rimanere*) — a casa. 5. Se noi (*dovere*) — studiare, (*studiare*) —. 6. Se oggi (*piovere*) —, noi non (*uscire*) —. 7. Se voi (*potere*) —, non (*volere*) — invitare degli amici? 8. Se Lei (*andare*) — al Teatro Argentina, (*vedere*) — quell'attrice. 9. Se Maria (*essere*) — qui oggi, noi (*potere*) — presentarla a Olga. 10. Se i biglietti (*costare*) — molto, io (*rimanere*) — a casa.

(2) *Supply the proper form of the required tense of the verb given in the infinitive:*

PRESENT INDICATIVE. 1. (*porre*) I ragazzi — i libri sullo scaffale. 2. (*volere*) Io non — incontrarlo. 3. (*dovere*) Noi — uscire di buon'ora. 4. (*potere*) Essi non — scrivere. 5. (*dovere*) I miei fratelli — ritornare da New York. 6. (*rimanere*) Io — spesso con loro. 7. (*volere*) Tu — troppe cose. 8. (*potere*) — tu darmi quell'informazione? 9. (*rimanere*) Le ragazze — contente. 10. (*potere*) Egli non — camminare.

PAST ABSOLUTE and PRESENT PERFECT. 1. (*volere*) Io — leggere quel romanzo. 2. (*porre*) Carlo — la lampada sulla tavola. 3. (*vedere*) Egli mi — con una signora. 4. (*rimanere*) Chi — coi ragazzi? 5. (*vedere*) Tu non li —.

6. (*volere*) Essi non —— dormire. 7. (*rimanere*) Esse non ——
a scuola. 8. (*volere*) Elena —— occupare il miglior posto.
9. (*porre*) Io li —— a letto. 10. (*rimanere*) Gli zii ——.
FUTURE.' 1. (*porre*) Io —— i calzini nel cassettone.
2. (*potere*) Nessuno —— farlo contento. 3. (*rimanere*) Voi
—— nello studio. 4. (*vedere*) Chi —— quello spettacolo?
5. (*volere*) Essi non —— sacrificarsi. 6. (*dovere*) I miei
amici —— essere a Milano. 7. (*potere*) Essi —— andare alla
mia banca. 8. (*rimanere*) Noi —— in America. 9. (*vedere*)
Voi non ci ——. 10. (*volere*) —— tu scrivermi spesso?

B.   Garibaldi e i Mille

I primi effetti della sconfitta dell'Austria si ebbero in
Emilia e in Toscana. Queste regioni si ribellarono ai loro
tiranni e dichiararono di unirsi al Piemonte con plebisciti
che ebbero luogo nei primi mesi del 1860. Napoleone
rispettò le conseguenze della libera manifestazione del voto
popolare, ma domandò in compenso, e ottenne dal Piemonte,
Nizza e la Savoia.

Il principale evento del 1860 fu però la conquista del
Regno delle Due Sicilie per opera di Garibaldi. Giuseppe
Garibaldi (1807–82), che in gioventù s'era arrolato tra i
patriotti della Giovane Italia e che s'era già coperto di
gloria nel quarantotto all'assedio di Roma e nella recente
guerra quale capo dei Cacciatori delle Alpi, concepì l'idea
di liberare l'Italia Meridionale dal giogo dei Borboni.

S'imbarcò da Genova con mille seguaci su due piroscafi, e
con essi sbarcò a Marsala, in Sicilia, dove la popolazione lo
ricevè in un delirio di patriottismo. L'impresa sembrava
pazzesca, ma la fortuna favorì la causa italiana per cui quei
prodi combatterono. Palermo [1] e poi tutta la Sicilia furono conquistate, mentre da ogni parte accorrevano volontari

---

[1] Names of cities are of feminine gender, irrespective of their ending.

a ingrossare le file dei garibaldini. Garibaldi fu proclamato dittatore in nome di Vittorio Emanuele e, passato sul continente, non trovò nessun ostacolo alla conquista di Napoli.

Cavour capì che quello era il momento d'intervenire e le truppe piemontesi entrarono negli Stati Papali, occuparono le Marche e l'Umbria, e si unirono all'esercito di Garibaldi mentre questi stava per attaccare l'esercito borbonico sul Volturno. La vittoria non poteva non arridere ai patriotti: i Borboni furono scacciati dall'Italia, e la penisola fu unita sotto lo scettro di Vittorio Emanuele II.

C. 1. Emilia and Tuscany rebelled against their tyrants. 2. A plebiscite took place in those regions in 1860. 3. They joined Piedmont. 4. This was an important event, but the most important [one] in that year was the expedition of the Thousand. 5. If that expedition had not taken place, Italy would have remained divided. 6. Garibaldi put himself at the head of a thousand men and sailed for Sicily. 7. He sailed from Genoa on May 5, 1860. 8. If he had not sailed, who could say when the Bourbons would have been expelled from Italy? 9. Italians can never (= will never be able to) forget what they owe to Garibaldi. 10. The Thousand landed at Marsala and were received with enthusiasm by the population.

D. 1. Garibaldi was a follower of Mazzini, but he understood that Italy could be united sooner under the leadership of Victor Emmanuel. 2. If he had remained faithful to Mazzini's ideas, he could not have fought (= he would not have been able to fight) for the king. 3. He wanted (*past absolute*) above all the unity and independence of his fatherland. 4. Many volunteers joined his army in Sicily and in the Neapolitan provinces. 5. They saw (*past absolute*) that the end of tyranny had arrived. 6. If Garibaldi's victories had not aroused their patriotism, they would not have fought so gallantly. 7. The last battle of that war took place on the banks of the river Volturno. 8. If I went to (in) Italy, I should want to see this river. 9. You will see this river in traveling from Rome to Naples. 10. Thanks to Garibaldi, Italy was united;

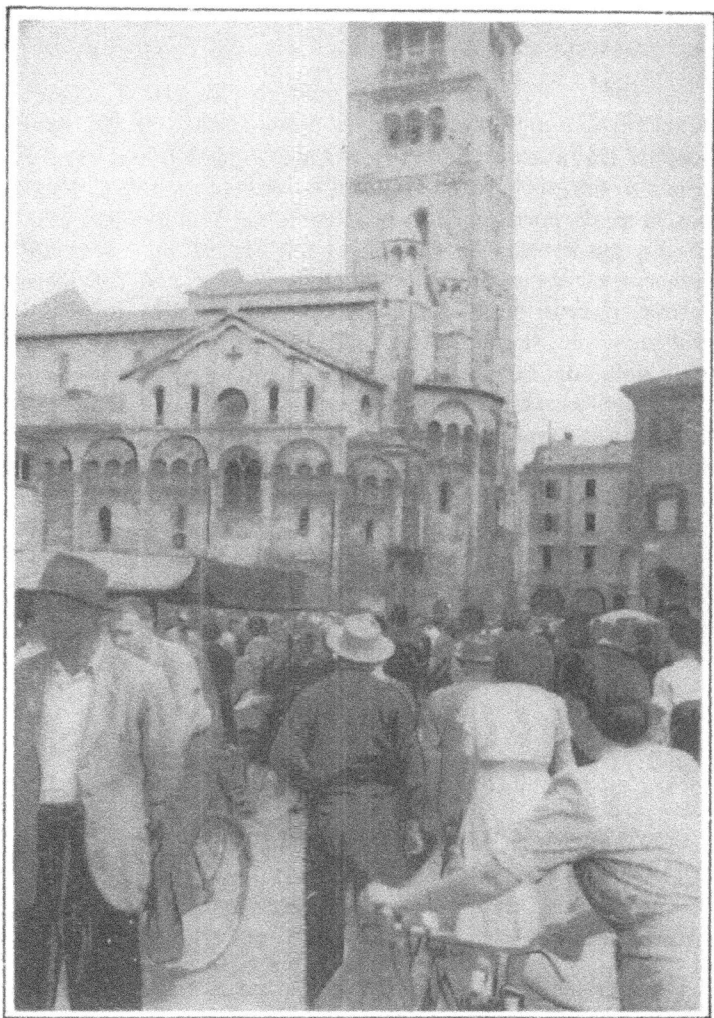

THE MARKET-PLACE AT MODENA

but Rome remained under the Pope, and the Venetian provinces remained under the yoke of Austria.[1]

E. *Oral.* 1. Quali furono i quattro patriotti che guidarono l'Italia nella lotta per l'indipendenza? 2. Di quale società era stato membro Garibaldi? 3. Dove s'era egli coperto di gloria? 4. Che idea concepì egli nel 1860? 5. Da quale porto partì la spedizione dei Mille? 6. Perchè questa spedizione fu chiamata dei Mille? 7. Su quanti piroscafi partirono i Mille? 8. Dove sbarcarono? 9. Come furono ricevuti in Sicilia? 10. Qual è la città principale dell'isola di Sicilia? 11. Per chi combattè Garibaldi? 12. Sarebbe riuscita la spedizione se i Siciliani non avessero ricevuto Garibaldi entusiasticamente? 13. Dove andò Garibaldi dopo aver conquistato la Sicilia? 14. Trovò egli ostacoli alla conquista di Napoli? 15. Che cosa pensò di fare Cavour? 16. Dove entrarono le truppe piemontesi? 17. Con quale esercito si unirono le truppe piemontesi? 18. Dove ebbe luogo l'ultima battaglia contro i Borbonici? 19. Con la vittoria si ebbe la completa unità d'Italia? 20. Quali parti non erano ancora unite al nuovo regno?

LESSON XLVII

156.   **Omission of the Definite Article**

Roma, capitale d'Italia	Rome, the capital of Italy
Vittorio Emanuele Terzo	Victor Emmanuel the Third

The definite article is omitted in Italian, though required in English: (*a*) Before a noun in apposition; (*b*) Before an ordinal numeral modifying a proper name (*see* § 133, 3).

157. Omission of the Indefinite Article. The indefinite article, though used in English, is omitted in Italian in the following cases:

---

[1] Use the definite article.

1. **Pisa, città di Toscana**   Pisa, a city of Tuscany

Often before a noun in apposition.

2. **Egli è americano.**   He is an American.
   Mio padre è avvocato.   My father is a lawyer.
But: **Egli è un buon avvocato.**   He is a good lawyer.

Before an unqualified predicate noun.

3. **Che peccato !**   What a pity !
   Quale idea !   What an idea !

After **che** or **quale**, in exclamations.

4. Before **cento** and **mille** (*see* § 75, 4).

5. After **da** in the sense of *in the manner of* (*see* § 151, 3).

158.   Verbal Adjective

1. **la lezione seguente**   the following lesson
   una macchina parlante   a talking machine
   gl'insegnanti   the teachers

When in English the present participle is used as an adjective, it is rendered in Italian, not by the form which we have called the participle, but by a verbal adjective, which can be formed from almost any Italian verb by adding to the verbal stem the endings –ante for the first conjugation, and –ente for the other two. Like all other adjectives, the verbal adjectives are inflected and may be used as nouns.

2. **un uccello che canta**   a singing bird

Another way of rendering the English present participle used as an adjective is that of changing the participle into a relative clause. With many verbs this form is preferable.

159.   The Verb *fare* with a Dependent Infinitive

Faccia aprire le porte.   Have the doors opened.
Si fece fare un abito.   He had a suit of clothes made.

The verb **fare** is used before an infinitive to express the idea that the action is to be done by somebody else. It renders such English expressions as *to have something done, to get something done,* etc. If a reflexive pronoun is understood in English (as in the second example), it must be expressed in Italian.

160.   **Conjunctive Pronouns with a Dependent Infinitive**

1. **Lo possiamo mandare.**   We can send it.
   Possiamo mandarlo.

   Gliene devo parlare.   I must speak of it to him.
   Devo parlargliene.

Several verbs, among which **dovere, potere, volere, osare** and **sapere,** have a sort of auxiliary function when followed by an infinitive. If the dependent infinitive has a pronoun object (or objects), the latter may either be appended to it, or precede the main verb.

2. **Lo *fecero* mandar via.**   They had him sent away.
   La vedo ammirare da tutti.   I see her admired by all.
   Sento dire molte cose.   I hear many things being said.
   Feci studiar la lezione a   I made this boy study his
   questo ragazzo.   lesson.
   Gliela feci studiare.   I made him study it.

On the other hand certain verbs, like **fare, lasciare, sentire, udire** and **vedere,** take the object of the dependent infinitive. Note, however, that if the object of either verb is a noun (3d example), it usually follows both verbs; and that if the main verb also has an object (4th and 5th examples), that object becomes indirect.

161. Study the inflection of **andare, bere, condurre, dare, fare,** and **stare** (*see* § 169, 16, 37, 55, 78, 132, 338.)

EXERCISE XLVII

A. (1) *Translate into Italian, rendering the English present
participle first by a verbal adjective, then by a relative clause:*
1. A sleeping girl. 2. The returning soldiers. 3. A talking
animal. 4. Some amusing stories. 5. The dying day.
6. The departing men. 7. The preceding page. 8. The
following poems.

(2) *Translate into Italian:* 1. They had a man sent to the
post office. 2. I must have my books sent here. 3. We
hear her singing. 4. Have the windows closed, please.
5. I must write it to him (*two ways*). 6. I shall have a dress
made. 7. Mary had a dress made for her little sister.
8. I see you working. 9. We may look at them (*two ways*).
10. What a fine day! 11. Who made you do that?
12. What a bad boy!

(3) *Supply the proper form of the required tense of the verb
given in the infinitive:*

PRESENT SUBJUNCTIVE. 1. (*bere*) Vuole ch'egh non —— che
acqua. 2. (*fare*) Desidero che tu —— come me. 3. (*condurre*) È impossibile che voi ci ——. 4. (*dare*) Mi ——
codesta penna, per favore. 5. (*stare*) Bisogna che essi ——
a casa. 6. (*andare*) Non credo che tu —— a cavallo.
7. (*bere*) Che vuole ch'essi —— ? 8. (*condurre*) Credo che
Carlo li —— sulla cattiva via.

PAST ABSOLUTE and PRESENT PERFECT. 1. (*dare*) Essi
ci —— un pacco. 2. (*bere*) Io —— alla loro salute. 3. (*condurre*) Incontrai (Ho incontrato) le signore e le —— al teatro.
4. (*fare*) Che —— Alberto? 5. (*stare*) Voi —— in campagna
tutta l'estate. 6. (*dare*) Tu non mi —— nulla. 7. (*fare*)
I ragazzi —— quel che la loro mamma aveva ordinato.

FUTURE. 1. (*bere*) Noi mangeremo e ——. 2. (*dare*) Che
cosa ti —— essi? 3. (*stare*) Io —— a Napoli nel mese di
marzo. 4. (*condurre*) Dove ci —— quest'uomo? 5. (*an-

dare) Non —— voi a Firenze la settimana ventura ?   6. (*fare*) Domani noi —— molte cose.   7. (*condurre*) Io vi —— a passeggiare sul Pincio.   8. (*andare*) Nessuno —— in città con loro.

B.   **Venezia e Roma**

Cavour morì poco dopo la proclamazione del nuovo regno, lasciando ai suoi successori la soluzione del problema di Venezia e di quello di Roma.   Gli Austriaci erano ancora nel Veneto, e il Papa regnava ancora a Roma, sotto la protezione d'un esercito francese.   Pio IX non solo aveva rifiutato di riconoscere il governo italiano, ma ne aveva anche scomunicato i capi.

Grande era il desiderio in tutta la penisola di veder completata l'unità della nazione, ma il nuovo governo dovè posporre ogni decisione per non rischiare le sorti della Patria in nuove guerre, e fu obbligato a opporsi con le armi a due tentativi, fatti da Garibaldi e dai suoi seguaci, di marciare su Roma.

Ma l'attesa non fu senza frutto.   Nel 1866, essendo scoppiata una guerra tra la Prussia e l'Austria, l'Italia riprese le armi contro l'antica avversaria, la quale dovè poco dopo cedere il Veneto.   Quattro anni più tardi un'altra occasione si presentò quando la Francia, trovandosi in guerra con la Germania, ritirò da Roma l'esercito che vi teneva.   Il 20 settembre 1870 le truppe italiane, dopo breve resistenza incontrata a Porta Pia, entrarono in Roma, e la Città Eterna fu proclamata capitale del nuovo regno.

C. 1. The great men of the Risorgimento made of Italy an important nation.   2. Unfortunately, Cavour did not see the complete unity of Italy.   3. He died in 1861, when he was only 51 years old.   4. What a sorrow that was[1] for all Italians !   5. Europe

---

[1] Translate, *was that.*

THE GRAND CANAL AND RIALTO BRIDGE, VENICE

had seen him prepare Italy for the struggle against Austria, and lead it to victory. 6. Thayer, a great American historian, thought that Cavour was the greatest statesman Europe had had in the past century. 7. His successor was Ricasoli, a good patriot, but a less able statesman than he. 8. He wanted to have the capital of Italy transferred to Rome, but he feared that the European nations would intervene again in the affairs of Italy. 9. Garibaldi attempted twice to (di) march on Rome. 10. The Italian government made him abandon his idea by (con) force of arms.

D. 1. Garibaldi led two expeditions against Rome, but without success. 2. Many in Italy thought that he was wrong in doing this. 3. Others wished that he would succeed. 4. They saw his little army disbanded by the Italian troops. 5. The government was obliged to arrest him and have him promise not to (di non) disturb the peace of Italy. 6. What a sad day was that for many patriots who desired Italian unity! 7. "We shall take Rome," they declared, "and stay there, when the opportune moment arrives." 8. "We shall lead an army into Rome and make the government proclaim a United Italy." 9. And the moment arrived when that prophecy came true. 10. On September 20, 1870 an Italian army entered Rome, led by General Cadorna, a veteran of the wars against Austria, and Rome was thenceforth the capital of Italy.

E. *Oral.* 1. In che anno morì Cavour? 2. Vide egli la completa unità della sua patria? 3. Chi fu il suo successore? 4. Quali problemi lasciò egli al suo successore? 5. Chi occupava Venezia? 6. Qual governo c'era ancora in Roma? 7. Che cosa aveva rifiutato Pio IX? 8. Chi aveva egli scomunicato? 9. Che cosa desideravano gl'Italiani? 10. Perchè il nuovo governo italiano dovè posporre ogni decisione? 11. Chi fece dei tentativi per prendere Roma? 12. Quante volte tentò egli di marciare su Roma? 13. Tra quali nazioni era scoppiata la guerra nel 1866? 14. Che cosa fece allora il governo italiano? 15. Quale fu il risultato di questa guerra per l'Italia? 16. In che anno scoppiò la guerra tra la Francia e la Germania? 17. Perchè ritirò la Francia i suoi soldati che erano in Roma? 18. Che fece allora il governo italiano? 19. In che giorno entrarono le truppe italiane nella Città Eterna? 20. Quale fu il risultato della presa di Roma?

LESSON XLVIII

162. Government of the Infinitive

The infinitive may depend upon a noun, an adjective, or a verb.

1. **casa da fittare** house to rent
   il bisogno di studiare the need of studying

If the infinitive depends upon a noun, the preposition **da** is used whenever purpose is implied; in all other cases **di** is generally used.

2. (a) **Son contento di partire.** I am glad to leave.
   È pesante a portare. It is heavy to carry.

An infinitive depending upon an adjective is usually preceded by **di** or **a**; very seldom by **da**.

(b) **Inutile parlare.** It is useless to talk.

With certain adjectives, such as **facile, difficile, utile, inutile, importante, giusto,** no preposition is used.

3. (a) **Devo lavorare.** I must work.
   Volevo parlargli. I wanted to talk to him.

A certain number of verbs take the infinitive without any preposition. The following are the most frequently used:

ardire	to dare	**dovere**	to be obliged
bastare	to suffice	**fare**	to make, have done
bisognare	to be necessary	**lasciare**	to let, allow

osare	to dare	sembrare	to seem
parere	to seem	sentire	to hear, feel
potere	to be able	udire	to hear
preferire	to prefer	vedere	to see
sapere	to know how	volere	to want,

(b) **Andò a comprare dei doni** — He went to buy some gifts.

Stetti ad aspettare. — I stood waiting.

Imparò a parlare italiano. — He learned to talk Italian.

An infinitive depending upon a verb of motion or rest, or a verb meaning the beginning, progress, or continuance of an action, or the verbs **imparare** and **insegnare** are regularly preceded by the preposition **a**.

(c) **Rifiutai di trattar quell'affare.** — I refused to transact that business.

Offrì di pagare. — He offered to pay.

Most other verbs take **di** before the following infinitive.

163.   Absolute Constructions

Finito il lavoro, partirono. — Having finished their work, they left.

Rimasta sola, ella cominciò a scrivere. — Having remained alone, she began to write.

Visti quei quadri, egli desiderò di comprarli. — Having seen those pictures, he wished to buy them.

Very frequently a past participle is used alone, in Italian, in place of the perfect participle. If the verb is transitive, the participle agrees in gender and number with its object; otherwise, with its subject.

164. Study the inflection of **chiudere, dire, leggere, mettere, prendere, rispondere, scrivere,** and **venire** (*see* § 169, 40, 91, 172, 175, 209, 275, 305, 371).

EXERCISE XLVIII

A. (1) *Insert the proper preposition if one is missing:*
1. Desideravo — camminare. 2. Devo — incontrarlo.
3. Lo sento — cantare. 4. Vado — studiare. 5. Voleva
— accompagnarmi. 6. Cominciarono — nuotare. 7. Lo
lascio — parlare. 8. Starò — udirli. 9. Ella mostrava
— capire. 10. Impariamo — remare. 11. Mi consigliò
— telefonarle. 12. Vuole — sacrificarsi per noi. 13. Con-
tinuerà — aspettare. 14. Rifiutò — venire. 15. Preferiva — non far nulla. 16. Non può — scendere. 17. Non
osavano — rispondere. 18. Desidera — vendere la sua
mobilia. 19. Gli scriva — venire. 20. Non bisogna —
cominciar male.

(2) *Replace the perfect participle by the absolute construction
in each of the following sentences:* 1. Essendo andati in campagna, volemmo divertirci. 2. Avendo comprato i libri,
desiderai di leggerli. 3. Avendo cominciato quelle cose,
dovei finirle. 4. Essendo venute le ragazze, la lezione
cominciò. 5. Avendo comprato quella casa, ne comprai
un'altra. 6. Avendo condotto i miei amici alla banca, li
presentai al cassiere.

(3) *Supply the proper form of the required tense of the verb
given in the infinitive:*
PRESENT INDICATIVE. 1. (*dire*) Noi non — chi sia stato.
2. (*leggere*) Io — questa novella italiana. 3. (*venire*) Tu
— sempre in ritardo. 4. (*dire*) Chi — queste cose?
5. (*leggere*) I ragazzi — in questo momento. 6. (*venire*)
Io — con Loro. 7. (*dire*) Tutti — che l'Italia è un bel
paese. 8. (*venire*) A che ora — il postino? 9. (*dire*) Tu
— che hanno torto. 10. (*venire*) I miei cugini — da
Bologna.
PAST ABSOLUTE and PAST PERFECT. 1. (*chiudere*) Gli
studenti — i libri. 2. (*dire*) Io — poche parole. 3. (*leg-*

R

gere) Elena —— la lettera che suo cugino le aveva scritta.
4. (*mettere*) Chi —— ogni cosa in ordine? 5. (*prendere*)
Maria e Olga —— delle frutta. 6. (*rispondere*) Io —— con
una lettera. 7. (*scrivere*) Le cartoline che essi —— dove
sono? (*or* dov'erano?) 8. (*venire*) Carlo —— due volte a
visitarci. 9. (*chiudere*) La lettera che io —— era scritta in
inglese. 10. (*dire*) Erano poche parole, ma io le —— volentieri.

PAST SUBJUNCTIVE and CONDITIONAL. 1. Se il signor
Cantoni vi (*invitare*) ——, voi (*venire*) ——? 2. Se io (*chiudere*) —— questa porta, Lei che (*dire*) ——? 3. Se Lei mi
(*scrivere*) ——, io le (*rispondere*) —— subito. 4. Se essi
(*avere*) —— tempo, (*venire*) ——. 5. Se noi (*potere*) ——
venire, (*venire*) ——. 6. Se Lei mi (*dare*) —— quel libro, io lo
(*prendere*) —— con piacere.

B.   **L'Italia dopo il Settanta**

Ottenuta l'unità politica, l'Italia dovè affrontare i gravi
problemi della ricostruzione interna e liquidare le tristi eredità del passato. Nelle province meridionali, dove per
secoli la popolazione aveva patito il malgoverno dei Borboni,
era generale l'analfabetismo e il disprezzo per le leggi e le
autorità: alla giustizia delle corti s'era sostituito in alcune
regioni il sistema delle vendette private.

La vigorosa azione del governo mise un termine a questo
stato di cose in pochi anni. Il sistema amministrativo e
giuridico fu riordinato, l'istruzione elementare fu fatta
obbligatoria, e, con lo sviluppo delle comunicazioni, le condizioni economiche della penisola vennero man mano migliorando.

Un fenomeno tipico della vita economica italiana negli
ultimi cinquant'anni è stato quello dell'emigrazione. Centinaia di migliaia d'Italiani si sono stabiliti in altri paesi
europei e nelle Americhe. Malgrado ciò, la popolazione del

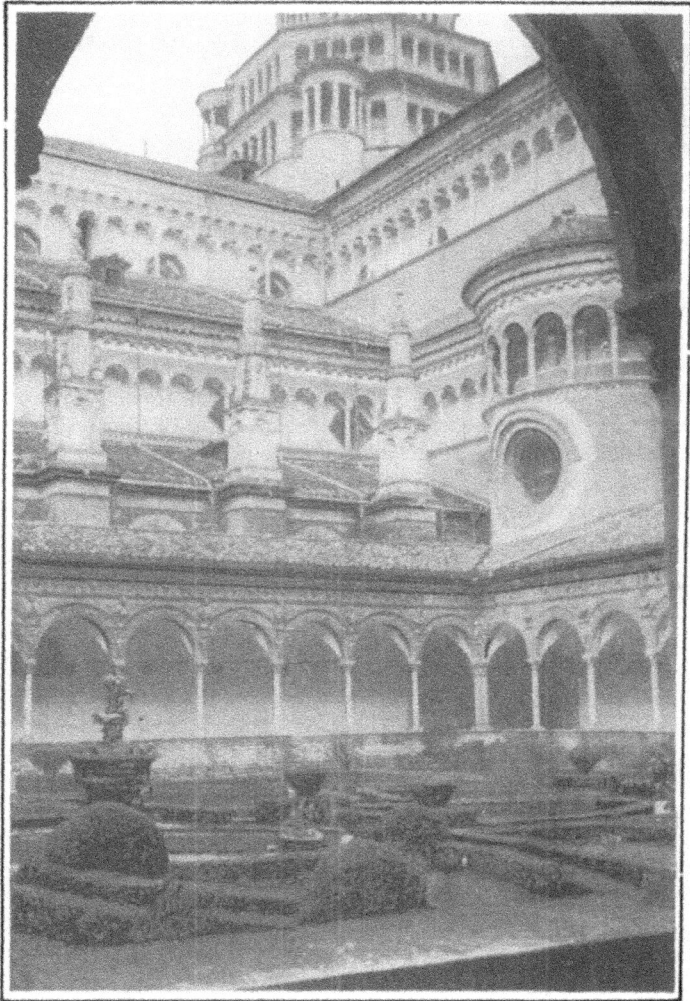

CERTOSA DI PAVIA

regno è andata sempre aumentando e aumenta tuttora, creando il bisogno d'espansione coloniale.

L'Italia, prima della seconda guerra mondiale, aveva tre colonie in Africa: l'Eritrea, sulla costa del Mar Rosso; la Somalia, sulla costa dell'Oceano Indiano; e la Libia, ceduta dalla Turchia in seguito alla guerra italo-turca del 1911–12, sul Mediterraneo.

C. 1. Having obtained their independence, Italians put every effort into the solution of their problems. 2. Centuries of misgovernment had left the country in a very wretched state. 3. Such was particularly the case in the Southern provinces. 4. Having lost all [1] faith in the justice of the courts, many still used to resort to private vengeance. 5. Illiteracy was very common, and crimes were in proportion to it.[2] 6. But Italians understood that it was necessary that these conditions be changed. 7. Schools were opened everywhere. 8. Railroads were built. 9. A new system of laws was adopted for all Italy. 10. Having done this, Italians strove to improve the economic and financial conditions of their country.

D. 1. Having transferred the capital to (in) the Eternal City, the government started to reorganize the country. 2. It was difficult to solve all the problems inherited from the old governments. 3. But the need of solving them was understood by the Italian statesmen. 4. In the last fifty years the country has made enormous progress. 5. Illiteracy has been fought with success, and the economic conditions have shown great improvement. 6. Today Genoa is the busiest harbor in the Mediterranean, and Turin and Milan are among the greatest industrial centers of Europe. 7. Italy's population increases very rapidly, although hundreds of thousands of Italians emigrate every year to (per) foreign countries. 8. Having settled in a foreign country, Italians usually distinguish themselves for their industry. 9. In America we are glad to see them becoming good citizens. 10. Their contribution to our material and intellectual progress has been very great.

[1] **Ogni.** [2] Use a disjunctive pronoun.

E. *Oral.* 1. Che cosa dovè affrontare l'Italia dopo il settanta? 2. In quali regioni d'Italia eran peggiori le condizioni? 3. Perchè eran peggiori? 4. Quali erano i problemi della nuova Italia? 5. Si rispettavano le leggi? 6. Che cosa s'era sostituito alla giustizia delle corti? 7. Chi mise un termine a questo stato di cose? 8. Che cosa riordinò il governo? 9. Come fu combattuto l'analfabetismo? 10. Che cosa fece possibile il miglioramento delle condizioni economiche del paese? 11. Qual è un fenomeno tipico della vita economica italiana? 12. Dove vanno gli emigranti italiani? 13. Rimangono tutti nel paese dove vanno? 14. Che bisogno crea l'aumento della popolazione in Italia? 15. Qual è il porto più attivo del Mediterraneo? 16. Quali sono le città più industriali d'Italia? 17 Quante colonie aveva l'Italia? 18. Dove erano queste colonie? 19. Come si chiamava la colonia italiana sulla costa del Mar Rosso? 20. Come si chiamava la colonia italiana ceduta dalla Turchia?

LESSON XLIX

165. **Augmentatives and Diminutives**

1. The meaning of an Italian noun, adjective, or adverb, may be modified by a suffix. Usually the noun thus modified keeps its gender, but occasionally a suffix of masculine ending, added to a feminine noun, makes it masculine. In adding the suffix, the final vowel of the word must be dropped, and if the final vowel is preceded by a c or a g, the original sound of these letters must be kept. **Stanza + ino = stanzino, barca + etta = barchetta, semplice + one = semplicione.**

2. un amico; un amicone   a friend; a great friend
     una donna; un donnone   a woman; an enormous woman
     una bottiglia; un bottiglione   a bottle; a big bottle
     una ragazza; una ragazzona   a girl; a big girl

The suffix denoting bigness is −one. It has a feminine form, −ona, which is used only with nouns or adjectives having both a masculine and a feminine form (see last example). In other cases, that is when no confusion might occur, a feminine noun takes the ending −one, and becomes masculine.

3.
una donna; una donnetta	a woman; a little woman
la campana; il campanello	the bell; the little bell
una commedia; una commediola	a play; a little play
Grazia; Graziella	Grace; little Grace
una casa; una casina	a house; a pretty little house
bello; bellino	beautiful; pretty
caro; carino	dear; darling
bene; benino	well; rather well
Olga; Olguccia	Olga; dear little Olga
una donna; una donnuccia	a woman; a silly little woman
una contadina; una contadinotta	a peasant woman; a sturdy peasant girl

The most important suffixes denoting smallness are:

−etto, −a; −ello, −a; −olo, −a, implying mere *smallness.*
−ino, −a, denoting *smallness* and *endearment.*
−uccio, −a, expressing *affection* if modifying a proper name or a name referring to a person; *pity* or *contempt,* if attached to a common noun.
−otto, −a, denoting *smallness* combined with *strength.*

4.
tempo; tempaccio	weather, nasty weather
roba; robaccia	stuff, goods; trash

The suffix −accio, −a conveys an idea of *intense contempt.*

5.
fratello brother	signorina	young lady, miss
sorella sister	libretto	libretto
	bambino baby	

Quite often the endings listed above lose their independent character and become inseparable parts of certain words.

6. These endings must be chosen according to precedent

and euphony. The ear is a sufficient guide in this matter to a native Italian, but the foreigner should use great discretion and avoid employing forms he has not already met.

166. Study the inflection of **chiedere, giungere, morire, nascere, parere, ridere, soffrire,** and **tenere** (*see* § 169, 39, 142, 177, 180, 190, 254, 31ᴇ, 350).

EXERCISE XLIX

A. (1) *Translate:* parolaccia, manina, figliuolo, poverello, piazzetta, cosuccia, bellino, inchiostraccio, stanzone, cosetta, Albertuccio, cappellino, benone, coltellino, contadinotto, spettacolaccio, saletta, scarpina, tovagliolino, vecchione.

(2) *Translate into Italian, using a suffix in each case:*
1. A contemptible vice. 2. A poor little house. 3. A little train. 4. That awful boy. 5. A poor little theater. 6. A pretty little theater. 7. Dear little Helen. 8. A nasty novel. 9. Some little rooms. 10. Extremely full. 11. A little dinner. 12. A great lord. 13. Rather proud. 14. Some little stores. 15. Dear little Mary. 16. A bad lawyer. 17. Rather light. 18. Rather good. 19. A big porter. 20. Some pretty little divans.

(3) *Supply the proper form of the required tense of the verb given in the infinitive:*
PRESENT INDICATIVE. 1. (*morire*) Gloria a quelli che —— per la Patria! 2. (*parere*) Molte cose —— facili che non lo sono. 3. (*tenere*) Queste ragazze —— la casa in ordine. 4. (*morire*) Il giorno ——. 5. (*parere*) Io non —— suo fratello. 6. (*tenere*) Che —— tu? 7. (*tenere*) Io non —— nulla. 8. (*morire*) Noi —— dal desiderio di veder nostra madre. 9. (*parere*) Sarà ricco, ma non ——.

PAST ABSOLUTE and PRESENT PERFECT. 1. (*chiedere*) Noi —— loro un favore 2. (*giungere*) Mia cugina —— col treno delle otto. 3. (*morire*) Quel poveretto —— senza vedere i suoi figliuoli. 4. (*nascere*) Carlo e Alberto —— a Roma. 5. (*parere*) Mi —— ch'egli fosse stanco. 6. (*ridere*) Al sentirlo parlar così, io —— di cuore. 7. (*soffrire*) Esse —— molto durante la guerra. 8. (*tenere*) Arturo —— l'automobile per un anno. 9. (*giungere*) Le mie sorelle non —— in tempo. 10. (*morire*) La sua nonna ——; non lo sapeva Lei? 11. (*ridere*) Egli non —— mai durante lo spettacolo. 12. (*soffrire*) Sua madre —— perchè egli era lontano.

FUTURE. 1. (*morire*). Quando io ——, lascerò quel po' che ho a mia sorella. 2. (*parere*) Questa casa non ti —— abbastanza grande. 3. (*tenere*) Chi la —— in ordine? 4. (*morire*) Egli —— senza soffrire. 5. (*parere*) Con questo cappello io —— più vecchio di quel che sono. 6. (*morire*) I nomi dei martiri del Risorgimento non —— mai.

B. L'Italia e la Guerra Mondiale

Quando nell'agosto del 1914 l'Austria e la Germania precipitarono l'Europa negli orrori della più immane guerra che la storia ricordi, l'Italia, che con queste due potenze aveva un'alleanza difensiva, dichiarando la propria neutralità si pronunziò contro la loro aggressione. Ma l'opinione pubblica, nella penisola, non pareva soddisfatta di ciò, e da ogni parte si chiedeva che il governo italiano dichiarasse guerra agl'Imperi Centrali con lo scopo d'assicurare il trionfo d'una giusta pace e di strappare dal dominio dell'Austria le province irredente del Trentino e della Venezia Giulia.

Fu nel maggio del 1915, quando la situazione strategica degli alleati sembrava più pericolosa, che l'Italia dichirò guerra all'Austria. Per circa tre anni e mezzo la lotta fu terribile tra le nevose cime delle Alpi, e l'Austria dovè più d'una volta ricorrere all'aiuto della Germania per difendere le sue linee. Spronato dall'esempio del suo re, che prese attiva parte durante tutte le ostilità, l'esercito italiano dette prova di vero eroismo in molte occasioni, e specialmente alla

LIVEROGNE, VAL D'AOSTA, ITALIAN ALPS

difesa del Piave, dopo il disastro di Caporetto. Nell'ottobre del 1918 da questo storico fiume fu lanciato l'assalto finale e, dopo dieci giorni di accanita lotta, l'esercito italiano riuscì a sconfiggere il nemico. Con la vittoria di Vittorio Veneto l'Italia ebbe finalmente i suoi naturali confini.

C. 1. Italy had a defensive alliance with Germany and Austria. 2. Without consulting Italy, the Central Powers unchained the World War. 3. This relieved Italy from its engagements, and the government of Rome declared its neutrality. 4. The invasion of Belgium, the destruction of cathedrals, libraries, monuments of art, so enraged public opinion that war was demanded.[1] 5. Besides, to every Italian patriot it seemed [2] that it was the duty of Italy to redeem Trento and Trieste. 6. On May 24, 1915, war was declared. 7. From every part of Italy, and even from distant countries, Italians answered with enthusiasm the [3] call of their Fatherland. 8. It was a long, terrible war, fought among the snowy summits of the Alps. 9. Cavour had said: "As for the conquest of Trento and Trieste, that will be for another generation." 10. These words were at the same time an admonition and a prophecy.

D. 1. It had seemed [2] that the moment had arrived [4] to give Italy her natural boundaries. 2. Among the mountains of Trentino and on the banks of the river Isonzo, victory after victory [5] favored Italian arms. 3. But, after years of struggle, a disaster took place. 4. Russia had betrayed her allies and made a separate peace with Germany and Austria. 5. This gave the Central Powers an opportunity to concentrate their forces for a terrific attack against the Italian lines. 6. A retreat was necessary, but, having reached the Piave, the Italian army held the line with extreme gallantry. 7. One year after the disaster of Caporetto, the Italian troops, under the command of General Diaz, gained [6] one of the most brilliant victories of the World War, the victory of

[1] Use the verb **chiedere**.
[2] Use the verb **parere**.
[3] Translate, *to the*.

[4] Use the verb **giungere**.
[5] Translate, *a victory after another*.
[6] Use the verb **ottenere**.

Vittorio Veneto. 8. Fortune has smiled on (a) Italy; her people, after having suffered for so many centuries, are united again in a powerful nation. 9. Shelley's words have at last become true.

> 10. Thou which wert once, and then didst cease to be,[1]
> Now art, and henceforth ever shalt be, free,
> If Hope, and Truth, and Justice can avail . . .

E. *Oral.* 1. Con quali governi era alleata l'Italia prima della guerra mondiale? 2. Che specie d'alleanza era quella? 3. In che anno cominciò la guerra mondiale? 4. Chi la provocò? 5. Perchè dichiarò l'Italia la propria neutralità? 6. Che cosa chiedeva l'opinione pubblica italiana? 7. Per quali nazioni erano le simpatie del popolo italiano? 8. Quando entrò in guerra l'Italia? 9. Per quanti anni lottò l'Italia in quella guerra? 10. Dove ebbero luogo le battaglie? 11. Quali territori voleva l'Italia redimere dal giogo dell'Austria? 12. Su qual mare è la città di Trieste? 13. Quale disastro ebbe luogo durante quella guerra? 14. Dove si ritirò l'esercito italiano? 15. Chi prese il comando dell'esercito italiano? 16. Quando ebbe luogo la vittoria finale contro l'Austria? 17. Che nome prese quella vittoria? 18. Dov'era il re d'Italia durante la guerra? 19. Come si chiama il re d'Italia? 20. Chi sa le parole che Shelley scrisse sull'Italia? — Le dica.

LESSON L

Review

A. *Continue the following:* 1. Io chiesi un favore, etc. 2. Io son nato in America, etc. 3. Io non volli vederlo, etc. 4. Io le scrissi una lettera, etc. 5. Io rimango contento, etc. 6. Io giunsi in tempo, etc. 7. Io non feci quel che dovevo fare, etc. 8. Io lessi quel libro, etc.

---

[1] Translate, *to be it.*

B. *Review Questions:* 1. What is an adjectival clause? 2. By what kind of pronouns are adjectival clauses introduced? 3. When does an adjectival clause take the subjunctive in Italian? 4. Tell about the infinitive used as a noun. 5. What is an adverbial clause? Give an example. 6. Mention six Italian conjunctions which take the subjunctive. 7. Is the subjunctive ever used in independent clauses? When? 8. Give three idiomatic uses of the preposition **da** and furnish examples. 9. Give an example of a conditional clause in English. 10. What tenses must be used in a conditional clause in Italian? 11. What forms of an Italian verb are always regular? 12. Mention two cases in which the definite article is omitted in Italian. 13. Mention two cases in which the indefinite article is omitted in Italian. 14. What is a verbal adjective, and how is it formed? 15. Give the verbal adjectives of **amare, credere** and **partire.** 16. How do you express in Italian such phrases as *to have something done?* 17. Can you express in a different way the phrase **lo possiamo mandare?** 18. What prepositions are used before an infinitive depending on a noun? 19. Mention five verbs which take a dependent infinitive without preposition. 20. Mention a verb which takes the dependent infinitive with the preposition **a.** 21. Mention a verb which takes the dependent infinitive with the preposition **di.** 22. Give an example of absolute construction. 23. Which is the augmentative suffix in Italian? 24. Mention four diminutive suffixes and explain their meanings.

C. *Supply the correct form of the present indicative of the verb given in the infinitive:* 1. (*rimanere*) Ce ne —— ventidue. 2. (*porre*) Noi —— i libri sullo scaffale. 3. (*bere*) Io —— volentieri una tazza di caffè. 4. (*dire*) Non credo a quel che essi ——. 5. (*venire*) Noi andiamo dai nostri amici, e i nostri amici —— da noi. 6. (*fare*) Essi —— ciò ch'io dico. 7. (*volere*) Tu —— sempre aver ragione. 8. (*dare*) Io —— del danaro a mio cugino. 9. (*morire*) I soldati —— con gloria. 10. (*udire*) Egli non —— quel che Lei dice.

D. *Supply the correct form first of the past absolute, then of the present perfect, of the verb given in the infinitive:* 1. (*scrivere*) Arturo non —— che poche parole. 2. (*rispondere*) Io gli —— lo stesso giorno. 3. (*fare*) Che cosa —— voi? 4. (*prendere*) I miei amici —— dell'arrosto di vitello. 5. (*mettere*) Chi —— la sedia vicino allo specchio? 6. (*dire*) Io non —— nulla di male. 7. (*rimanere*) Quei signori non —— molto contenti. 8. (*condurre*) Il capitano —— i suoi soldati. 9. (*parere*) La cosa non mi —— giusta. 10. (*tenere*) Essi non ci ——.

E. *Supply the correct form of the past subjunctive and of the conditional of the verb given in the infinitive:* 1. Se voi (*fare*) —— ciò, voi (*morire*) ——. 2. Se Loro (*essere*) —— contenti, io li (*condurre*) —— con me. 3. Se Maria (*stare*) —— a casa, ella (*potere*) —— studiare. 4. Se io non (*avere*) —— bisogno di bere, io non (*bere*) ——. 5. Se la cameriera non (*porre*) —— i miei libri in ordine, io non (*potere*) —— lavorare. 6. Se Lei mi (*dare*) —— codesto libro, io lo (*leggere*) —— volentieri. 7. Se i miei amici (*avere*) —— danaro, essi (*andare*) —— in Italia. 8. Se noi (*partire*) —— alle otto, a che ora (*giungere*) ——? 9. Se io le (*dire*) —— chi è stato, (*essere*) —— Lei contento? 10. Se io (*potere*) —— viaggiare, (*venire*) —— con Lei.

F. *Complete the following sentences inserting the correct form of the verb given in the infinitive:* 1. (*venire*) Non vogliono che io ——. 2. (*potere*) Peccato che egli non —— viaggiare! 3. (*dire*) Non so quel ch'egli ——. 4. (*uscire*) Temei ch'ella ——. 5. (*uscire*) Temo ch'ella ——. 6. (*bere*) Voglio ch'egli —— la sua medicina. 7. (*stare*) Temo che i miei parenti non —— a casa a quest'ora. 8. (*dare*) Che vuole che io le ——? 9. (*fare*) Bisogna ch'essa —— ogni cosa. 10. (*volere*) Mario credeva che io —— dormire. 11. (*volere*) Mario crede che voi —— dormire. 12. (*condurre*) Peccato che egli non ci ——!

G. *Translate into Italian, using a suffix in each case:* 1. A contemptible little novel. 2. A pretty little skirt. 3. Two large gloves. 4. An ugly hand. 5. Some kittens. 6. Some little hens. 7. Little Alberta. 8. A little box. 9. A big box. 10. Some toy soldiers. 11. A young dressmaker. 12. Two ugly old shoes. 13. A pretty little rug. 14. Some little pockets. 15. Rather delightful. 16. A bad pen. 17. The very common people. 18. Rather small. 19. An ugly fashion. 20. A great master.

H. *Write in Italian a letter of about one hundred words, telling your professor how you expect to spend the coming vacation. Such a letter should begin with* **Egregio Sig. Professore** (*My dear Professor*), *and end with* **Con distinti saluti, devotissimo (–a)** (*With best wishes, sincerely yours*).

POEMS

1

Buon giorno, Lunedì;
come sta Martedì?
Bene, Mercoledì;
andiam da Giovedì
per dire a Venerdì
che bisogna che Sabato
si pensi alla Domenica.

2

Trenta giorni hanno settembre,
april, giugno e poi novembre;
di ventotto ce n'è uno;
gli altri sette n'han trentuno.

3

Fratelli d'Italia,
l'Italia s'è desta;
dell'elmo di Scipio
s'è cinta la testa:
dov'è la vittoria?
le porga la chioma,
chè schiava di Roma
Iddio la creò !

— Goffredo Mameli

253

4. Che fai tu, luna, in ciel?

Che fai tu, luna, in ciel? dimmi, che fai,
silenzïosa luna?
Sorgi la sera, e vai,
contemplando i deserti, indi ti posi.
Ancor non sei tu paga
di rïandare i sempiterni calli?
Ancor non prendi a schivo, ancor sei vaga
di mirar queste valli?

— Giacomo Leopardi

5. Preghiera

Alla mente confusa
di dubbio e di dolore,
soccorri, o mio Signore,
col raggio della Fè.

Sollevala dal peso
che la declina al fango:
a Te sospiro e piango,
mi raccomando a Te.

Sai che la vita mia
si strugge a poco a poco,
come la cera al fuoco,
come la neve al sol.

All'anima che anela
di ricovrarti in braccio,
rompi, Signore, il laccio
che le impedisce il vol.

— Giuseppe Giusti

6. Pianto antico

L'albero a cui tendevi
la pargoletta mano,
il verde melograno
da' bei vermigli fior,

nel muto orto solingo
rinverdì tutto or ora,
e giugno lo ristora
di luce e di calor.

Tu, fior della mia pianta
percossa e inaridita,
tu, dell'inutil vita
estremo, unico fior,

sei nella terra fredda,
sei nella terra negra;
nè il sol più ti rallegra,
nè ti risveglia amor.

— *Giosuè Carducci*

7. Fanciulla, che cosa è Dio?

Nell'ora che pel bruno firmamento
comincia un tremolio
di punti d'oro, d'atomi d'argento,
guardo e dimando: — Dite, o luci belle,
ditemi cosa è Dio'
— Ordine — mi rispondono le stelle.

Quando all'april la valle, il monte, il prato,
i margini del rio,
ogni campo dai fiori è festeggiato,

s

guardo e dimando: — Dite, o bei colori,
ditemi cosa è Dio?
— Bellezza — mi rispondono quei fiori.

Quando il tuo sguardo innanzi a me scintilla
amabilmente pio,
io chiedo al lume della tua pupilla:
— Dimmi, se il sai, bel messagger del core,
dimmi che cosa è Dio?
E la pupilla mi risponde: — Amore.

— *Aleardo Aleardi*

8. Le stagioni

Dicea la Primavera: — Io porto amore
e ghirlande di fiori e di speranza. —

Dicea l'Estate: — Ed io, col mio tepore,
scaldo il seno fecondo all'abbondanza. —

Dicea l'Autunno: — Io spando a larga mano
frutti dorati alla collina e al piano. —

Sonnecchiando dicea l'Inverno annoso:
— Penso al tanto affannarvi, e mi riposo.

— *Renato Fucini*

9. Fides

Quando brillava il vespero vermiglio,
e il cipresso pareva oro, oro fino,
la madre disse al piccoletto figlio:
Così fatto è lassù tutto un giardino.

Il bimbo dorme, e sogna i rami d'oro;
  gli alberi d'oro, le foreste d'oro;
  mentre il cipresso nella notte nera
  scagliasi al vento, piange alla bufera.

                  — *Giovanni Pascoli*

10. Ave Maria!

Ave Maria piena di grazia, eletta
fra le spose e le vergini sei tu;
sia benedetto il frutto, o benedetta,
di tue materne viscere, Gesù.
Prega per chi adorando a te si prostra,
prega pel peccator, per l'innocente
e pel debole oppresso, e pel possente,
misero anch'esso, tua pietà dimostra.
Prega per chi sotto l'oltraggio piega
la fronte e sotto la malvagia sorte;
per noi tu prega
sempre e nell'ora della morte nostra.
Ave Maria . . . nell'ora della morte . . .
Amen.

                  — *Arrigo Boito*

11. Momento

Quando, lettrice mia, quando vedrai
impazzir per le strade il carnovale,
oh non scordarti, non scordarti mai
che ci son dei morenti all'ospedale!

Quando, bella e gentil, tu salirai
di liete danze alle sonanti sale,
volgiti indietro e la miseria udrai,
la miseria che piange in sulle scale.

Quando ti riderà negli occhi belli,
come un raggio di sol giocondo, amore,
pensa che amor non ride ai poverelli.

Quando ti specchierai, ti dica il core,
che una perla rapita ai tuoi capelli,
solo una perla può salvar chi muore.

— *Olindo Guerrini*

12. La Carità

Il presidente d'una società
che protegge le bestie maltrattate,
s'intese domandar la carità:
— Ho fame, ho fame, signorino mio,
mi raccomando, non m'abbandonate,
datemi un soldo per l'amor di Dio!
— Non ti posso dar niente,
— gli disse il presidente, —
io non proteggo che le bestie sole . . .
— E allora — gli rispose il poverello,
levandosi il cappello —
fatel per queste povere bestiole.

— Adapted from *Trilussa*

13. Falce di luna calante

O falce di luna calante
che brilli su l'acque deserte,
o falce d'argento, qual messe di sogni
ondeggia al tuo mite chiarore qua giù!

Aneliti brevi di foglie,
di fiori, di flutti, dal bosco
esalano al mare: non canto, non grido,
non suono, pel vasto silenzïo va.

Oppresso d'amor, di piacere,
 il popol de' vivi s'addorme ...
O falce calante, qual messe di sogni
ondeggia al tuo mite chiarore qua giù !
                        — *Gabriele D'Annunzio*

14. Maggiolata

Maggio risveglia i nidi,
 maggio risveglia i cuori;
 porta le ortiche e i fiori,
 i serpi e l'usignol.

Schiamazzano i fanciulli
 in terra, e in ciel li augelli:
 le donne han nei capelli
 rose, ne gli occhi il sol.

Tra colli, prati e monti
 di fior tutto è una trama:
 canta, germoglia ed ama,
 l'acqua, la terra, il ciel.

E a me germoglia in cuore
 di spine un bel boschetto;
 tre vipere ho nel petto
 e un gufo entro il cervel.
                        — *Giosuè Carducci*

15. Tanto gentile ...

Tanto gentile e tanto onesta pare
la donna mia quand'ella altrui saluta,
ch'ogne lingua deven tremando muta,
e li occhi no l'ardiscon di guardare.

Ella si va, sentendosi laudare,
benignamente d'umiltà vestuta;
e par che sia una cosa venuta
di cielo in terra a miracol mostrare.

Mostrasi sì piacente a chi la mira,
che dà per li occhi una dolcezza al core,
che 'ntender no la può chi no la prova.

E par che de la sua labbia si mova
un spirito soave pien d'amore,
che va dicendo a l'anima: Sospira.

— *Dante Alighieri*

APPENDIX

I. AUXILIARY VERBS

167. SIMPLE TENSES

Infinitive

essere *to be*   avere *to have*

Present Participle

essendo *being*   avendo *having*

Past Participle

stato *been*   avuto *had*

Indicative Mood

PRESENT

I am, etc.		*I have, etc.*	
sono	siamo	ho	abbiamo
sei	siete	hai	avete
è	sono	ha	hanno

PAST DESCRIPTIVE

I was being, used to be, etc.		*I was having, used to have, etc.*	
ero	eravamo	avevo	avevamo
eri	eravate	avevi	avevate
era	erano	aveva	avevano

PAST ABSOLUTE

I was, etc.		*I had, etc.*	
fui	fummo	ebbi	avemmo
fosti	foste	avesti	aveste
fu	furono	ebbe	ebbero

FUTURE

I shall be, etc.		*I shall have, etc.*	
sarò	saremo	avrò	avremo
sarai	sarete	avrai	avrete
sarà	saranno	avrà	avranno

Subjunctive Mood

PRESENT

(that) I (may) be, etc.		*(that) I (may) have, etc.*	
sia	siamo	abbia	abbiamo
sia	siate	abbia	abbiate
sia	siano	abbia	abbiano

PAST

(that) I (might) be, etc.		*(that) I (might) have, etc.*	
fossi	fossimo	avessi	avessimo
fossi	foste	avessi	aveste
fosse	fossero	avesse	avessero

Conditional Mood

PRESENT

I should or would be, etc.		*I should or would have, etc.*	
sarei	saremmo	avrei	avremmo
saresti	sareste	avresti	avreste
sarebbe	sarebbero	avrebbe	avrebbero

Imperative

Be, etc.	*Have, etc.*
sii	abbi
siamo	abbiamo
siate	abbiate

COMPOUND TENSES

Perfect Infinitive

essere stato *to have been* avere avuto *to have had*

Perfect Participle

essendo stato *having been*   avendo avuto *having had*

Indicative Mood

PRESENT PERFECT

I have been, etc.   *1 have had, etc.*

sono stato (–a), etc.   ho avuto, etc.

PAST PERFECT

I had been, etc.   *I had had, etc.*

ero stato (–a), etc.   avevo avuto, etc.

SECOND PAST PERFECT

I had been, etc.   *I had had, etc.*

fui stato (–a), etc.   ebbi avuto, etc.

FUTURE PERFECT

I shall have been, etc.   *I shall have had, etc.*

sarò stato (–a), etc.   avrò avuto, etc.

Subjunctive Mood

PRESENT PERFECT

I (may) have been, etc   *I (may) have had, etc.*

sia stato (–a), etc.   abbia avuto, etc.

PAST PERFECT

I (might) have been, etc.   *I (might) have had, etc.*

fossi stato (–a), etc.   avessi avuto, etc.

Conditional Mood

PERFECT

I should have been, etc.   *I should have had, etc.*

sarei stato (–a), etc.   avrei avuto, etc.

II. REGULAR VERBS

168. SIMPLE TENSES

I	II	III
	Infinitive	
compr-**are** *to buy*	vend-**ere** *to sell*	fin-**ire** *to finish*
	Present Participle	
compr-**ando** *buying*	vend-**ɛndo** *selling*	fin-**ɛndo** *finishing*
	Past Participle	
compr-**ato** *bought*	vend-**uto** *sold*	fin-**ito** *finished*

Indicative Mood

PRESENT

I buy, do buy, am buying, etc.	*I sell, do sell, am se ling, etc.*	*I finish, do finish, am finishing, etc.*
compr-**o**	vend-**o**	fin-**isc-o**
compr-**i**	vend-**i**	fin-**isc-i**
compr-**a**	vend-**e**	fin-**isc-e**
compr-**iamo**	vend-**iamo**	fin-**iamo**
compr-**ate**	vend-**ete**	fin-**ite**
compr-**ano**	vend-**ono**	fin-**isc-ono**

PAST DESCRIPTIVE

I was buying, used to buy, etc.	*I was selling, used to sell, etc.*	*I was finishing, used to finish, etc.*
compr-**avo**	vend-**evo**	fin-**ivo**
compr-**avi**	vend-**evi**	fin-**ivi**
compr-**ava**	vend-**eva**	fin-**iva**
compr-**avamo**	vend-**evamo**	fin-**ivamo**
compr-**avate**	vend-**evate**	fin-**ivate**
compr-**avano**	vend-**evano**	fin-**ivano**

Past Absolute

I bought, etc.	*I sold, etc*	*I finished, etc.*
compr-ai	vend-ei (-ɛtti)	fin-ii
compr-asti	vend-esti	fin-isti
compr-ɔ	vend-è (-ɛtte)	fin-ì
compr-ammo	vend-emmo	fin-immo
compr-aste	vend-este	fin-iste
compr-*arono*	vend-**erono** (-ɛttero)	fin-*irono*

Future

I shall buy, etc.	*I shall sell, etc.*	*I shall finish, etc*
comprer-ɔ	vender-ɔ	finir-ɔ
comprer-ai	vender-ai	finir-ai
comprer-à	vender-à	finir-à
comprer-emo	vender-emo	finir-emo
comprer-ete	vender-ete	finir-ete
comprer-anno	vender-anno	finir-anno

Subjunctive Mood

Present

(that) I (may) buy, etc.	*(that) I (may) sell, etc.*	*(that) I (may) finish, etc.*
compr-i	vend-a	fin-isc-a
compr-i	vend-a	fin-isc-a
compr-i	vend-a	fin-isc-a
compr-iamo	vend-iamo	fin-iamo
compr-iate	vend-iate	fin-iate
compr-ino	vend-ano	fin-*isc*-ano

Past

(that) I (might) buy, etc.	*(that) I (might) sell, etc.*	*(that) I (might) finish, etc.*
compr-assi	vend-essi	fin-issi
compr-assi	vend-essi	fin-issi
compr-asse	vend-esse	fin-isse
compr-*assimo*	vend-*essimo*	fin-*issimo*
compr-aste	vend-este	fin-iste
compr-*assero*	vend-*essero*	fin-*issero*

Conditional Mood
PRESENT

I should buy, etc.	*I should sell, etc.*	*I should finish, etc.*
comprer-εi	vender-εi	finir-εi
comprer-esti	vender-esti	finir-esti
comprer-εbbe	vender-εbbe	finir-εbbe
comprer-**emmo**	vender-**emmo**	finir-**emmo**
comprer-**este**	vender-**este**	finir-**este**
comprer-**εbbero**	vender-**εbbero**	finir-**εbbero**

Imperative

Buy, etc.	*Sell, etc.*	*Finish, etc.*
compr-**a**	vend-**i**	fin-**isc-i**
compr-**iamo**	vend-**iamo**	fin-**iamo**
compr-**ate**	vend-**ete**	fin-**ite**

COMPOUND TENSES

parlare *to speak*   **partire** *to depart*

Perfect Infinitive

avere parlato *to have spoken*   εssere partito *to have departed*

Perfect Participle

avεndo parlato *having spoken*   essendo partito *having departed*

Indicative Mood
PRESENT PERFECT

I have spoken, etc.	*I have departed, etc.*
hɔ parlato, etc.	sono partito (–a), etc.

PAST PERFECT

I had spoken, etc.	*I had departed, etc.*
avevo parlato, etc.	εro partito (–a), etc.

SECOND PAST PERFECT

I had spoken, etc.	*I had departed, etc.*
ebbi parlato, etc.	fui partito (–a), etc.

FUTURE PERFECT

I shall have spoken, etc.	*I shall have departed, etc.*
avrò parlato, etc.	sarò partito (–a), etc.

Subjunctive Mood

PRESENT PERFECT

I (may) have spoken, etc.	*I (may) have departed, etc.*
abbia parlato, etc.	sia partito (–a), etc.

PAST PERFECT

I (might) have spoken, etc.	*I (might) have departed, etc.*
avessi parlato, etc.	fossi partito (–a), etc.

Conditional Mood

PERFECT

I should have spoken, etc.	*I should have departed, etc.*
avrei parlato, etc.	sarei partito (–a), etc.

III. IRREGULAR VERBS

169. All forms not listed below are regular. For the conjugation of the irregular past absolute, see §§ 108–109; for the tense formation, see § 154. Abbreviations used: *fut.* future; *impve.* imperative; *p. abs.* past absolute; *p. part.* past participle; *pres. ind.* present indicative; *pres. subj.* present subjunctive. Verbs preceded by * are conjugated with essere. Verbs preceded by ° sometimes take essere, sometimes avere.

*1. **accadere** to happen (*impersonal*); *see* **cadere**
 2. **accedere** to accede; *see* **concedere**

3. *accendere* to light; *p. abs.* accesi, accendesti, etc.; *p. part.* acceso.

4. **accludere** to enclose; *see* **alludere**

5. **accogliere** to receive; *see* **cogliere**

*6. **accorgersi** to perceive; *see* **scorgere**

*7. **accorrere** to run up; *see* **correre**

8. **accrescere** to increase; *see* **crescere**

*9. **addirsi** (= **addicersi**) to suit; *see* **dire**

10. *addurre* (= **adducere**) to convey; *pres. ind.* adduco, etc.; *p. abs.* addussi, adducesti, etc.; *p. part.* addotto; *fut.* addurrò; *pres. subj.* adduca, adduciamo, adduciate, adducano; *impve.* adduci, adduciamo, adducete

11. *affiggere* to stick, fasten; *p. abs.* affissi, affiggesti, etc.; *p. part.* affisso

12. *affliggere* to afflict; *p. abs.* afflissi, affliggesti, etc.; *p. part.* afflitto

13. **aggiungere** to add; *see* **giungere**

14. *alludere* to allude; *p. abs.* allusi, alludesti, etc.; *p. part.* alluso

15. **ammettere** to admit; *see* **mettere**

*16. *andare* to go; *pres. ind.* vado *or* vɔ, vai, va, andiamo, andate, vanno; *fut.* andrɔ; *pres. subj.* vada, andiamo, andiate, vadano; *impve.* va', andiamo, andate

17. *annettere* to annex; *p. abs.* annessi *or* annettei, annettesti, etc.; *p. part.* annèsso

*18. *apparire* to appear; *pres. ind.* appaio *or* apparisco, appari *or* apparisci, appare *or* apparisce, appariamo, apparite, appaiono *or* appariscono; *p. abs.* apparsi *or* apparvi *or* apparii, apparisti, etc.; *p. part.* apparso *or* apparito; *pres. subj.* appaia *or* apparisca, appariamo, appariate, appaiano *or* appariscano; *impve.* appari *or* apparisci, appariamo, apparite

19. **appartenere** to belong; *see* **tenere**

20. *appendere* to hang; appesi, appendesti, etc ; *p. part.* appeso

21. **apporre** (= **apponere**) to affix; *see* **porre**

22. **apprendere** to learn; *see* **prendere**

23. **aprire** to open; *p. abs.* apersi *or* aprii, apristi, etc.; *p. part.* aperto

24. **ardere** to burn; *p. abs.* arsi, ardesti, etc.; *p. part.* arso

*25. **ascendere** to ascend; *see* **scendere**

26. **aspergere** to sprinkle; *see* **spargere**

27. **assalire** to assail, assault; *see* **salire**

28. **assolvere** to absolve; *p. abs.* assolsi *or* assolvei *or* assolvetti, assolvesti, etc.; *p. part.* assoluto *or* assolto

29. **assumere** to assume; *p. abs.* assunsi, assumesti, etc.; *p. part.* assunto

*30. **astenersi** to abstain; *see* **tenere**

31. **astrarre** (= **astraere**) to abstract; *see* **trarre**

32. **attendere** to attend, wait; *see* **tendere**

33. **attingere** to draw up; *see* **tingere**

*34. **avvedersi** to perceive; *see* **vedere**

*35. **avvenire** to happen (*impersonal*); *see* **venire**

36. **benedire** to bless; *see* **dire**

37. **bere** (= **bevere**) to drink; *pres. ind.* bevo; *p. abs.* bevvi *or* bevei *or* bevetti, bevesti, etc.; *p. part.* bevuto; *fut.* berrò *or* beverò; *pres. subj.* beva; *impve.* bevi, beviamo, bevete

*38. **cadere** to fall; *p. abs.* caddi, cadesti, etc.; *fut.* cadrò

39. **chiedere** to ask; *pres. ind.* chiedo *or* chieggo, chiedi, chiede, chiediamo, chiedete, chiedono *or* chieggono; *p. abs.* chiesi, chiedesti, etc.; *p. part.* chiesto; *pres. subj.* chieda *or* chiegga; *impve.* chiedi, chiediamo, chiedete

40. **chiudere** to close; *p. abs.* chiusi, chiudesti, etc.; *p. part.* chiuso

41. **cingere** to gird, embrace; *p. abs.* cinsi, cingesti, etc.; *p. part.* cinto

42. **cogliere** *or* **corre** to gather; *pres. ind.* colgo, cogli, coglie, cogliamo, cogliete, colgono; *p. abs.* colsi, cogliesti, etc.; *p. part.* colto; *pres. subj.* colga; *impve.* cogli, cogliamo, cogliete

43. **commettere** to commit; *see* **mettere**

44. **commuovere** to move, affect; *see* **muovere**

*45. **comparire** to appear; *see* **apparire**

46. **compiacere** to please; *see* **piacere**

47. **compiangere** to pity; *see* **piangere**
48. **comporre** (= **componere**) to compose; *see* **porre**
49. **comprendere** to comprehend; *see* **prendere**
50. *comprimere* to compress; *p. abs.* compressi, comprimesti, etc.; *p. part.* compresso
51. *concedere* to concede, grant; *p. abs.* concessi *or* concedei *or* concedetti, concedesti, etc.; *p. part.* concesso *or* conceduto
52. **concludere** *or* **conchiudere** to conclude; *see* **alludere**
53. **concorrere** to concur; *see* **correre**
*54. **condolersi** to complain, condole with; *see* **dolere**
55. **condurre** (= **conducere**) to conduct; *see* **addurre**
56. **configgere** to drive in; *see* **figgere**
57. **confondere** to confound; *see* **fondere**
58. **congiungere** to join, match; *see* **giungere**
59. **connettere** to connect; *see* **annettere**
60. *conoscere* to know; *p. abs.* conobbi, conoscesti, etc.
61. **contendere** to contend; *see* **tendere**
62. **contenere** to contain; *see* **tenere**
63. **contorcere** to twist; *see* **torcere**
64. **contradire** to contradict; *see* **dire**
65. **contraffare** (= **contraffacere**) to counterfeit; *see* **fare**
66. **contrarre** (= **contraere**) to contract; *see* **trarre**
*67. **convenire** to agree; *see* **venire**
68. **convincere** to convince; *see* **vincere**
69. **coprire** to cover; *see* **aprire**
70. **correggere** to correct; *see* **reggere**
°71. *correre* to run; *p. abs.* corsi, corresti, etc.; *p. part.* corso
72. **corrispondere** to correspond; *see* **rispondere**
73. **corrompere** to corrupt; *see* **rompere**
74. **costringere** to force; *see* **stringere**
75. *costruire* to construct, build; *p. abs.* costrussi, costruisti, etc.; *p. part.* costrutto *or* costruito
°76. *crescere* to grow, raise; *p. abs.* crebbi, crescesti, etc.
77. *cuocere* to cook; *pres. ind.* cuocio, cuoci, cuoce, cociamo, cocete, cuociono; *p. abs.* cossi, cocesti, etc.; *p. part.* cotto; *pres. subj.* cuocia; *impve.* cuoci, cociamo, cocete

78. *dare* to give; *pres. ind.* do, dai, dà, diamo, date, danno; *p. abs.* diedi *or* detti, desti, etc.; *p. part.* dato; *fut.* darò; *pres. subj.* dia, diamo, diate, diano *or* dieno; *impve.* da', diamo, date

79. *decidere* to decide; *p. abs.* decisi, decidesti, etc.; *p. part.* deciso

*80. **decrescere** to decrease; *see* **crescere**

81. **dedurre** (= **deducere**) to deduce, deduct; *see* **addurre**

82. **deludere** to delude, beguile; *see* **alludere**

83. **deporre** (= **deponere**) to depose, bear witness; *see* **porre**

84. **deprimere** to depress; *see* **comprimere**

85. **deridere** to deride; *see* **ridere**

86. **descrivere** to describe; *see* **scrivere**

87. *difendere* to defend; *p. abs.* difesi, difendesti, etc.; *p. part.* difeso

88. **diffondere** to diffuse; *see* **fondere**

*89. **dipendere** to depend; *see* **appendere**

90. **dipingere** to paint; *see* **pingere**

91. *dire* (= *dicere*) to say, tell; *pres. ind.* dico, dici, dice, diciamo, dite, dicono; *p. abs.* dissi, dicesti, etc.; *p. part.* detto; *fut.* dirò; *pres. subj.* dica, diciamo, diciate, dicano *impve.* di', diciamo, dite

92. *dirigere* to direct; *p. abs.* diressi, dirigesti, etc.; *p. part.* diretto

*93. **discendere** to descend; *see* **scendere**

94. **dischiudere** to disclose, open; *see* **chiudere**

95. **disciogliere** to untie; *see* **sciogliere**

96. **discorrere** to talk; *see* **correre**

97. *discutere* to discuss; *p. abs.* discussi, discutesti, etc.; *p. part.* discusso

98. **disfare** (= **disfacere**) to undo; *see* **fare**

99. **disgiungere** to disjoin, separate; *see* **giungere**

100. **disilludere** to disappoint; *see* **illudere**

101. **disperdere** to disperse; *see* **perdere**

*102. **dispiacere** to displease; *see* **piacere**

103. **disporre** (= **disponere**) to dispose; *see* **porre**

104. **dissuadere** to dissuade; *see* **persuadere**

T

105. **distendere** to stretch; *see* **tendere**
106. *distinguere* to distinguish; *p. abs.* distinsi, distinguesti, etc.; *p. part.* distinto
107. **distogliere** *or* **distorre** to dissuade, divert from; *see* **togliere**
108. **distrarre** (= **distraere**) to distract, divert; *see* **trarre**
109. **distruggere** to destroy; *see* **struggere**
*110. **divenire** to become; *see* **venire**
111. *dividere* to divide; *p. abs.* divisi, dividesti, etc.; *p. part.* diviso
*112. *dolere* to ache, pain; *pres. ind.* dolgo, duoli, duole, doliamo, dolete, dolgono; *p. abs.* dolsi, dolesti, etc.; *fut.* dorrò; *pres. subj.* dolga, doliamo, doliate, dolgano
°113. *dovere* to have to, be obliged, must; *pres. ind.* devo *or* debbo, devi, deve, dobbiamo, dovete, devono *or* debbono; *fut.* dovrò; *pres. subj.* deva *or* debba, dobbiamo, dobbiate, devano *or* debbano
114. **effondere** to pour out; *see* **fondere**
115. **eleggere** to elect; *see* **leggere**
116. *elidere* to elide; *p. abs.* elisi, elidesti, etc.; *p. part.* eliso
117. **eludere** to elude; *see* **alludere**
*118. *emergere* to emerge; *p. abs.* emersi, emergesti, etc.; *p. part.* emerso
119. **emettere** to emit; *see* **mettere**
120. *ergere* to erect, raise; *p. abs.* ersi, ergesti, etc.; *p. part.* erto
121. **erigere** to erect, raise; *see* **dirigere**
122. **escludere** to exclude; *see* **alludere**
123. *esigere* to exact, cash; *p. part.* esatto
124. *espellere* to expel; *p. abs.* espulsi, espellesti, etc.; *p. part.* espulso
125. *esplodere* to explode; *p. abs.* esplosi, esplodesti, etc.; *p. part.* esploso
126. **esporre** (= **esponere**) to expose; *see* **porre**
127. **esprimere** to express; *see* **comprimere**
128. **estendere** to extend; *see* **tendere**
129. **estinguere** to extinguish; *see* **distinguere**

130. **estrarre** (= **estraere**) to extract; *see* **trarre**

*131. *evadere* to evade; *p. abs.* evasi, evadesti, *etc.*; *p. part.* evaso

132. *fare* (= *facere*) to do, make; *pres. ind.* faccio *or* fo, fai, fa, facciamo, fate, fanno; *p. abs.* feci, facesti, *etc.*; *p. part.* fatto; *fut.* farò; *pres. subj.* faccia, facciamo, facciate, facciano; *impve.* fa', facciamo, fate

133. *fendere* to split; *p. part.* fesso

134. *figgere* to fix; *p. abs.* fissi, figgesti, *etc.*; *p. part.* fitto

135. *fingere* to feign, pretend; *see* **cingere**

136. *fondere* to melt; *p. abs.* fusi, fondesti, *etc.*; *p. part.* fuso

137. **frammettere** to interpose, insert; *see* **mettere**

138. *frangere* to break; *p. abs.* fransi, frangesti, *etc.*; *p. part.* franto

139. **frapporre** (= **frapponere**) to interpose, insert, *see* **porre**

140. *friggere* to fry; *p. abs.* frissi, friggesti, *etc.*; *p. part.* fritto

141. *giacere* to lie; *pres. ind.* giaccio, giaci, giace, giaciamo *or* giacciamo, giacete, giacciono; *p. abs.* giacqui, giacesti, *etc.*; *pres. subj.* giaccia; *impve.* giaci, giaciamo *or* giacciamo, giacete

142. *giungere* to arrive, [1] join (*the hands*); *p. abs.* giunsi, giungesti, *etc.*; *p. part.* giunto

143. **illudere** to delude, beguile; *see* **alludere**

144. **immergere** to immerse, plunge; *see* **emergere**

145. **imporre** (= **imponere**) to impose; *see* **porre**

146. **imprimere** to imprint, impress; *see* **comprimere**

147. **incidere** to cut; *see* **decidere**

148. **includere** to include; *see* **alludere**

*149. **incorrere** to incur; *see* **correre**

150. **increscere** to cause sorrow; *see* **crescere**

151. **incutere** to strike; *see* **discutere**

152. **indurre** (= **inducere**) to induce; *see* **addurre**

153. *inferire* to infer; *p. abs.* infersi *or* inferii, inferisti, *etc.*; *p. part.* inferto *or* inferito

154. **infliggere** to inflict; *see* **affliggere**

155. **infondere** to infuse; *see* **fondere**

156. **intendere** to intend, understand; *see* **tendere**

---

[1] giungere in the sense of *to arrive*, takes the auxiliary essere.

157. **intercɛdere** to intercede; *see* **cɛdere**
158. **interdire** (= **interdicere**) to interdict, prohibit; *see* **dire**
159. **interporre** (= **interponere**) to interpose; *see* **porre**
160. **interrompere** to interrupt; *see* **rompere**
*161. **intervenire** to intervene; *see* **venire**
162. **intraprɛndere** to undertake; *see* **prɛndere**
163. *intridere* to temper; *p. abs.* intrisi, intridesti, etc.; *p. part.* intriso
164. **introdurre** [1] (= **introducere**) to introduce; *see* **addurre**
*165. *intrudersi* to intrude; *p. abs.* intrusi, intrudesti, etc.; *p. part.* intruso
166. **invadere** to invade; *see* **evadere**
167. **invɔlgere** to wrap; *see* **vɔlgere**
*168. **irrompere** to rush in upon; *see* **rompere**
169. **iscrivere** to inscribe; *see* **scrivere**
170. **istruire** to instruct; *see* **costruire**
171. *lɛdere* to hurt, offend; *p. abs.* lɛsi, ledesti, etc.; *p. part.* lɛso
172. *lɛggere* to read; *p. abs.* lɛssi, leggesti, etc.; *p. part.* lɛtto
173. **maledire** to curse; *see* **dire**
174. **mantenere** to maintain; *see* **tenere**
175. *mettere* to put; *p. abs.* misi *or* messi, mettesti, etc. *p. part.* messo
176. *mɔrdere* to bite; *p. abs.* mɔrsi, mordesti, etc.; *p. part.* mɔrso
*177. *morire* to die; *pres. ind.* muɔio, muɔri, muɔre, moriamo, morite, muɔiono; *p. part.* mɔrto; *fut.* morirɔ *or* morrɔ; *pres. subj.* muɔia, moriamo, moriate, muɔiano; *impve.* muɔri, moriamo, morite
178. *muɔvere or mɔvere* to move; *pres. ind.* muɔvo *or* mɔvo, muɔvi *or* mɔvi, muɔve *or* mɔve, moviamo, movete, muɔvono *or* mɔvono; *p. abs.* mɔssi, movesti, etc.; *p. part.* mɔsso; *pres. subj.* muɔva *or* mɔva, moviamo, moviate, muɔvano *or* mɔvano; *impve.* muɔvi *or* mɔvi, moviamo, movete
179. *mungere* to milk; *p. abs.* munsi, mungesti, etc.; *p. part.* munto

---

[1] For other verbs with the prefix **intra** or **intro,** see the simple verb.

180. **nascere** to be born; *p. abs.* nacqui, nascesti, etc.; *p. part.* nato

181. **nascondere** to hide, conceal; *p. abs.* nascosi, nascondesti, etc.; *p. part.* nascosto

182. *nuɔcere or nɔcere* to hurt, prejudice; *pres. ind.* nɔccio, nuɔci, nuɔce, nociamo, nocete, nɔcciono; *p. abs.* nɔcqui, nocesti, etc.; *pres. subj.* nɔccia, nociamo, nociate, nɔcciano; *impve.* nuɔci *or* nɔci, nociamo, nocete

*183. **occorrere** to be necessary; (*impersonal*); *see* **correre**

184. **offendere** to offend; *see* **difendere**

185. *offrire* to offer; *p. abs.* offersi *or* offrii, offristi, etc.; *p. part.* offerto

186. **omettere** to omit; *see* **mettere**

187. **opporre** (= **opponere**) to oppose; *see* **porre**

188. **opprimere** to oppress; *see* **comprimere**

189. **ottenere** to obtain; *see* **tenere**

*190. *parere* to seem, appear; *pres. ind.* paio, pari, pare, paiamo, parete, paiono; *p. abs.* parvi *or* parsi, paresti, etc.; *p. part.* parso; *fut.* parrɔ; *pres. subj.* paia, paiamo, pariate, paiano

191. **percorrere** to run over; *see* **correre**

192. **percuɔtere** to strike; *see* **scuɔtere**

193. *perdere* to lose; *p. abs.* persi *or* perdei *or* perdetti, perdesti, etc.; *p. part.* perso *or* perduto

194. **permettere** to permit; *see* **mettere**

195. *persuadere* to persuade; *p. abs.* persuasi, persuadesti, etc.; *p. part.* persuaso

196. **pervenire** to arrive at; *see* **venire**

197. *piacere* to please; *pres. ind.* piaccio, piaci, piace, piacciamo, piacete, piacciono; *p. abs.* piacqui, piacesti, etc.; *pres. subj.* piaccia, piacciamo, piacciate, piacciano; *impve.* piaci, piacicamo, piacete

198. *piangere* to cry, weep; *p. abs.* piansi, piangesti, etc.; *p. part.* pianto

199. *pingere* to paint; *p. abs.* pinsi, pingesti, etc.; *p. part.* pinto

200. *piɔvere* to rain (*impersonal*); *p. abs.* piɔvve

201. *pɔrgere* to present, offer; *p. abs.* pɔrsi, porgesti, etc.; *p. part.* pɔrto

202. *porre* (= *ponere*) to put; *pres. ind.* pongo, poni, pone, poniamo, ponete, pongono; *p. abs.* posi, ponesti, etc.; *p. part.* posto; *fut.* porrò; *pres. subj.* ponga, poniamo, poniate, pongano; *impve.* poni, poniamo, ponete

203. **posporre** (= **posponere**) to postpone; *see* **porre**

204. **possedere** to own, possess; *see* **sedere**

*205. *potere* to be able, may, can; *pres. ind.* posso, puoi, può, possiamo, potete, possono; *fut.* potrò; *pres. subj.* possa, possiamo, possiate, possano

206. *prediligere* to prefer; *p. abs.* predilessi, prediligesti, etc.; *p. part.* prediletto

207. **predire** (= **predicere**) to predict; *see* **dire**

*208. **prefiggersi** to take into one's head; *see* **affiggere**

209. *prendere* to take; *p. abs.* presi, prendesti, etc.; *p. part.* preso

210. **preporre** (= **preponere**) to prefer; *see* **porre**

211. **prescegliere** to choose from among; *see* **scegliere**

212. **prescrivere** to prescribe; *see* **scrivere**

213. **presedere** to preside; *see* **sedere**

214. **presumere** to presume; *see* **assumere**

215. **pretendere** to pretend; *see* **tendere**

216. **prevedere** to foresee; *see* **vedere**

217. **prevenire** to anticipate; *see* **venire**

218. **produrre** (= **producere**) to produce; *see* **addurre**

219. **profferire** to utter; *see* **inferire**

220. **profondere** to pour out; *see* **fondere**

221. **promettere** to promise; *see* **mettere**

222. **promuovere** *or* **promovere** to promote; *see* **muovere**

223. **proporre** (= **proponere**) to propose; *see* **porre**

*224. **prorompere** to burst out; *see* **rompere**

225. **proscrivere** to proscribe; *see* **scrivere**

226. *proteggere* to protect; *p. abs.* protessi, proteggesti, etc.; *p. part.* protetto

*227. **provenire** to proceed from; *see* **venire**

228. **provvedere** to provide; *see* **vedere**

229. *pungere* to sting; *p. abs.* punsi, pungesti, etc.; *p. part.* punto

230. **racchiudere** to include; *see* **chiudere**
231. **raccogliere** to gather; *see* **cogliere**
232. *radere* to shave; *p. abs.* rasi, radesti, etc.; *p. part.* raso
233. **raggiungere** to overtake; *see* **giungere**
*234. **rapprendere** to congeal; *see* **prendere**
235. **rattenere** to restrain; *see* **tenere**
236. **rattorcere** to wring; *see* **torcere**
*237. **rattrarsi** (= **rattraersi**) to shrink; *see* **trarre**
*238. **ravvedersi** to repent; *see* **vedere**
239. **ravvolgere** to wrap up; *see* **volgere**
240. **recidere** to cut off; *see* **decidere**
241. **redigere** to write; *see* **esigere**
242. *redimere* to redeem; *p. abs.* redensi, redimesti, etc.; *p. part.* redento
243. *reggere* to support; *p. abs.* ressi, reggesti, etc.; *p. part.* retto
244. *rendere* to render; *p. abs.* resi, rendesti, etc.; *p. part.* reso
245. **reprimere** to repress; *see* **comprimere**
246. **respingere** to push back; *see* **spingere**
247. **restringere** *or* **ristringere** to restrain; *see* **stringere**
*248. **retrocedere** to retrocede; *see* **cedere**
*249. **ricadere** to fall again; *see* **cadere**
250. **richiedere** to request; *see* **chiedere**
251. **riconoscere** to recognize; *see* **conoscere**
252. **ricoprire** to cover again; *see* **coprire**
*253. **ricorrere** to run again, have recourse; *see* **correre**
254. *ridere* to laugh; *p. abs.* risi, ridesti, etc.; *p. part.* riso
255. **ridire** (= **ridicere**) to say again; *see* **dire**
256. **ridurre** (= **riducere**) to reduce; *see* **addurre**
257. **rifare** (= **rifacere**) to do again, make again; *see* **fare**
258. *riflettere* to reflect; *p. part.* riflettuto *or* riflesso
259. **rifrangere** to refract; *see* **frangere**
*260. *rimanere* to remain; *pres. ind.* rimango, rimani, rimane, rimaniamo, rimanete, rimangono; *p. abs.* rimasi, rimanesti, etc.; *p. part.* rimasto; *fut.* rimarrò; *pres. subj.* rimanga, rimaniamo, rimaniate, rimangano; *impve.* rimani, rimaniamo, rimanete

261. **rimettere** to replace, set again; *see* **mettere**
*262. **rimordere** to bite again, feel remorse; *see* **mordere**
263. **rimpiangere** to regret; *see* **piangere**
*264. **rinascere** to be born again; *see* **nascere**
265. **rinchiudere** to shut in, enclose; *see* **chiudere**
*266. **rincrescere** to regret (*impersonal*); *see* **crescere**
267. **rinvenire** to find again; *see* **venire**
.268. **ripercuotere** to repercuss, strike back; *see* **percuotere**
269. **riporre** (= **riponere**) to put again; *see* **porre**
270. **riprendere** to retake, recover; *see* **prendere**
271. **riprodurre** (= **riproducere**) to reproduce; *see* **addurre**
272. **riscuotere** to collect; *see* **scuotere**
273. **risolvere** to resolve; *see* **assolvere**
*274. **risorgere** to rise up again; *see* **sorgere**
275. *rispondere* to answer, reply; *p. abs.* risposi, rispondesti, etc.; *p. part.* risposto
*276. **ristare** to cease; *see* **stare**
277. **ristringere** to restrain; *see* **stringere**
278. **ritenere** to retain; *see* **tenere**
279. **ritrarre** (= **ritraere**) to draw; *see* **trarre**
*280. **riuscire** to succeed; *see* **uscire**
281. **rivedere** to see again; *see* **vedere**
282. **rivivere** to live again; *see* **vivere**
283. **rivolgere** to turn; *see* **volgere**
284. *rodere* to gnaw; *p. abs.* rosi, rodesti, etc.; *p. part.* roso
285. *rompere* to break; *p. abs.* ruppi, rompesti, etc.; *p. part.* rotto
°286. *salire* to ascend, climb; *pres. ind.* salgo, sali, sale, saliamo, salite, salgono; *pres. subj.* salga, saliamo, saliate, salgano; *impve.* sali, saliamo, salite
287. *sapere* to know, know how; *pres. ind.* so, sai, sa, sappiamo, sapete, sanno; *p. abs.* seppi, sapesti, etc.; *fut.* saprò; *pres. subj.* sappia, sappiamo, sappiate, sappiano; *impve.* sappi, sappiamo, sappiate
*288. **scadere** to fall due; *see* **cadere**
289. *scegliere* to select; *pres. ind.* scelgo, scegli, sceglie, scegliamo, scegliete, scelgono; *p. abs.* scelsi, scegliesti,

etc.; *p. part.* scelto; *pres. subj.* scelga, scegliamo, scegliate, scelgano; *impve.* scegli, scegliamo, scegliete

290. *scendere* to descend; *p. abs.* scesi, scendesti, etc.; *p. part.* sceso

291. schiudere to disclose; *see* chiudere

292. *scindere* to separate; *p. abs.* scissi, scindesti, etc.; *p. part.* scisso

293. *sciogliere* to untie; *pres. ind.* sciolgo, sciogli, scioglie, sciogliamo, sciogliete, sciolgono; *p. abs.* sciolsi, sciogliesti, etc.; *p. part.* sciolto; *pres. subj.* sciolga, sciogliamo, sciogliate, sciolgano; *impve.* sciogli, sciogliamo, sciogliete

294. scommettere to bet; *see* mettere

295. scomparire to disappear; *see* apparire

296. scomporre (= scomponere) to undo; *see* porre

297. sconfiggere to defeat; *see* figgere

298. sconnettere to disconnect; *see* annettere

299. sconoscere to pay with ingratitude; *see* conoscere

300. scontorcere to contort, twist; *see* torcere

301. sconvolgere to overturn; *see* volgere

302. scoprire to discover; *see* aprire

303. *scorgere* to perceive; *p. abs.* scorsi, scorgesti, etc.; *p. part.* scorto

304. scorrere to flow; *see* correre

305. *scrivere* to write; *p. abs.* scrissi, scrivesti, etc.; *p. part.* scritto

306. *scuotere* to shake; *pres. ind.* scuoto, scuoti, scuote, scotiamo, scotete, scuotono; *p. abs.* scossi, scotesti, etc.; *p. part.* scosso; *fut.* scoterò; *pres. subj.* scuota, scotiamo, scotiate, scuotano; *impve.* scuoti, scotiamo, scotete

307. *sedere* to sit; *pres. ind.* siedo *or* seggo, siedi, siede, sediamo, sedete, siedono *or* seggono; *pres. subj.* sieda *or* segga, sediamo, sediate, siedano *or* seggano; *impve* siedi, sediamo, sedete

308. *seppellire* to bury; *p. part.* seppellito *or* sepolto

309. smettere to cease; *see* mettere

310. smuovere to move; *see* muovere

311. socchiudere to half shut; *see* chiudere

312. **soccorrere** to assist; *see* **correre**
313. **soddisfare** (= **soddisfacere**) to satisfy; *see* **fare**
314. *soffrire* to suffer; *p. abs.* soffersi or soffrii, soffristi, etc.; *p. part.* sofferto
315. **soggiungere** to add; *see* **giungere**
*316. *solere* to be accustomed; *pres. ind.* sɔglio, suɔli, suɔle. sogliamo, solete, sɔgliono; *pres. subj.* sɔglia, sogliamo. sogliate, sɔgliano; *p. part.* sɔlito
317. **sɔlvere** to untie; *see* **assɔlvere**
318. **sommergere** to submerge; *see* **emergere**
319. **sopprimere** to suppress; *see* **comprimere**
*320. *sorgere* to arise; *p. abs.* sorsi, sorgesti, etc.; *p. part.* sorto
321. **sorprendere** to surprise; *see* **prendere**
322. **sorreggere** to support; *see* **reggere**
323. **sorridere** to smile; *see* **ridere**
324. **sospendere** to suspend; *see* **pendere**
325. **sospingere** to push; *see* **spingere**
326. **sostenere** to support; *see* **tenere**
327. **sottintendere** to leave to understand; *see* **tendere**
328. **sovvenire** to aid; *see* **venire**
329. *spandere* to shed; *p. part.* spanto
330. *spargere* to shed, scatter; *p. abs.* sparsi, spargesti, etc.; *p. part.* sparso
*331. *sparire* to disappear; *p. abs.* sparii or sparvi, sparisti, etc.
332. *spegnere or spengere* to extinguish; *pres. ind.* spengo, spengi, spenge, spengiamo, spengete, spengono; *p. abs.* spensi, spengesti, etc.; *p. part.* spento
333. *spendere* to spend; *p. abs.* spesi, spendesti, etc.; *p. part.* speso
*334. **sperdersi** to disappear; *see* **perdere**
335. **spiacere** to displease; *see* **piacere**
336. *spingere* to push; *p. abs.* spinsi, spingesti, etc.; *p. part.* spinto
337. **sporgere** to hold out; *see* **porgere**
*338. *stare* to stay, stand, be; *pres. ind.* stɔ, stai, sta, stiamo, state, stanno; *p. abs.* stetti, stesti, etc.; *pres. subj.* stia, stiamo, stiate, stiano; *fut.* starɔ; *impve.* sta', stiamo, state

339. **stendere** to stretch out; *see* **tendere**
340. **storcere** to wrest, twist; *see* **torcere**
341. *stringere* to bind fast; *p. abs.* strinsi, stringesti, etc.; *p. part.* stretto
342. *struggere* to melt, pine away; *p. abs.* strussi, struggesti, etc.; *p. part.* strutto
*343. **succedere** to succeed, happen; *see* **concedere**
344. **supporre** (= **supponere**) to suppose; *see* **porre**
345. *svellere* to root out; *pres. ind.* svello *or* svelgo, svelli *or* svelgi, svelle *or* svelge, svelliamo *or* svelgiamo, svellete *or* svelgete, svellono *or* svelgono; *p. abs.* svelsi, svelgesti, etc.; *p. part.* svelto; *pres. subj.* svelga, svelliamo, svelliate, svelgano; *impve.* svelli, svelliamo, svellete
*346. **svenire** to faint away; *see* **venire**
347. **svolgere** to unfold; *see* **volgere**
348. *tacere* to pass over in silence, not to say; *pres. ind.* taccio, taci, tace, taciamo, tacete, tacciono; *p. abs.* tacqui, tacesti, etc.; *pres. subj.* taccia, taciamo, taciate, tacciano; *impve.* taci, taciamo, tacete
349. *tendere* to tend; *p. abs.* tesi, tendesti, etc.; *p. part.* teso
350. *tenere* to hold, have; *pres. ind.* tengo, tieni, tiene, teniamo, tenete, tengono; *p. abs.* tenni, tenesti, etc.; *fut.* terrò; *pres. subj.* tenga, teniamo, teniate, tengano; *impve.* tieni, teniamo, tenete
351. *tergere* to dry; *p. abs.* tersi, tergesti, etc.; *p. part.* terso
352. *tingere* to dye; *p. abs.* tinsi, tingesti, etc.; *p. part.* tinto
353. *togliere or torre* to take from; *pres. ind.* tolgo, togli, toglie, togliamo, togliete, tolgono; *p. abs.* tolsi, togliesti, etc.; *p. part.* tolto; *pres. subj.* tolga, togliamo, togliate, tolgano; *impve.* togli, togliamo, togliete
354. *torcere* to twist, writhe; *p. abs.* torsi, torcesti, etc.; *p. part.* torto
355. **tradurre** (= **traducere**) to translate; *see* **addurre**
356. **trafiggere** to run through; *see* **figgere**
357. **transigere** to come to terms; *see* **esigere**
358. *trarre* (= *traere*) to draw, pull; *pres. ind.* traggo, trai, trae, traiamo, traete, traggono; *p. abs.* trassi, traesti,

etc.; *p. part.* tratto; *fut.* trarrò; *pres. subj.* **tragga,** traiamo, traiate, traggano; *impve.* trai, traiamo, traete

359. **trascorrere** to pass over; *see* **correre**

360. **trascrivere** to transcribe; *see* **scrivere**

361. **trasmettere** to transmit, send; *see* **mettere**

*362. **trasparire** to shine forth; *see* **apparire**

363. **trattenere** to entertain; *see* **tenere**

364. **travedere** to see dimly; *see* **vedere**

365. *uccidere* to kill; *p. abs.* uccisi, uccidesti, etc.; *p. part.* ucciso

366. *udire* to hear; *pres. ind.* odo, odi, ode, udiamo, udite, odono; *pres. subj.* oda, udiamo, udiate, odano; *impve.* odi, udiamo, udite

367. **ungere** to grease; *p. abs.* unsi, ungesti, etc.; *p. part.* unto

*368. *uscire* to go out; *pres. ind.* esco, esci, esce, usciamo, uscite, escono; *pres. subj.* esca, usciamo, usciate, escano; *impve.* esci, usciamo, uscite

*369. *valere* to be worth; *pres. ind.* valgo, vali, vale, valiamo, valete, valgono; *p. abs.* valsi, valesti, etc.; *p. part.* valso; *fut.* varrò; *pres. subj.* valga, valiamo, valiate, valgano

370. *vedere* to see; *p. abs.* vidi, vedesti, etc.; *p. part.* visto *or* veduto; *fut.* vedrò

*371. *venire* to come; *pres. ind.* vengo, vieni, viene, veniamo, venite, vengono; *p. abs.* venni, venisti, etc.; *p. part.* venuto; *fut.* verrò; *pres. subj.* venga, veniamo, veniate, vengano; *impve.* vieni, veniamo, venite

372. *vincere* to win; *p. abs.* vinsi, vincesti, etc.; *p. part.* vinto

*373. *vivere* to live; *p. abs.* vissi, vivesti, etc.; *p. part.* vissuto

ᵒ374. *volere* to will, wish, want; *pres. ind.* voglio, vuoi, vuole; vogliamo, volete, vogliono; *p. abs.* volli, volesti, etc.; *fut.* vorrò; *pres. subj.* voglia, vogliamo, vogliate, vogliano; *impve.* vogli, vogliamo, vogliate

375. *volgere* to turn, revolve; *p. abs.* volsi, volgesti, etc.; *p. part.* volto

VOCABOLARIO

I. La classe

1. La matita. 2. La carta. 3. Il calamaio. 4. La
lettera. 5. La penna (penna stilografica). 6. La lavagna.
7. La finestra. 8. Il professore. 9. La sedia. 10. I
libri. 11. Il tavolino. 12. Il cestino. 13. Il banco.
14. L'alunno. 15. Il quaderno. 16. L'alunna. 17. La
panca. 18. Il gesso. 19. La bacchetta. 20. La busta.
21. Il cassino. 22. La riga.

II. La casa [1]

A. 1. Il tetto. 2. Il fumaiolo. 3. Il muro. 4. La
porta. 5. La finestra. 6. La cantina. 7. L'erba.
8. L'albero. 9. I fiori. 10. Il marciapiede. 11. La via.
B. 1. La terrazza. 2. Il muro. 3. Il marciapiede.
4. La porta. 5. Il portone. 6. Il cortile. 7. La finestra.
8. Il balcone. 9. La bottega (il magazzino).

III. Il salotto

1. La luce elettrica. 2. La finestra. 3. La cortina.
4. La parete. 5. La porta. 6. Il candeliere. 7. Il
quadro. 8. L'orologio. 9. Il pianoforte. 10. La libreria.
11. La mensola del caminetto. 12. Il caminetto. 13. La
poltrona. 14. Il tappeto. 15. La sedia. 16. Il divano.
17. Il libro. 18. La tavola. 19. Il pavimento.

---

[1] Corresponds to No. IX of *Heath's Modern Language Wall Charts.*

IV. Vestiario e parti del corpo umano [1]

A. 1. Il cappello. 2. Il colletto. 3. La giacca. 4. La manica. 5. Il bottone. 6. La cravatta. 7. La camicia. 8. Il panciotto. 9. Il fazzoletto. 10. Il polsino. 11. La tasca. 12. I pantaloni. 13. I guanti. 14. La scarpa. 15. Il calzino.

B. 1. L'ombrellino (l'ombrello). 2. Il cappello. 3. Il nastro. 4. La piuma. 5. L'orecchino. 6. La collana. 7. La giacchetta. 8. La cravatta. 9. Il guanto. 10. La cintura. 11. La gonnella. 12. La calza. 13. La fibbia. 14. La scarpina.

C. 1. Il mento. 2. L'occhio. 3. La fronte. 4. I capelli. 5. La tempia. 6. Il naso. 7. La bocca. 8. L'orecchio. 9. Il capo (la testa). 10. Il labbro (*pl.* le labbra). 11. Il collo. 12. La guancia. 13. La mascella. 14. La spalla. 15. Il petto (contiene i polmoni e il cuore). 16. Il braccio (*pl.* le braccia). 17. L'addome (contiene lo stomaco, il fegato, i reni e gl'intestini). 18. La mano. 19. L'anca. 20. Le dita della mano. 21. La coscia. 22. Il ginocchio (*pl.* le ginocchia). 23. La gamba. 24. Il piede. 25. I diti del piede.

V. *A.* Il piroscafo [2]

1. La bandiera nazionale. 2. L'albero. 3. Il fumaiolo. 4. La poppa. 5. La coperta. 6. L'ancora. 7. I passeggieri. 8. La passerella. 9. Il cameriere. 10. La valigia. 11. Il finestrino. 12. La prua. 13. Il molo. 14. I bauli.

B. Il treno

1. La sala d'aspetto. 2. I viaggiatori. 3. Lo spaccio dei biglietti. 4. Le carrozze *o* i vagoni (di prima classe, di

[1] No. X of *Wall Charts.*   [2] No XII.

seconda classe, di terza classe, la carrozza letti, la carrozza ristorante). 5. Il conduttore. 6. La carrozza postale. 7. Il carro bagagli. 8. Il tender. 9. Il binario. 10. La locomotiva. 11. La valigia. 12. Il facchino. 13. Il baule. 14. L'ufficio dei bagagli. 15. La banchina.

VI. La famiglia [1]

1. La finestra. 2. La madre. 3. Il padre. 4. La sedia. 5. La tavola. 6. Il nonno. 7. La nonna. 8. La figlia. 9. Il figlio. 10. Il cane. 11. Il gatto.

VII. Il ristorante [2]

1. La tovaglia. 2. La tavola. 3. Il tovagliolo. 4. Il coltello. 5. Il piatto. 6. La bottiglia. 7. Le frutta. 8. I fiori. 9. Il pane (panino). 10. Il cucchiaio. 11. La forchetta. 12. Il cameriere. 13. L'appendipanni. 14. La paglia. 15. L'ombrello. 16. Il capotto (pastrano). 17. Il bastone.

VIII. La camera [3]

1. La coperta. 2. Il letto. 3. Il guanciale. 4. La federa. 5. Il lenzuolo. 6. Il cassettone. 7. Lo specchio. 8. La luce elettrica. 9. La brocca. 10. La catinella. 11. Il lavabo. 12. La saponiera (il sapone). 13. Il porta asciugamani. 14. L'asciugamano. 15. Lo spazzolino pei denti. 16. La sedia. 17. Il cassetto. 18. Il canterano. 19. Il quadro. 20. La lampada. 21. La scrivania. 22. Il calamaio. 23. La penna. 24. La carta.

IX. La campagna [4]

1. La pala. 2. La carriola. 3. La falce. 4. La forca. 5. Il rastrello. 6. L'aratro. 7. La zappa. 8. Il pozzo.

[1] No. II. [2] No. VI. [3] No. IV. [4] No. VIII.

9. I cavalli.   10. Il prato.   11. Le vacche.   12. Il campo lavorato.   13. L'orto (di verdure e alberi fruttiferi).
14. La strada.   15. La casa.   16. L'autorimessa (il garage).   17. Gli alberi.   18. Il carretto.   19. Il carro.
20. La siepe.   21. Il giardino (di fiori).   22. Le galline.
23. Lo stagno.   24. La patata.   25. Il fagiolo.   26. La barbabietola.   27. La carota.   28. Il cavolo.   29. Il ravanello.   30. La rapa.   31. Il pisello.   32. La lattuga.
33. Il pomodoro.

X. La cucina [1]

1. La caffettiera.   2. Il tegame (la cazzeruola).   3. Il fornello.   4. Il forno.   5. Il grembiule.   6. La cuoca.
7. La teiera.   8. La marmitta.   9. La bottiglia del latte.
10. La padella.   11. Il forchettone.   12. Il coltello (da cucina).   13. Il bicchiere.

XI. La via [2]

Le parole in parentesi quadra si riferiscono alle cose che si fanno o si vendono, e alle persone che le fanno o le vendono.

1. Il teatro.   2. La libreria [il libraio, il libro].   3. La calzoleria [il calzolaio, la scarpa].   4. La sartoria [il sarto, il vestito].   5. La cappelleria [il cappellaio, il cappello].
6. Il cinematografo.   7. La farmacia [il farmacista, le medicine].   8. La banca.   9. La panetteria [il panettiere, il pane].   10. La macelleria [il macellaio, la carne].   11. La bottega dei commestibili.   12. L'automobilista (lo chauffeur).   13. L'automobile.   14. L'autocarro.   15. Il marciapiede.   16. La guardia.   17. Il manovratore.   18. Il conduttore.   19. Il lastrico.   20. Il binario del tram.
21. Il tram.

XII. Il teatro [3]

1. Il bigliettinaio.   2. Lo sportello.   3. Il portinaio.
4. Il lubbione.   5. La galleria.   6. I palchi.   7. La

---

[1] No. V.   [2] No. VII.   [3] No. XIII.

platea. 8. I posti distinti. 9. Le poltrone. 10. Il sipario. 11. Le quinte. 12. Lo spettatore. 13. L'usciere. 14. L'orchestra. 15. I musicanti. 16. L'attore. 17. L'attrice. 18. Il palcoscenico.

XIII. Gli animali [1]

Le parole in parentesi quadra si riferiscono al nato dell'animale.

1. Il cane, la cagna [il cagnolino]. 2. Il gatto, la gatta [il gattino]. 3. Il cavallo, la giumenta [il puledro]. 4. L'asino, l'asina [l'asinello]. 5. La vacca, il toro [il vitello]. 6. Il montone la pecora [l'agnello]. 7. Il capro, la capra [il capretto]. 8. Il maiale, la scrofa [il maialetto]. 9. Il coniglio. 10. Il gallo. 11. La gallina [il pulcino]. 12. Il tacchino. 13. L'oca. 14. L'anitra. 15. Il colombo. 16. L'aquila. 17. L'elefante. 18. Il leone, la leonessa [il leoncino]. 19. La tigre 20. L'orso, l'orsa [l'orsacchiotto]. 21. Il lupo, la lupa [il lupicino]. 22. Il cervo. 23. La volpe. 24. La scimmia. 25. Il ratto. 26. Il topo.

XIV. L'ufficio

1. Il tagliacarte. 2. La penna. 3. Il cassino (la gomma). 4. La matita. 5. Il calamaio 6. Il telefono. 7. La scrivania. 8. Il cestino. 9. La sedia girante. 10. Il capufficio (sta dettando una lettera). 11. La carta geografica. 12. La macchina da scrivere. 13. La stenografa (sta scrivendo sotto dettato). 14. L'archivio. 15. L'impiegato. 16. Il tavolino. 17. Il giornale. 18. Il libro di cassa. 19. Il calendario. 20. L'orologio. 21. Il ragioniere. 22. Il libro mastro. 23. La macchina per sommare.

[1] No. XI.

U

ABBREVIATIONS

adj.	adjective	*p.*	past
adv.	adverb	*p. abs.*	past absolute
art.	article	*p. des.*	past 'descriptive
conj.	conjunction	*part.*	participle
demonstr.	demonstrative	*pl.*	plural
f.	feminine	*poss.*	possessive
imp.	impersonal	*prep.*	preposition
impve.	imperative	*pres.*	present
ind.	indicative	*pron.*	pronoun
inter.	interrogative	*rel.*	relative
irr.	irregular	*subj.*	subjunctive
m.	masculine	*superl.*	superlative
n.	noun	*v.*	verb

* Verbs conjugated with ɛssere.

° Verbs conjugated with ɛssere only if used intransitively.

Open and stressed e is indicated by the symbol ɛ; open and stressed o is indicated by the symbol ɔ. Vowels italicized or having a written accent are stressed. In words in which the position of the stress is not indicated, it rests on the next-to-the-last vowel. Italicized s and z are voiced.

Nouns ending in –o are masculine, and those ending in –a are feminine, unless otherwise indicated. Proper nouns which are spelled the same way in Italian as in English are omitted; information about them is contained in the text. For numerals see Lessons XXI and XXXIX. The preposition commonly used with a verb or an adjective is shown in parentheses after the word.

GENERAL VOCABULARY

ITALIAN-ENGLISH

A

a, ad to, at, toward, as, on, in
abbaiare to bark
abbandonare to abandon
abbastanza enough
abbattere to overthrow
abbondanza abundance
abdicare to abdicate
abilità ability
abitante *m.* inhabitant
abito suit of clothes
abolire to abolish
****abortire** to miscarry, fail
accanito stubborn, furious
accettare (di) to accept
accompagnare to accompany
accordare to grant
****accorrere** *irr. v.* to run, run up
acqua water
addome *m.* abdomen
****addormirsi** to fall asleep
aderire to adhere; — **a** join
adesso now
adorare to adore
adottare to adopt
adottivo adoptive
****adunarsi** to assemble
****affannarsi (a)** to strive
affare *m.* business
affermare to affirm
affermativamente affirmatively

affidare to entrust
affinchè in order that
affresco fresco
affrettare to hasten
affrontare to face
aggressione *f.* aggression
agognare to covet, long to
agosto August
aiutare to help
aiuto help
albergo hotel
albero tree; mast; — **fruttifero** fruit-bearing tree
Alberto Albert
alcuno some, any
alleanza alliance; **Santa A—,** Holy Alliance
alleato ally
allora then, at that time; **da —** **in poi** thenceforth
alma soul
almeno at least
Alpi *f. pl.* Alps
alto high, tall
altro other; *adv.* otherwise; **ogni —,** any other
altrove elsewhere, anywhere else
altrui other, others
alunno, alunna pupil
amabilmente amiably, kindly
amante *m. or f.* lover
amare to love, like

289

amaro bitter
ambizioso ambitious
americano American
amico, amica friend
ammalato ill
ammesso admitted
amministrativo administrative
ammirare to admire
ammirazione *f.* admiration
amore *m.* love
analfabetismo illiteracy
anca hip
anche also; quand'anche even
  when, even if
ancora anchor
ancora still, yet; — una volta
  once more
andare *irr. v.* to go
anelare to long
anelito panting, breath
anello ring
angolo corner
anima soul
animale *m.* animal
animo soul
anitra duck
annesso annexed
anno year; l'— passato last year;
  l'— venturo next year
annoso old
antico ancient, old
aperto open, opened
apostolo apostle
apparecchiare to set, prepare
appartenere *irr. v.* to belong
appena hardly, as soon as
appendipanni *m.* clothes-hanger
appetito appetite
appiè at the foot of
applaudire to applaud
appoggio support

appuntamento appointment
aprile *m.* April
aprire *irr. v.* to open
aquila eagle
aratro plough
archivio filing cabinet
ardente ardent
ardire to dare
Argentina Argentine
argento silver
armi *f. pl.* arms
armonia harmony
arrestare to arrest
arridere *irr. v.* to smile upon
*arrivare (a) to arrive
arrolare to enroll
arrosto roast
artista *m. or f.* artist
artistico artistic
Arturo Arthur
ascetico ascetic
asciugamano towel
ascoltare to listen, listen to
asino donkey
aspettare to wait, wait for
aspirare (a) to wish for
aspirazione *f.* aspiration
assalto attack
assedio siege
assegno check
assicurare to assure, make sure
assistente *m. or f.* assistant
assoluto absolute
atomo atom
attaccare to attack
attesa expectation
attirare to attract, draw
attivo active, busy
atto act
attore *m.* actor
attrice *f.* actress

attualmente now, at the present time

attuare to realize

audace bold, audacious

augello bird

aumentare to increase

aumento increase

austriacó Austrian

autocarro lorry

automobile *f.* automobile, car

automobilista *m.* chauffeur

autorimessa garage

autorità authority

autunno autumn

avanti che before

ave hail

avere *irr. v.* to have; — appetito *or* fame be hungry; — bisogno di need; — fretta be in a hurry; — l'abitudine di be used to; — luogo take place; — paura be afraid; — ragione be right; — torto be wrong

avvento advent, coming

avversario adversary, enemy

avvilirsi to be discouraged

azione *f.* action, activity; stock

azzurro blue

B

babbo daddy

bacchetta rod, pointer

bagaglio baggage

bagno bath, bathing

balcone *m.* balcony

banca bank

banchina quay, platform

banco bench; bank

bandiera flag, banner

barbabietola beet

barca boat

base *f.* basis, element; a — di on a basis of; in — a upon

basso low

bastone *m.* stick, cane

battaglia battle; campo di —, battlefield

battere to beat

baule *m.* trunk

bellezza beauty

bello beautiful, handsome, fine

benchè although

bene well; *before a numeral* more than

benedire *irr. v.* to bless

benignamente benignantly

bere *irr. v.* to drink

bestia beast, animal

bestiola little beast

bianco white

biblioteca library

bicchiere *m.* glass

bidello school janitor

bigliettinaio ticket seller

biglietto ticket; — di banca paper money

bimbo baby

binario rails, track

*bisognare *imp. v.* to be necessary

bisogno need

bocca mouth

Borboni *m. pl.* Bourbons

borbonico Bourbonic

borgo hamlet, village

boschetto grove

bosco wood

bottega store, shop; — di commestibili grocery store

bottiglia bottle

bottone *m.* button

braccialetto bracelet

braccio arm
bramare to long for
brano passage (*of a book*)
breve short
brillare to shine
brocca pitcher
bronchite *f.* bronchitis
bruno dark
brutale brutal
bue *m.* ox
bufera hurricane, storm
buono good
burro butter
busta envelope

C

cabina stateroom
cacciatore *m.* hunter
caduta fall, downfall
caffè *m.* coffee
caffettiera coffee-pot
calamaio inkstand
calante waning
calendario calendar
calle *m.* way
calmo calm
calore *m.* heat
calza stocking
calzino sock
calzolaio shoemaker
calzoleria shoemaker's shop
cambiale *f.* note
cambiare to change
camera bedroom
cameriera maid
cameriere *m.* waiter, steward
camicetta shirt waist
camicia shirt
Camillo Camillus
caminetto fireplace

camminare to walk
cammino walk
campagna country; campaign;
   in —, in *or* to the country
campanello bell
campo field; — di battaglia
   battlefield
cancellare to erase, cancel
candeliere *m.* candlestick
cane *m.* dog
cantare to sing
canterano chest of drawers
cantina cellar
canto song
cantonata corner
cantone *m.* canton
capello hair
capezzale *m.* bolster
capire to understand
capitale *adj. or f. n.* capital
capitano captain
capo head, leader; a — di at the
   head of; da un — all'altro from
   one end to the other
capolavoro masterpiece
cappellaio hatter
cappelleria hat shop
cappello hat
cappotto overcoat
capriccioso capricious
capro, capra goat
capufficio manager
carboneria society of the Carbonari
carcere *m. or f.* prison; imprisonment
carico loaded
carità charity
Carlo Charles
carne *f.* meat
carnovale *m.* carnival

caro dear, expensive
carota carrot
carretto cart
carriola wheelbarrow
carro wagon
carrozza coach; — letti sleeping
car; — ristorante dining car
carta paper; — geografica map
cartolina post card
casa house, home
cassa cash; — di risparmio savings department
cassetto drawer
cassettone m. chiffonier
cassiere cashier
cassino eraser, board-rubber
catinella washbasin
cattivo bad
causa cause
causare to cause
cavallo horse; andare a —, to
ride horseback
cavolo cabbage
cazzeruola pot, casserole
cedere to yield, submit, give up
celebre celebrated, famous
cena supper
censimento census
centinaio about a hundred
centrale central
cera wax
cercare to seek
cerchio circle
certamente certainly
cervello brain
cervo stag, deer
cestino basket, waste-basket
che (che cosa) what? rel. pron.
who, which, that; conj. that,
than
chè for

checchè whatever
chi who, whom; he who, he whom
chiacchiera chatter, idle talk
chiamare to call; mi chiamo I
call myself = my name is
chiarore m. light
chiedere irr. v. to ask
chiesa church
chioma head of hair
chiudere to close, shut
chiunque whoever
chiuso (p. part. of chiudere) closed
ci pron. us, to us, ourselves; adv.
there
cielo heaven, sky
ciglio eyelash
cima summit, top
cinematografo moving-picture
theater
cinto (p. part. of cingere) girded
cintura belt
ciò this, that; oltre a —, besides
cipresso cypress
circa about, nearly
citare to mention
città city; in —, in or to the city
ciuco ass
civile civil, civilized
classe f. class
codesto that
cognata sister-in-law
cognato brother-in-law
cognome m. surname
colazione f. breakfast; lunch
collana necklace
colle m. hill
colletto collar
collina hill
collo neck
colombo pigeon
colonia colony

coloniale colonial
colore *m.* color
colpire to strike, punish
coltello knife
comando command
combattere to fight
come as, like, how
cominciare to begin, start
commedia comedy
commerciale commercial
commercio commerce
commovente touching
comodamente comfortably
comodo comfortable
compagnia company
compenso reward, compensation
compleanno birthday
completare to complete
completo complete
comprare to buy
comune common
comunicazione *f.* communication
con with
concedere *irr. v.* to grant
concepire to conceive
condizione *f.* condition
condurre *irr. v.* to conduct, lead
conduttore *m.* conductor
confinare to bound, border
confine *m.* boundary
*confondersi *irr. v.* to become confused
conforto comfort
confuso (*p. part. of* confondere) confused
congresso congress, convention
coniglio rabbit
conoscenza acquaintance; fare la — di to become acquainted with
conoscere *irr. v.* to know, be acquainted with

conquista conquest
conquistare to conquer
consegnare to hand
conseguenza consequence
conservare to keep
considerare to consider
consigliare to advise
consiglio advice
contadino farmer
contare to count, number
contatto contact
conte *m.* count
contea county
contemplare to contemplate
contemporaneo contemporary
contenere *irr. v.* to contain
*contentarsi (di) to be contented with
contento (di) glad, satisfied
continente *m.* continent
continuare to continue
conto account; — corrente checking account
contribuire to contribute
contro against
convenzionale conventional
coordinato co-ordinated
coperta cover, blanket; deck
coperto *p. part of* coprire
copiare to copy
coprire *irr. v.* to cover
corallo coral
core *m.* heart
corte *f.* court
cortile *m.* courtyard, patio
cortina curtain
corto short
cosa thing, affair; *in place of* che —? what?
coscia thigh
coscienza conscience

così so, thus
costa coast
costà there
costare to cost
costì there
costituzione *f.* constitution
costretto (*p. part. of* costringere)
   forced
costruire to construct, build
cravatta necktie
creare to create
credente *m.* believer
credenza sideboard
credere to believe
*crollare to crumble
crollo downfall
crude cruel
crudelmente cruelly
cucchiaino teaspoon
cucchiaio spoon
cucina kitchen
cucire to sew
cugino, –a cousin
cui whom, which; il —, whose
cultura culture
cuoco, cuoca cook
cuore *m.* heart
cura cure; care, concern

D

da by, from, with; to *or* at the
   house of
danaro money
Daniele Daniel
danza dance
dare *irr. v.* to give
dato che granted that
davanti a before, in front of
de (*in Dante*) = da

debole weak
decembre *m.* December
decisione *f.* decision
declinare to bend
dedicare to dedicate
delirio delirium, frenzy
delizioso delightful, delicious
deluso frustrated
democratico democratic
denotare to designate
dente *m.* tooth
depositare to deposit
deposito deposit
descrizione *f.* description
deserto *n. or adj.* desert
desiderare to desire, wish
desiderio desire
desinare *m.* dinner
desistere to desist
despotismo despotism
destare to awaken, arouse
destinare to destine
destinazione *f.* destination
desto awakened
dettare to dictate
dettato dictation
detto called
deven (*in Dante*) = divien, *from*
   divenire
di of, than, in
dia (*pres. subj. of* dare) give
dica (*pres. subj. of* dire) say
dichiarare (di) to declare
dichiarazione *f.* declaration
diecina about ten
dieta lattea milk diet
dietro a behind
difendere *irr. v.* to defend
difensivo defensive
difesa defense
difficile difficult

dignitoso dignified
diligente diligent
dimandare *see* **domandare**
dimenticare to forget
dimmi (*impve. of* **dire**) tell me
dimostrare to demonstrate, show
dinastico dynastic
Dio God
dipingere *irr. v.* to paint
dire (di) *irr. v.* to say, tell
direzione *f.* direction
diritto right
disarmare to disarm
disastro disaster
discordia discord
discorso speech
disfatta defeat
*****disinteressarsi** to take no further interest in
disonore *m.* dishonor
*****dispiacere** *irr. v.* to displease; **mi dispiace** I am sorry
disporre *irr. v.* to dispose
disprezzo scorn, disrespect
disse (*p. abs. of* **dire**) said
dissipare to disperse
distanza distance, space
distinto distinguished
dite (*impve. of* **dire**) say
dito finger
dittatore *m.* dictator
divano divan, sofa
*****divenire** *irr. v.* to become
*****diventare** to become
diverso different; **diversi** several
*****divertirsi** to amuse oneself, have a good time
divino divine
divisione *f.* division
diviso (*p. part. of* **dividere**) divided
dizionario dictionary

dolcezza sweetness; sweet feeling
dolore *m.* woe, grief, sorrow
domanda demand
domandare to ask
domani tomorrow
domare to subdue
domenica Sunday
dominare to rule over
dominio rule, dominion
donna woman, lady; **prima —**, leading lady
dono gift
dopo, dopo che after, afterward; **poco dopo** soon afterward
dorato golden
dormire to sleep
dorso back
dove where
°dovere *irr. v.* must, to be obliged, have to, owe
dovunque everywhere
dubbio doubt
dubitare to doubt
ducato duchy
duce *m.* leader
duomo cathedral
durante during
*****durare** to last
duraturo lasting
duro hard, stiff

E

e, ed and
eccezione *f.* exception
ecco here is (are), there is (are)
eco echo
economico economic
educazione *f.* education
effetto effect
egli he

egregio egregious; dear
elefante *m.* elephant
elegante elegant
elementare elementary
Elena Helen
eletto chosen
elettrico electric
ella she; Ella you
elmo helmet
eludere *irr. v.* to evade
Emanuele Emmanuel
emettere *irr. v.* to issue
emigrante *m. or f.* emigrant
emigrazione *f.* emigration
empiere to fill
energicamente energetically
*entrare (in) to enter
entro within
entusiasmo enthusiasm
entusiasticamente enthusiastically
epoca time
erba grass
eredità inheritance
eroicamente heroically
eroico heroic
eroismo heroism
esalare to exhale
esatto exact
esca bait; fuel
escire *see* uscire
esempio example
esercito army
esigere *irr. v.* to exact, demand
esilio exile
espansione *f.* expansion
espressione *f.* expression
espulso (*p. part. of* espellere) expelled
essa she, it
essenziale essential

*essere *irr. v.* to be; — in ritardo be late
esso he, it, him
estate *f.* summer
estendere to grow
estero foreign
esteso large
estremo utmost
età age
eterno eternal
Europa Europe
europeo European
evento event
eventuale eventual
evitare to avoid
evocare to evoke

F

fa ago
facchino porter
facile easy
facilitare to facilitate
facilmente easily
fagiolo bean
fai (*pres. ind. of* fare) you do
falce *f.* scythe, sickle
fame *f.* hunger; aver —, to be hungry
famiglia family
famoso famous
fanatico fanatic
fanciullo child
fango mire, mud
fare *irr. v.* to do, make; say; — caso di pay attention to; — colazione take breakfast (lunch); — la conoscenza di become acquainted with
farina flour, meal
farmacia pharmacy, drug store

farmacista *m.* druggist
fasciare to bind
fatto fact; (*p. part. of* fare) made
favore *m.* favor; per —, please
favorire to favor
fazzoletto handkerchief
fe' *see* fede
febbraio February
febbre *f.* fever
fece *p. abs. of* fare
fecondo fecund, fertile
fede *f.* faith
fedele faithful
fedeltà fidelity; loyalty
federa pillow-case
fegato liver
felice happy
Felice Felix
femmina female
fenomeno phenomenon
Ferdinando Ferdinand
ferocia fierceness
ferrovia railroad
festeggiare to fête, feast
fibbia buckle
fides (*Latin*) faith
fieno hay
fiero fierce
figlia daughter
figlio son, child
figliuolo child
fila row
finale final
finalmente finally, at last
finchè until
fine *f.* end
finestra window
finestrino little window, porthole
finire to finish, end
fino fine
fino a until

fiore *m.* flower, blossom
Firenze *f.* Florence
firma signature
firmamento firmament, sky
firmare to sign, endorse
fiume *m.* river
flutto wave
foglia leaf
foglio sheet of paper
fondare to found
fondatore *m.* founder
fondazione *f.* foundation
fondo background
fonte *f* source; cause
forca pitchfork; execution
forchetta fork
forchettone *m.* large fork
foresta forest
formare to form
fornello stove
forno oven
forte strong
fortezza fortress
fortuna fortune
fortunatamente fortunately
forza strength
fra among, between, within
Francesco Francis
francese French
Francia France
francobollo stamp
frase *f.* sentence
fratellanza brotherhood
fratello brother
freddo cold
fretta haste
fronte *f.* front; forehead
fruttifero fruit-bearing
frutto fruit; senza —, in vain
fuggire to flee
fulmine *m.* thunderbolt

fumaiolo chimney, smoke-stack
fuoco fire

G

galantuomo honest; n. honest man
galleria gallery
gallina hen
gallo rooster
gamba leg
garibaldino Garibaldine, of Garibaldi
gattino kitten
gatto cat
generale adj. or n. m. general
genere m. kind; — umano mankind
genero son-in-law
geniale genial
gennaio January
Genova Genoa
gente f. people
gentile kind, gentle
geografia geography
geograficamente geographically
geografico geographic
Germania Germany
germogliare to sprout, bud
gesso chalk
Gesù Jesus
ghirlanda garland
già already
giacca or giacchetta coat
giallo yellow
giardino garden
ginocchio knee
Gioacchino Joachim
giocondo joyful
giogo yoke
gioielleria jewelry
gioielliere m. jeweler

giornale m. journal, newspaper
giornata day
giorno day
giovane young; n. young man
Giovanni John
giovare to help, assist
giovedì m. Thursday
gioventù f. youth
giovinezza youth
girare to turn
giù down
giugno June
*giungere irr. v. to arrive
giuramento oath
giurare to swear
giuridico juridical, judicial
Giuseppe Joseph
giustizia justice
giusto just
gli art. the; pron. to him
gloria glory
golfo gulf, bay
gomma eraser, rubber
gonnella skirt
governare to govern
governo government
grado rank, degree
grammatica grammar
grande large, big, great
granduca m. grand duke
granducato grand duchy
grano wheat
grave weighty, difficult
grazia grace
grazie thanks
grembiule m. apron
grido cry
grigio gray
gruppo group
guancia cheek
guanciale m. pillow

guanto glove
guardare to look, look at
guardia policeman
guarigione f. recovery
guarire to recover
guerra war
gufo owl
Guglielmo William
guida guide, leadership
guidare to guide
guscio shell

I

i the
Iddio God
idea idea
ideale ideal
idealismo idealism
identificare to identify
ieri yesterday; — sera last night
ignoranza ignorance
il the; pron. it
*imbarcarsi to embark
immane ruthless
immediato immediate
immortale immortal
imparare to learn
impaziente impatient
*impazzire to go mad
impedire to imped , hinder
imperiale imperial
impero empire
impeto impetus
impiegato clerk
importante important
*importare to matter
impossibile impossible
impresa undertaking
impugnare to seize
in in, into; —su upon

inaridire to wither, dry up
incantevole enchanting
incendio conflagration, fire
inchiostro ink
includere irr. v. to include
incontrare to meet
indi then, afterward
indiano Indian
indietro back, backward
indipendente independent
indipendenza independence
indirizzo address
industria industry
industriale industrial
inferiore inferior
informazione f. information
Inghilterra England
inglese English
ingoiare to swallow
ingrossare to engross, enlarge
innanzi a before
innocente innocent
insalata salad
insegnare to teach
insensibile indifferent
insieme together
insuccesso failure
insulare insular
insurrezione f. insurrection
intanto meanwhile
integerrimo most upright
integro righteous, upright
intelletto intellect, mind
intelligente intelligent
intendere irr. v. to understand;
    hear
intento intent, aim, intention
interessante interesting
interessare to interest
interesse m. interest
interno internal

*intervenire *irr. v.* to intervene
intervento intervention
intese *p. abs. of* intendere
intestini *m. pl.* bowels
inutile useless
invano vainly, in vain
inverno winter
invitare to invite
invito invitation
invocare to invoke
io I
irredento unredeemed
isola island
ispirare to inspire
ispirazione *f.* inspiration
istruzione *f.* instruction, education
Italia Italy
italiano Italian
italico Italic
italo (*poetic*) Italian
ivi there

L

la *art.* the; *pron.* her, it, you
là there
labbia (*in Dante*) = labbra
labbro lip
laccio tie
lago lake
lampada lamp
lanciare to launch
largo broad; a larga mano generously
lasciare to leave; let, allow
lassù there above
lastrico pavement
latte *m.* milk
lattuga lettuce
laudare *see* lodare
lavabo washstand

lavagna blackboard
lavare to wash
lavorare to work; plow
lavoro work
Lazio Latium
le *art.* the; *pron.* them, you, to
  her, to you
legge *f.* law
leggere *irr. v.* to read
leggiero light, not heavy
legno wood
lei her; Lei you
lentamente slowly
lento slow
lenzuolo sheet
leone *m.* lion
lettera letter; — raccomandata
  registered letter
letterato man of letters, writer
letteratura literature
letto bed
lettrice *f. of* lettore reader
lettura reading
levare to raise
lezione *f.* lesson
li them, you
li (*in Dante*) = gli
lì there
liberale liberal
liberare to free
liberatore *m.* liberator
liberazione *f.* liberation
libero free
libertà liberty
Libia Lybia
libico Lybian
libraio bookseller
libreria bookcase; bookshop
libro book; — di lettura reader;
  — mastro ledger
lieto gay

linea line
lìngua tongue; language
linguaggio language, talk
liquidare to settle
lira lira
lo *art.* the; *pron.* him, it
locale local
locomotiva locomotive
lodare to praise
Lombardia Lombardy
lontano distant, far
loro them, to them; *poss.* their,
theirs; **Loro** you
lotta struggle, fighting
lottare to struggle, fight
lubbione *m.* second gallery
luce *f.* light
luglio July
lui him
Luigi Louis
lume *m.* light
luna moon
lunedì *m.* Monday
lungo long
luogo place; **aver —,** to take
place
lupo wolf

M

ma but
macchina machine; **— da scri-**
vere typewriter
macellaio butcher
macelleria butcher shop
madre *f.* mother
maestro, maestra teacher
magazzino store, shop
maggio May
maggiolata May song
maggiore greater

magnifico magnificent
mai ever, never; **quanto —, as**
ever, extremely
maiale *m.* pig
malcontento discontent
male *n. m.* evil; *adj.* bad, wrong
malgoverno misgovernment
malgrado in spite of
maltrattare to illtreat
malvagio wicked
mamma mamma
mancanza lack
mancare to lack
mandare to send
mangiare to eat
manica sleeve
manifestazione *f.* manifestation
mano *f.* hand; **a larga —,** generously; **man —,** little by little
manovratore *m.* motorman, en-
gineer
Marche *f. pl.* Marches
marciapiede *m.* sidewalk
marciare to march
mare *m.* sea
Margherita Margaret
margine *m.* edge, bank
Maria Mary
Mario Marius
marmitta pot
marrone brown
martedì *m.* Tuesday
martire *m. or f.* martyr
marzo March
mascella jaw
massa mass, majority
massimo very great; **al —,** at the
most
mastro *see* libro
materialmente materially
materno motherly

matita pencil

mattina morning; di —, in the morning

mattone *m.* floor-tile

maturo mature, ripe

me me

medicina medicine

medico physician

meglio better

melograno pomegranate

membro member

memento (*Latin*) remember

memorando memorable

memore mindful

memoria memory; a —, by heart

menare to lead

meno less; a — che non unless

mensola del caminetto mantelpiece

mente *f.* mind

mento chin

mentre while

mercoledì *m.* Wednesday

meridionale Southern

merito merit

mese *m.* month

messaggero messenger

messe *f.* harvest

messo (*p. part. of* mettere) put

metodo method

mettere *irr. v.* to put

mezzanotte *f.* midnight

mezzo *n.* means; *adj.* half

mezzogiorno noon

mi me, to me, myself

Michelangelo Buonarroti Michelangelo

Michele Michael

migliaio about a thousand

miglio mile

migliorare to improve, better

migliore better, best

Milano Milan

militare to serve

minacciare (di) to threaten

ministro minister

minuta bill of fare

minuto minute

mio my, mine

mirabilmente admirably

miracolo miracle

mirare to gaze, gaze at

miseria misery, distress, poverty

misero wretched, miserable

misurare to measure

mite mild

mittente *m. or f.* sender

mobile *m.* piece of furniture

mobilia furniture

moda fashion; di —, fashionable

moderazione *f.* moderation

modista milliner

modo manner; in tal —, thus

moglie *f.* wife

molo quay, dock

molto *adj.* much, many; *adv.* very

momento moment

monarchia monarchy

monarchico monarchic

mondiale *adj.* world- (*used as an adjective in compound words*)

mondo world; in tutto il —, the world over

moneta coin

monte *m.* mountain

montone *m.* ram

moralmente morally

morbido soft

morente dying

*morire *irr. v.* to die

morte *f.* death

mostrare to show

mɔtto motto
mɔvere *irr. v.* to move
movimento movement
muɔre (*pres. ind. of* morìre) dies
muro wall
musɛo museum
musicante *m. or f.* musician
mutare to change
muto silent

N

nacque (*p. abs. cf* nascere) was born
Napoleone Napoleon
napoleɔnico Napoleonic
napoletano Neapolitan
Napoli *f.* Naples
*nascere *irr. v.* to be born
nascita birth, birthday
naso nose
nastro ribbon   [offspring
nato (*p. part of* nascere) born,
natura nature
naturale natural
nazionale national
nazione *f.* nation
nè ... nè neither ... nor
ne *pron.* of him, of her, of it, of them; some; *adv.* therefrom
negare to deny
negɔzio store
negro (*poetic*) black
nemico enemy
nero black
nessuno not any, not one, nobody
neutralità neutrality
neve *f.* snow
*nevicare to snow
nevoso snowy̆
nido nest

niɛnte nothing
nipote *m. or f.* nephew, niece, grandson, granddaughter, grandchild
Nizza Nice
nɔ no; (*in Dante*) = non
nɔbile noble
noce *f.* nut
nɔcere *irr. v.* to hurt, harm
noi we, us
nome *m.* name
non not
nɔnna grandmother
nɔnno grandfather
nɔstro our, ours
nɔtte *f.* night
novella story, short story
novembre *m.* November
'ntender (*in Dante*) = intendere
nulla nothing
numero number
numeroso numerous
nuɔra daughter-in-law
nuotare to swim
nuɔvo new

O

o or
obbligare to oblige
obbligatɔrio obligatory, compulsory
obbligazione *f.* obligation, bond
ɔca goose
occasione *f.* occasion, instance
occhiali *m. pl.* spectacles
ɔcchio eye
occupare to occupy
ocɛano ocean
ɔde *f.* ode
odiare to hate

odore *m.* smell, scent
offrire (di) *irr. v.* to offer
oggetto object
oggi today
ogne (*in Dante*) = ogni
ogni (*invariable*) every; — altro
   any other; da — parte from
   everywhere
ognora always
oltraggio outrage, affront
oltre beyond; — a ciò besides
ombrellino parasol
ombrello umbrella
onda wave
ondeggiare to waver, move like
   waves
onesto honest, pure
onore *m.* honor
onta disgrace
opera work; opera; per — di by,
   through
opinione *f.* opinion
opporre *irr. v.* to oppose
opposizione *f.* opposition
oppresso oppressed
ora *n.* hour; di buon' — early;
   adv. now; or —, just now
orario time table
orchestra orchestra
ordinare (di) to order
ordine *m.* order
orecchino earring
orecchio ear
organizzare to organize
organizzatore *m.* organizer
organizzazione *f.* organization
orgoglio pride
orgoglioso proud
oro gold
orologio watch, clock
orribile horrible

orrido horrid
orrore *m.* horror
orso bear
ortica nettle
orto kitchen garden, orchard
osare to dare
ospedale *m.* hospital
osservare to observe
osso bone
ostacolo obstacle
ostilità hostility
ottenere *irr. v.* to obtain
ottobre *m.* October
ove where

P

pacco parcel, package
pace *f.* peace
padella frying-pan
padre *m.* father
padrona mistress
padrone *m.* master
paese *m.* country
pagare to pay
paglia straw, straw hat
pago contented, satisfied
paio pair
pala shovel
palazzo palace
palco box; —scenico stage
panca seat
panciotto waistcoat
pane *m.* bread
panetteria bakery
panettiere *m.* baker
panino roll
pantaloni *m. pl.* trousers
papa *m.* pope
papale papal
parente *m. or f.* relative
parentesi *f.* parenthesis

*parere *irr. v.* to seem, appear
parete *f.* wall
pargoletto *n.* baby; *adj.* baby (hand)
parimente likewise
parlamento parliament
parlare to speak
parola word
parte *f.* part, side; **da ogni —,** from everywhere
partecipare to take part; belong
parteggiare to side
*partire to depart, leave
partito party
passaggio alley
*passare to pass; spend
passarella gang plank
passato past
passeggiare to take a walk
passeggiero passenger
pastrano overcoat
patata potato
patibolo scaffold
patire to suffer, endure
patria country, fatherland
patriotta *m.* patriot
patriottico patriotic
patriottismo patriotism
pavimento floor
pazzesco foolhardy
peccatore *m.* sinner
peggiore worse, worst
pelliccia fur, fur coat
penisola peninsula
penna pen; **— stilografica** fountain pen
pensare to think
per *prep.* for, through, per; *conj.* in order to; **— quanto** however
perchè why, because, in order that

percosso struck
perdere *irr. v.* to lose, waste, miss
perdita loss
perfezione *f.* perfection
pericoloso dangerous
periglio peril
periodo period
perla pearl
però however
perorare to defend
persecuzione *f.* persecution
persona person
pesante heavy
pescare to fish
pescatore *m.* fisherman
pesce *m.* fish
peso weight, burden
petto breast
pezzo piece
piacente pleasing
piangere *irr. v.* to weep, cry
piano plain; floor; **al — terreno** on the ground floor; **al — superiore** on the upper floor
pianoforte *m.* piano
pianta plant, tree
pianto tears, weeping
piatto dish
piazza square
piccoletto very little, very young
piccolo little, small
piede *m.* foot
piegare to bend, bow
Piemonte *m.* Piedmont
piemontese Piedmontese
pieno full
pietà pity
pietra stone
pigliare to catch, take
pigro lazy
pio pious, sweet

Pio Pius
*piovere *imp. irr. v.* to rain
pipa pipe
piroscafo steamer; — a petrolio
oil burner
pisello pea
pittore *m.* painter
pittura painting
più more, any more
piuma plume, feather
platea parquet floor (*in theater*)
plebeo common person, plebeian
plebiscito, plebiscite
poco (po') little, not much, few;
a — a —, little by little; dopo
—, soon afterward; tra —, in
a little while; un po' di a little,
some
poesia poetry, poem
poeta *m.* poet
poi then, afterward; *see* allora
poichè since, because
politico political
polizia police
pollaio chicken yard
pollo chicken
polmone *m.* lung
polsino cuff
poltrona armchair
pomeriggio afternoon
pomodoro tomato
ponte *m.* bridge
popolare popular
popolazione *f.* population
popolo people
poppa poop
porgere *irr. v.* to offer
porre *irr. v.* to put
porta door, gate
porta asciugamani towel rack
portare to bring, bear, carry, wear

portinaio janitor, doorman
porto harbor
portone *m.* gate, driveway
posare to set, set down
posporre *irr. v.* to postpone
possente powerful, mighty
possibile possible
posso (*pres. ind. of* potere) I can
posta post, post office
postino letter carrier
posto place; (*p. part. of* porre)
placed
potenza power
°potere *irr. v.* to be able, be allowed,
can, may; non — non to have to
potere *m.* power; venire al —, to
assume authority
poverello poor one
povero poor
pozzo well
pranzo dinner; sala da —, dining
room
praticare to go with
pratico practical
prato meadow
°precipitare to precipitate, plunge
precisamente precisely
preciso precise, definite
preferire to prefer
pregare to pray
preghiera prayer
prendere *irr. v.* to take; — a
schivo take a dislike to
preparare to prepare
presa taking, capture
prescrizione *f.* prescription
presentare to present, introduce
presidente *m.* president
prestare to lend
presto soon; ben —, very soon
pretesto pretext

prezioso precious
prezzo price
prigione *f.* prison
prigionia imprisonment
prima, prima di first, before; di
—, former
primavera spring
primo first
principale principal
principalmente principally, mainly
principe *m.* prince
•principiare to start, begin
principio beginning, start; touch;
al —, at first
privato private
probabile probable
problema *m.* problem
proclamare to proclaim, declare
proclamazione *f.* proclamation
procurare (di) to procure
prode *m.* brave man
professione *f.* profession
professore *m.* professor
profeta *m.* prophet
profondo profound, deep
progetto project, plan
progresso progress
pronto ready, prompt
pronunziare to pronounce, utter
propaganda propaganda
propizio propitious
proponeva (*p. des. of* proporre)
proposed
proprio own
prosa prose
•prostrarsi to prostrate oneself
proteggere *irr. v.* to protect
protezione *f.* protection
prova proof
provare to experience; find out
provincia province

provocare to provoke
prua prow
pubblicare to publish
pubblico public
Puglia Apulia
puledro colt
pulire to clean
punto point, dot
può (*pres. ind. of* potere) can
pupilla pupil (*of the eyes*)
purchè provided that
pure also, yet
purità purity
purtroppo unfortunately

Q

qua here
quaderno exercise book
quadro *n.* picture, painting; *adj.*
square
qualche some, any
quale which, as, what; il —, who,
whom, which, that; — tale
just as
qualità quality
quando when; — anche even
when, even if
quanto how much, how many; —
mai as ever
quantunque although
quasi almost
quello that
questi this, the latter
questo this, the latter
qui here
quinta wing (*of a theater*)

R

raccomandare (di) to recommend
racconto story
radice *f.* root

Raffaello Raphael
ragazza girl
ragazzo boy
raggio ray
ragguagliare to put together
ragione *f.* reason; aver —, to be right
ragioniere *m.* bookkeeper
raglio braying
rallegrare to delight; cheer up
rammentare (di) to remind
ramo branch
rapa turnip
rapido rapid, fast
rapire to snatch, take
rappresentante *m.* representative
rappresentare to represent
rastrello rake
ratto rat
ravanello radish
razza race
re *m.* king
realizzare to realize
reazione *f.* reaction
recente recent
recisamente decisively
recitare to recite; act
redenzione *f.* redemption
redimere *irr. v.* to redeem
regione *f.* region
regnare to reign
regno kingdom
regola rule
remare to row
rene *m.* kidney
repubblica republic
repubblicano republican
resistenza resistence
restare to remain
restaurare to restore
restaurazione *f.* restoration

restituire to restore
resto rest
rete *f.* net
*riandare *irr. v.* to repass; go over
*ribellarsi to rebel
ricco rich
ricevere to receive
ricevuta receipt
riconoscere *irr. v.* to recognize
ricordare to remember; record
ricordo memory; record
ricorrere *irr. v.* to resort
ricostituire to reconstruct, recon-
    stitute
ricostruzione *f.* reconstruction
*ricovrarsi to seek refuge
ridare *irr. v.* to return, give back
ridere *irr. v.* to laugh, smile
*rientrare to re-enter, return
*riferirsi to refer
rifiutare to refuse, reject
rifiuto refusal
*rifugiarsi to take refuge
riga ruler
rigo line
riguardo regard, respect
*rimanere *irr. v.* to remain
rinverdire to grow green again
rio brook
riordinare to set in order, reform
ripetere to repeat
*riposarsi to take a rest
riposo rest
ripristinare to restore
rischiare (di) to risk
riscuotere *irr. v.* to cash; collect
rispettare to respect
rispondere *irr. v.* to answer
ristorante *m.* restaurant
ristorare to restore
risultato result

risvegliare to awake
ritardo delay; essere in —, to be late; venire in —, come late
ritirare to draw, draw out; withdraw
ritornare to return
riuscire *irr. v.* to succeed
rivedere *irr. v.* to see again
rivelare to reveal
rivolta rebellion, revolt
rivoltoso insurgent
rivoluzionario revolutionary
rivoluzione *f.* revolution
Roma Rome
romano Roman
romanzo novel
rompere *irr. v.* to break
rosa rose
rosso red
rovesciare to overthrow
rovescio wrong side
rovinare to ruin, spoil
rubino ruby
ruscello brook

S

sabato Saturday
sacrificare to sacrifice
sacrifizio sacrifice
sacro sacred, holy
sai (*pres. ind. of* sapere) you know
sala hall, room; — da pranzo dining room; — d'aspetto waiting room '
*salire to rise, climb
salotto parlor
salutare to greet
salute *f.* health
saluto greeting
salvare to save

santo *n.* saint; *adj.* holy
sapere *irr. v.* to know, know how
sapone *m.* soap
saponiera soap box
Sardegna Sardinia
sarta dressmaker
sarto tailor
sartoria tailor shop
Savoia Savoy
sbagliare to be mistaken
sbaglio mistake
sbarcare to land
scacciare to drive away, expel
scaffale *m.* bookshelf
*scagliarsi to dash
scala stairs
scaldare to warm up
scarpa shoe
scarpina low shoe
scatola box
scelto (*p. part. of* scegliere) chosen
*scendere *irr. v.* to descend, come down
scettro scepter
scheggia splinter
scherzo joke, jest
schiacciare to crush
schiamazzare to brawl, clamor
schiavo slave
schivo shy; prendere a —, to take a dislike to
scimmia ape, monkey
scintillare to sparkle
scolastico academic, scholastic
scomunicare to excommunicate
sconfiggere *irr. v.* to defeat
sconfitta defeat
scoperta discovery
scopo aim, scope
*scoppiare to break out
*scordarsi to forget

scorso last, past
scrittore *m.* writer
scrivania desk
scrivere *irr. v.* to write
scuola school
scusare to excuse
se if, whether
sè himself, herself, itself, yourself, yourselves, themselves; da —, alone
secolo century
secondo according
sede *f.* seat
sedere to sit, sit down
sedia chair; — a dondolo rocking chair
segreto secret
seguace *m.* follower
seguente following
seguire (a) to follow
seguito result; in — a as a result of
selvatico wild
*sembrare to seem, appear, look like
sempiterno everlasting, eternal
sempre always, continually; — più more and more
seno bosom
senso sense, good sense
sentire to feel, hear
senza, senza che without
separatamente separately
sera evening; ieri —, last night
serietà earnestness, seriousness
serpe *m. or f.* snake
servitù servitude
servo, serva servant, slave
seta silk
settembre *m.* September
settentrionale Northern

settimana week
sfida challenge
sfortunato unfortunate
sforzo effort
sguardo glance
si himself, herself, itself, yourself, yourselves, themselves, one, oneself
sì yes, so
Sicilia Sicily
siciliano Sicilian
sicuro sure
sidereo starry
siepe *f.* hedge
signora lady, madam, Mrs.
signore *m.* gentleman, sir, lord, Mr.
signoria lordship
signorina miss, young lady
signorino little lord, dear sir
silenzio silence
silenzioso silent
Silvia Sylvia
simbolico symbolic
simpatia sympathy
sipario curtain
sistema *m.* system
situazione *f.* situation
smeraldo emerald
sminuzzare to parcel
soave sweet, pleasant, charming
*soccombere to fall; yield
soccorrere *irr. v.* to help, give aid to
società society
soddisfare *irr. v.* to satisfy
soffocare to stifle
soffrire *irr. v.* to suffer
sognare to dream
sogno dream
solamente only

soldato soldier
soldo penny
sole *m.* sun, sunlight
solingo lonely
solino collar
solito usual; di —, usually
sollevare to relieve; *sollevarsi to
  rise up in arms
solo alone, only
soluzione *f.* solution
Somalia Somaliland
sommare to add
sommossa riot, rebellion
sonante resounding
sonnecchiare to doze
sorcio mouse
sorella sister
sorgere *irr. v.* to rise
sorte *f.* destiny
sorvegliare to watch
sospetto suspected
sospettoso suspicious
sospirare to sigh
sostanza substance
sostegno support, prop
sostituire to substitute
sotto under
sovrano sovereign
spaccio di biglietti ticket office
spagnolo Spanish
spalla shoulder
spandere *irr. v.* to pour out
spaventare to frighten
spazzolino little brush
*specchiarsi to look at oneself
specchio mirror
speciale special
specialmente especially
specie *f.* kind, sort
spedizione *f.* expedition
speranza hope

sperare to hope
spergiuro perjurer
spesso often
spettacolo show
spettatore *m.* spectator
spiaggia shore
spiegare to explain
spina thorn
spirito spirit
splendido splendid
spodestare to oust
spolverare to dust
sponda shore
sportello door (*of a car*); window
  (*of an office*)
sposa bride
sposalizio wedding
spronare to spur
stabilimento di bagni bath house
stabilire to establish
stagione *f.* season
stagno pond
stalla stable, barn
stamani this morning
stanco (di) tired
stanotte tonight, last night
stanza room; — da bagno bathroom
*stare *irr. v.* to stay, stand, be;
  — per be about
stasera this evening, tonight
staterello little state
stato state
statua statue
statuto constitution
stazione *f.* station
stella star
stenografa stenographer
stesso same, self
stirpe *f.* family
stomaco stomach

storia history
storico historic
strada road, street
straniero foreign; *n.* foreigner, stranger; foreign enemy
straordinario unusual
strappare to wrest
strategico strategic
stretto narrow, close
•struggersi *irr. v.* to pine away
studente *m.* student
studiare to study
studio study
studioso studious
su on, upon
subito at once
successo success
successore *m.* successor
suddito subject
suo his, her, hers, its, your, yours
suocera mother-in-law
suocero father-in-law
suonare to sound, play, ring
suono sound
superbia haughtiness
superiore superior, upper; *see* piano
svago amusement
sviluppo development
Svizzera Switzerland

T

tacchino turkey
tagliacarte *m.* paper cutter
tagliare to cut
tale such, this
tanto so much, so many
tappeto rug
tardi late
tasca pocket

tavola table
tavolino little table, stand
tazza cup
te thee, you
teatro theater
tedesco German
tegame *m.* stewpan
teiera teapot
telefonare to telephone
telefono telephone
temere (di) to fear
temperatura temperature
tempia temple
tempo time, weather; a —, on time
tendere *irr. v.* to hold out
tenere *irr. v.* to keep, hold, have; — in conto take into account
tentare to attempt
tentativo attempt
tepore *m.* heat
termine *m.* term; end
terra earth, ground
terrazza flat roof
terremoto earthquake
terreno *see* piano
terribile terrible
territorio territory
terrore *m.* terror
tesi *f.* thesis
testa head; alla — di at the head of
tetto roof
Tevere *m.* Tiber
ti thee (you), to thee (you), thyself (yourself)
tigre *f.* tiger
tipico typical
tirannia tyranny
tirannizzare to tyrannize
tiranno tyrant
tirare to pull, haul

tɔpo mouse
Torino Turin
tormento torment
*tornare (a) to return
tɔro bull
tɔrto wrong
torturare to torture
Toscana Tuscany
tovaglia tablecloth
tovagliɔlo napkin
tra between, among, within
tradizione f. tradition
traduzione f. translation
tragedia tragedy
tram m. street car
trama woof, weft
trasfigurazione f. transfiguration
trattare to transact
trattato treaty
trattenere irr. v. to prevent. hold
traversata crossing ⟦(back)
tremare to tremble, quiver
tremolio quivering
trɛno train; — diretto express
  train; in —, in a train
trionfante in triumph
trionfo triumph
triste sad
trɔno throne
trɔppo too, too much, too many
trovare to find
truppa troop
tu thou, you
tuo thy, thine, your, yours
turco Turkish
tutto all, whole; tutti e due both
tuttora even now; continuously

U

uccɛllo bird
udire irr. v. to hear

ufficiale m. officer
ufficio office
ultimatum (Latin) ultimatum
ultimo latter, last
umanità humanity
umano human
umiltà humility, humbleness
un, uno, una a, an, one; l'—
  l'altro each other; a — a —,
  one by one
unghia nail, claw
unico only
unire to unite, join
unità unity
università university
uɔmo man; — di stato statesman
uɔvo egg
usare to use
uscɛre m. usher
*uscire irr. v. to go out, come out,
  issue
uscita exit
usignɔlo nightingale
utile useful

V

va (pres. ind. of andare) goes
vacca cow
vaglia m. money order
vago fond
vagone m. car (of a train)
valigia valise, suitcase
valle f. valley
vantaggio advantage
vantaggioso advantageous
varco way, passage, ford
vasto vast
Vaticano Vatican
vecchiaia old age
vɛcchio old
vedere irr. v, to see

vendere to sell
vendetta vengeance, revenge
venerdì Friday; di V— Santo
    Good Friday
Veneto Venetia
Venezia Venice
Venezia Giulia Julian Venetia
*venire *irr. v.* to come, come about
vento wind
venturo coming
veramente really
verbo verb
verde green
verdura vegetables
vergine virgin
vermiglio vermilion, ruddy, rosy
vero true, real   [ward
verso *n.* line of poetry; *prep.* to-
vespero evening, twilight
veste *f.* dress
vestire to dress, attire
vestito suit of clothes
vestuta (*in Dante*) = vestita, *from*
    vestire
vettura carriage
vetturino driver
vi *pron.* you, to you, yourself,
    yourselves; *adv.* there
via street, way, path, road
viaggiare to travel
viaggiatore *m.* traveler
viaggio journey, trip
vicino neighboring
vicino a near
vigilanza vigilance
vigoroso vigorous
villano peasant

Vincenzo Vincent
violento violent
violino violin
vipera viper
virtù *f.* virtue
viscere *m.* bosom
visitare to visit, call on
vita life
vitello calf, veal
vittima victim
vittoria victory
Vittorio Victor
vittorioso victorious
vivo alive, living
vizio vice
voi you
*volare to fly
volentieri gladly, willingly
°volere *irr. v.* to want, wish, be
    willing
*volgersi *irr. v.* to turn
volo flight
volontario *n.* volunteer; *adj.* vol-
    untary
volpe *f.* fox
volta time; turn; una —, once;
    ancora una —, once more
vostro your, yours
voto vote
vuoto empty

Z

zappa hoe
zero zero
zia aunt
zio uncle

A

a un, uno, una
abandon abbandonare
ability abilità
able abile; to be —, potere
about circa, quasi; to bring —,
  portare a conclusione
above sopra
absolute assoluto
abuse abuso
accept accettare (di)
accompany accompagnare
accomplish attuare
according to secondo
acquire acquistare
act n. atto; v. recitare
action azione f.
active attivo
actor attore m.
actress attrice f.
address indirizzo
administration amministrazione f.
admirably mirabilmente
admire ammirare
admonition ammonizione f.
adopt adottare
Adriatic Adriatico
adventurous avventuroso
advice consiglio
advise consigliare (di)
affair affare m.
affirmatively affermativamente
afraid see be

after dopo, dopo che; soon —,
  poco dopo
afternoon pomeriggio
afterward poi
again di nuovo
against contro; (before a pron.)
  contro di
age età
ago fa
aid aiuto
aim proposito, scopo
Albert Alberto
all tutto; — Americans tutti gli
  Americani
alliance alleanza
allied alleato
ally alleato
almost quasi
alone solo
Alps Alpi f. pl.
also anche, pure
although benchè, quantunque
always sempre
ambassador ambasciatore m.
American americano
amnesty amnistia
among tra
amuse divertire
amusement svago
an see a
and e, ed
animal animale m.
another un altro
answer rispondere irr. v. 275

antiquity antichità
any di + *def. art.;* alcuno, qualche, un po' di; *see* § 61
anything *see* § 33
appetite appetito
applaud applaudire
appointment appuntamento
April aprile *m.*
architect architetto
ardent ardente
ark arca
arm braccio (*pl.* le braccia)
armchair poltrona
arms armi *f. pl.*
army esercito
arouse destare
arrest arrestare
arrive arrivare, giungere *irr. v.* 142
art arte *f.*
Arthur Arturo
artist artista *m. or f.*
artistic artistico
as come, da; — for in quanto a
ask domandare (di)
assemble adunare
assistant assistente *m.*
assume assumere *irr. v.* 29
assure assicurare
at a, ad; — last finalmente; — once subito
attack attacco
attempt *n.* tentativo; *v.* tentare (di)
attention attenzione *f.*; to pay — to far caso di
August agosto
aunt zia
Austrian austriaco
automobile automobile *f.*
autumn autunno

avail valere *irr. v.* 369
avenge vendicare
avoid evitare (di)

B

back dorso
bad cattivo
baggage bagaglio
bait esca
balcony balcone *m.*
bank banca; (*of a river*) sponda
bark abbaiare
barn stalla
base basare
bath bagno
bath house stabilimento di bagni
battle battaglia
battlefield campo di battaglia
bay golfo
be essere *irr. v.* § 167; stare *irr. v.* 338; — able potere *irr. v.* 205; — afraid aver paura; — born nascere *irr. v.* 180; — hot far caldo *see* § 141; — hungry aver appetito; — in a hurry aver fretta; — late essere in ritardo; — necessary bisognare *imp. v.*; — obliged dovere *irr. v.* 113; — right aver ragione; — used to aver l'abitudine di; — willing volere *irr. v.* 374; — worth valere *irr. v.* 369; — wrong aver torto
bear portare
beat battere
beautiful bello; *see* § 87
beauty bellezza
because perchè
become diventare; — true avverarsi

bed letto
bedroom camera
before (*place*) davanti a; (*time*) prima, prima che, avanti che
begin cominciare (a)
beginning princípio
behind dietro a
Belgium Belgio
believe credere
bell campanello
belong appartenere *irr. v.* 19
besides inoltre
best il migliore
betray tradire
better *adj.* migliore; *adv.* meglio
between tra
beyond oltre
big grande; *see* § 87
bill of fare minuta
birthday compleanno
black nero
blackboard lavagna
bloody sanguinoso
blow soffiare
blue azzurro
boat barca
bombard bombardare
bond obbligazione *f.*
bone osso
book libro; exercise —, quaderno
bookshelf scaffale *m.*
born nato; to be—, nascere *irr. v.* 180; he was—, nacque
both tutti e due
boundary confine *m.*
Bourbons Borboni *m. pl.*
box scatola; (*of a theater*) palco
boy ragazzo
bracelet braccialetto
break rompere *irr. v.* 285; of a broken heart di crepacuore

breakfast colazione *f.*
brilliant brillante
bring portare; — about portare a conclusione
bronchitis bronchite *f.*
brook ruscello
brother fratello
brother-in-law cognato
brown marrone
brutal brutale
build costruire
burst out scoppiare
business affari *m. pl.*
busy attivo, occupato
but ma
butter burro
buy comprare
by da

C

call *n.* chiamata; *v.* chiamare; — a convention convocare un congresso; — upon visitare
calm calmo
can potere *irr. v.* 205
capital capitale *f.*
capricious capriccioso
captain capitano
car automobile *f.*; (*of a train*) carrozza, vagone *m.*
card cartolina
care for curarsi di
carriage vettura
carry portare
case caso
cash riscuotere *irr. v.* 272
cashier cassiere *m.*
cat gatto, –a
catch pigliare
cathedral cattedrale *f.*
cause *n.* causa; *v.* causare

cease cessare (di)
census censimento
cent soldo; per —, per cento
center n. centro; v. concentrare
central centrale
century secolo
chair sedia; arm—, poltrona;
  rocking —, sedia a dondolo
chalk gesso
change cambiare
Charles Carlo
check assegno
checking account conto corrente
chicken pollo
chicken yard pollaio
chiffonier cassettone m.
child figlio
church chiesa
citizen cittadino
city città; in or to the —, in città
civilized civile
class classe f.
clean pulire
clerk impiegato
close adj. stretto; v. chiudere
closed chiuso   [irr. v. 40
coat giacca, giacchetta
coffee caffè m.
coin moneta
collar colletto
collection collezione f.
color colore m.
colt puledro
come venire irr. v. 371; — down
  scendere irr. v. 290; — true
  avverarsi
comedy commedia
comfortable comodo
coming venturo
command comando
commerce commercio

commercial commerciale
common comune
complete completo
concentrate concentrare
conclude concludere irr. v. 52
condition condizione f.
conduct condurre irr. v. 55
conductor conduttore m.
conference conferenza
congress congresso
conquest conquista
consecrate consacrare
consider considerare
constitution statuto
consult consultare
contact contatto
contemporary contemporaneo
contrary contrario; on the —, al
  contrario, viceversa
contribution contribuzione f.
convention congresso; call a —,
  convocare un congresso
cook cuoco, cuoca
cool fresco
co-ordinated coordinato
copy copiare
coral corallo
corner cantonata, angolo
cost costare
count contare, dipendere irr. v. 89
country campagna; (fatherland)
  paese m., patria; in or to the —,
  in campagna
courage coraggio
court corte f.
cousin cugino, cugina
cover coprire irr. v. 69
cow vacca
create creare
crime delitto
criticize criticare

Y

cross valicare, passare
crossing traversata
crowd folla
crown corona
cruelty crudeltà
cup tazza
cure guarigione *f.; v.* guarire

D

daddy babbo
danger pericolo
dare osare
date data
daughter figlia
daughter-in-law nuora
day giorno, giornata
dear caro
death morte *f.*
December decembre *m.*
declare dichiarare (di)
deep profondo
defensive difensivo
delicious delizioso
delightful delizioso
demand domandare (di), chiedere
   (di) *irr. v.* 39
democratic democratico
depart partire
deposit *n.* deposito; *v.* depositare
descend scendere *irr. v.* 290
describe descrivere *irr. v.* 86
desire desiderare (di)
desk scrivania
despotism despotismo
destination destinazione *f.*
destine destinare
destruction distruzione *f.*
dictate dettare
dictionary dizionario
die morire *irr. v.* 177
diet dieta; milk —, dieta lattea

different diverso
difficult difficile (a)
diligent diligente
dining room sala da pranzo
dinner pranzo, desinare *m.*
direct diretto
disarm disarmare
disaster disastro
disband sbandare
discouraging sconfortante
dish piatto
displease dispiacere *irr. v.* 102
dissatisfaction malcontento
distant lontano
distinguish distinguere *irr. v.* 106
disturb disturbare
divan divano
divided diviso
do fare *irr. v.* 132; *see* §§ 24 *and* 33
dog cane *m.*
door porta; (*of a car*) sportello
doubt dubitare
down giù; come —, scendere *irr*
   v. 290
downfall caduta
draw ritirare
dream sogno
dress veste *f.*
dressmaker sarta
drink bere *irr. v.* 37
drive scacciare
driver vetturino
duck anitra
during durante
dust spolverare
duty dovere *m.*

E

each ciascuno; — other l'un
   l'altro; *see* § 97, 4

eager bramoso
early di buon'ora, presto
earring orecchino
earthquake terremoto
easy facile (a)
eat mangiare
echo eco
economic economico
effort sforzo
egg uovo (pl. le uova)
Egypt Egitto
elegant elegante
emerald smeraldo
emigrate emigrare
Emmanuel Emanuele
emperor imperatore m.
empire impero
empty vuoto
enchanting incantevole
encouragement incoraggiamento
end n. fine f.; v. finire (di)
endorse firmare
enemy nemico
engagement impegno
England Inghilterra
English inglese
enlightened dotto
enormous enorme
enough abbastanza
enrage irritare
enter entrare (in)
enthusiasm entusiasmo
entrance entrata
entrust affidare
epoch epoca
erase cancellare
especially specialmente
establish costituire
eternal eterno; Eternal City Città
  Eterna
Europe Europa

European europeo
even anche, finanche
evening sera; this —, stasera
event evento
ever mai
every ogni
everything ogni cosa
everywhere dovunque
evoke evocare
exact esatto
example esempio
except eccetto
exception eccezione f.
exercise esercizio; — book quaderno
exile esilio; (exiled) esule m.
exit uscita
expedition spedizione f.
expel scacciare, espellere irr. v.
  124
expensive caro
explain spiegare
express esprimere irr. v. 127
express train treno diretto
expression espressione f.
extreme estremo

F

facilitate facilitare
faith fede f., fiducia
faithful fedele
family famiglia
famous famoso
far lontano
farmer contadino
fascinating affascinante
fashion moda
fashionable di moda
fast rapido
father padre m.

father-in-law suocero
fatherland patria
favor favorire, arridere (a) *irr.*
   v. 254
fear temere
February febbraio
feeling sentimento
fellow-patriot compatriotta *m.*
Ferdinand Ferdinando
fever febbre *f.*
few: a —, pochi
field campo
fight combattere
financial finanziario
find trovare
fine bello; *see* § 87
finger dito (*pl.* le dita)
finish finire
first *adj.* primo; *adv.* prima
fish *n.* pesce *m.*; *v.* pescare
fisherman pescatore *m.*
flag bandiera
flee fuggire
flight fuga
floor pavimento, piano; **on the**
   ground —, al pian terreno;
   on the upper —, al piano
   superiore
Florence Firenze *f.*
flower fiore *m.*
follow seguire
follower seguace *m.*
for *prep.* per, da; *conj.* perchè
force *n.* forza; *v.* forzare
foreign, foreigner straniero
forget dimenticare (di)
fork forchetta
former quegli, quello
fortunately fortunatamente
fortune fortuna
found fondare

foundation fondazione *f.*
fountain pen penna stilografica
France Francia
Francis Francesco
free *adj.* libero; *v.* liberare
French francese
fresco affresco
friend amico, amica
from da
front fronte *f.*; **in — of** davanti a
fruit frutto (*pl.* le frutta)
full pieno
fur, fur coat pelliccia
furniture mobilia; **piece of —,**
   mobile *m.*

G

gain guadagnare, acquistare
gallantly valorosamente
gallantry valore *m.*
general *n.* generale *m.*; *adj.*
   generale
generally generalmente
generation generazione *f.*
generous generoso
genius genio
Genoa Genova
gentleman signore *m.*
geographical geografico
German tedesco
Germany Germania
gift dono
girl ragazza
give dare *irr. v.* 78; **— me** mi dia
glad contento (di)
gladly volentieri
glass bicchiere *m.*
glorious glorioso
glory gloria
glove guanto

go andare *irr. v.* 16; — out
  uscire *irr. v.* 368
goat capra
God Dio
gold oro
good buono; *see* § 87
govern governare
government governo
grammar grammatica
grandchild nipote *m. or f.*
granddaughter nipote *f.*
grandfather nonno
grandmother nonna
grandson nipote *m.*
grant accordare; —ed that dato
  che
gray grigio
great grande; *see* § 87
greatly grandemente
Greek greco
green verde
greet salutare
greetings saluto
Gregory Gregorio
ground *see* floor
group gruppo
guilty colpevole, convinto
gulf golfo

H

half *n.* metà; *adj.* mezzo
hall sala
hamlet borgo
hand *n.* mano *f.*; *v.* consegnare
handkerchief fazzoletto
handsome bello; *see* § 87
happen accadere *irr. v.* 1
harbor porto
hard duro, (*difficult*) difficile
hasten affrettare

hat cappello
hate odiare
haul tirare
have avere *irr. v.* § 167; tenere
  irr. v. 350; — a good time
  divertirsi
hay fieno
he egli, esso
head capo, testa; at the — of
  a capo di
hear udire *irr. v.* 366; sentire
heart cuore *m.*; by —, a memoria;
  of a broken —, di crepacuore
heavy pesante
Helen Elena
help *n.* aiuto; *v.* aiutare (a)
hen gallina
henceforth da ora in poi
her lei, essa, la; *poss.* suo
here qua, qui; — is, — are ecco
hero eroe *m.*
hers suo
herself lei stessa, se stessa, si
hesitate esitare
high alto
him lui, esso, lo
himself lui stesso, se stesso, si
his suo
historian storico
history storia
hold tenere *irr. v.* 350, mantenere
  irr. v. 174
home casa; at —, a casa
honest onesto; the Honest King
  il Re Galantuomo
hope *n.* speranza; *v.* sperare (di)
horror orrore *m.*
horse cavallo
hostile ostile
hot caldo; it is —, fa caldo
hotel albergo

hour ora
house casa
how come; — **much** quanto; —
many quanti
however però
humanity umanità
hungry affamato; **to be** —, aver
appetito
hunter cacciatore *m.*
hurry fretta; **to be in a** —, aver
fretta

I

I io
idea idea
idealist idealista *m. or f.*
identify identificare
if se
ill ammalato
illiteracy analfabetismo
imagine immaginare (di)
imminent imminente
impatient impaziente
important importante
impossible impossibile
improve migliorare
improvement miglioramento
in in; (*after a superl.*) di; (*before
the name of a city*) a
increase aumentare
independence indipendenza
independent indipendente
indirect indiretto
industrial industriale
industry operosità, industria
influence influenza
information informazione *f.*
inhabitant abitante *m.*
inherit ereditare
ink inchiostro
inspire ispirare

instance esempio; **for** —, per
esempio .
instead of invece di
insular insulare
insurgent insorgente
intellectual intellettuale
intelligent intelligente
intend intendere *irr. v.* 156,
avere l'intenzione di
interest interesse *m.*
interesting interessante
international internazionale
intervene intervenire *irr. v.* 161
into in
intransigent intransigente
introduce presentare
invasion invasione *f.*
invitation invito
invite invitare (a)
island isola
issue emettere *irr. v.* 119
it esso, essa, lo, la (*not translated
if subject of an imp. v.*)
Italian italiano
Italy Italia
its suo
itself sè, se stesso, se stessa, si

J

janitor portinaio; (*of a school*)
bidello
January gennaio
jeweler gioielliere *m.*
jewelry gioielleria
John Giovanni
join unirsi a; — **an army** arrolarsi
in un esercito
Josephine Giuseppina
journey viaggio
joy gioia

July luglio
June giugno
just giusto
justice giustizia
justly giustamente

K

keep tenere *irr. v.* 350
kind *n.* specie *f.*; *adj.* gentile
king re *m.*; **the Honest King** il Re Galantuomo; **King Bomba** Re Bomba
kingdom regno
kitchen cucina
kitten gattino
knee ginocchio
knife coltello
know sapere *irr. v.* 287; conoscere *irr. v.* 60; see § 111

L

lady signora; **leading** —, prima donna; **young** —, signorina
lamp lampada
land *n.* terra; *v.* sbarcare
language lingua
large grande; *see* § 87
last *v.* durare; *adj.* ultimo, passato, scorso; **at** —, finalmente
lasting duraturo
late tardi
Latium Lazio
latter questi, questo
laugh ridere *irr. v.* 254
law legge *f.*
lawyer avvocato
lazy pigro
lead menare, condurre *irr. v.* 55
see lady
leader capo, duce *m.*, guida

leadership guida
learn imparare (a)
least il meno
leave (*something*) lasciare; (*depart*) partire
lend prestare
Leo Leone
less meno
lesson lezione *f.*
letter lettera; **registered** —, lettera raccomandata
letter carrier postino
liberal liberale
liberation liberazione *f.*
liberator liberatore *m.*
liberty libertà
library biblioteca
life vita
light *n.* luce *f.*; *adj.* leggiero
lighten lampeggiare *imp. v.*
like *v.* amare; **I** — = **it pleases me** mi piace; *conj.* come
line rigo, linea; (*of poetry*) verso
lip labbro (*pl.* le labbra)
lira lira
listen, listen to ascoltare
literature letteratura
little piccolo; poco; **a** —, un po' di
live vivere *irr. v.* 373
loaded carico
locomotive locomotiva
long lungo
long for bramare
look, look at guardare; — **for** cercare; — **like** sembrare
lord signore *m.*
lose perdere *irr. v.* 193
loss perdita
love *n.* amore *m.*; *v.* amare
low basso
lunch colazione *f*

M

machine macchina
madam signora
magic magico
magnificent magnifico
maid cameriera
main principale
make fare *irr. v.* 132
mamma mamma
man uomo (*pl.* uomini)
many molti; so —, tanti
map carta geografica
March marzo
march marciare
Mary Maria
marry sposare
martyrdom martirio
mass massa
masterpiece capolavoro
material materiale
May maggio
may potere *irr. v.* 205
me mi, me
medicine medicina
Mediterranean Mediterraneo
meet incontrare; fare la cono-
    scenza di
member membro
memorize imparare a memoria
memory memoria
method metodo
Michelangelo Michelangelo
midnight mezzanotte *f.*
Milan Milano
mile miglio
military militare
milk latte *m.*
milliner modista
mind mente *f.*
mine mio

minister ministro; prime —,
    primo ministro
minute minuto
mirror specchio
misgovernment malgoverno
miss *n.* signorina; *v.* perdere
mistake sbaglio
moment momento
monarchical monarchico
monarchy monarchia
money danaro; paper —, biglietti
    di banca
money order vaglia *m.*
month mese *m.*
monument monumento
more più; — and —, sempre
    più
morning mattina; this —, stamani
most il più; at the —, al massimo
mother madre *f.*
mother-in-law suocera
motto motto
mountain monte *m.*, montagna
movement movimento
Mr. signor
Mrs. signora
much molto; so —, tanto
museum museo
must dovere *irr. v.* 113, biso-
    gnare *imp. v.*
my mio
myself me stesso me stessa, mi

N

name nome *m.*
napkin tovagliolo
Naples Napoli *f.*
Napoleon Napoleone
narrow stretto
nation nazione *f.*

national nazionale
natural naturale
Neapolitan napoletano
near vicino, vicino a
nearly quasi
necessary necessàrio; be —, bisognare *imp. v.*
necktie cravatta
need bisogno, necessità; *v.* aver bisogno di
negation negazione *f.*
neighboring vicino
neither ... nor nè ... nè
nephew nipote *m.*
net rete *f.*
neutrality neutralità
never mai
new nuovo
next venturo
niece nipote *f.*
night notte *f.*; last —, ieri sera; stanotte
no no; (*before a noun*) nessuno; — one nessuno
noble nobile
nobody nessuno
none nessuno
noon mezzogiorno
nor nè
Northern settentrionale
not non; — one, — any nessuno
note cambiale *f.*
nothing niente, nulla
novel romanzo
November novembre *m.*
now adesso, ora

O

oath giuramento
obligation obbligazione *f.*

obliged obbligato; be —, dovere *irr. v.* 113
object oggetto
observe osservare
obstacle ostacolo
obtain ottenere *irr. v.* 189
occasion occasione *f.*
occupy occupare
ocean oceano
October ottobre *m.*
ode ode *f.*
of di
offence reato
offer offrire *irr. v.* 185
office ufficio
officer ufficiale *m.*
often spesso
oil olio; petrolio; — burner piroscafo a petrolio
old vecchio, antico
on su
once una volta; at —, subito
one un, uno, una; *imp.* si
oneself se stesso, si
only *adj.* unico, solo; *adv.* solamente, soltanto; non ... che; not — ... but non solo ... ma
open aprire *irr. v.* 23
open *p. part.* aperto
opening apertura
openly apertamente
opinion opinione *f.*
opportune opportuno, propizio
opportunity opportunità
or o
order *n.* ordine *m.*; *v.* ordinare; in — that perchè, affinchè; in — to per
organize organizzare
origin origine *f.*

Y*

other altro
our nostro
ourselves noi stessi, ci
overcoat cappotto
owe dovere *irr. v.* 113
ox bue *m.* (*pl.* buoi)

P

package pacco
page pagina
painter pittore *m.*
painting pittura, quadro
pair paio (*pl.* le paia)
papal papale
paper carta
parcel pacco
pardon *n.* perdono; *v.* scusare;
  pres. subj. scusi
parish priest parroco
parquet platea
parliament parlamento
parlor salotto
part parte *f.*
particularly particolarmente
pass passare
passenger passeggiero
past passato, scorso
path cammino
patriot patriotta *m.*; fellow —,
  compatriotta *m.*
patriotism patriottismo
patron protettore *m.*
pay pagare; — attention to fare
  caso di
pea pisello
peace pace *f.*
pearl perla
pen penna
pencil matita
peninsula penisola

people gente *f.;* (*population*)
  popolo; (*imp.*) si; *see* § 128, 4
perfect oneself perfezionarsi
perfidious perfido
period periodo
perseverance perseveranza
person persona
physician medico
picture quadro
piece pezzo; — of furniture
  mobile *m.*
Piedmont Piemonte *m.*
Piedmontese piemontese
pig maiale *m.*
Pius Pio
place *n.* posto; *v.* mettere *irr. v.*
  175; take —, aver luogo
plain pianura
plan piano, progetto
play suonare
please per favore
pleasure diletto, piacere *m.*
plebiscite plebiscito
pocket tasca
poem poesia
poet poeta *m.*
poetry poesia
police polizia
political politico
poor povero
pope papa *m.*
popular popolare
population popolazione *f.*
porter facchino
possible possibile
post posta; — card cartolina;
  — office posta
potato patata
power potenza, potere *m.;* temporal —, potere temporale
powerful potente

praise lodare
pray pregare (di)
precede precedere
precious prezioso
prefer preferire
prepare preparare
prescription prescrizione *f.*
present *n.* dono; *v.* presentare
pretext pretesto
prevent impedire (di)
prey preda
price prezzo
priest *see* parish
prime primo
prince principe *m.*
princess principessa
prison prigione *f.*
private privato
probable probabile
probably probabilmente; *see* § 50
problem problema *m.*
proclaim proclamare
professor professore *m.*
progress progresso
promise promettere *irr. v.* 221
prompt pronto (a)
pronounce pronunziare
prophecy profezia
prophet profeta *m.*
proportion proporzione *f.*
proposal proposta
prose prosa
protect proteggere *irr. v.* 226
proud orgoglioso
prove provare (di)
provided that purchè
province provincia
public pubblico
publish pubblicare
pull tirare
pupil alunno, −a

put mettere *irr. v.* 175, porre
irr. v. 202

Q

quality qualità
quarter quarto
queen regina

R

railroad ferrovia
rain piovere *imp. irr. v.* 200
Raphael Raffaello
rapid rapido
rapidly rapidamente
reach raggiungere *irr. v.* 233
reaction reazione *f.*
read leggere *irr. v.* 172
reader libro di lettura
reading lettura
ready pronto (a)
real vero
realize realizzare
reason ragione *f.*
rebel rivoltarsi
receipt ricevuta
receive ricevere
recent recente
recite recitare
recognize riconoscere *irr. v.* 251
recover guarire
recovery guarigione *f.*
red rosso
redeem redimere *irr. v* 242
redeemed redento
refuse rifiutare
régime regime *m.*
region regione *f.*
registered *see* letter
reign regno; — of Terror il Terrore
relative parente *m. or f.*

relieve liberare
remain rimanere *irr. v.* 260
remember ricòrdare, ricordarsi di
reorganize riorganizzare
repeal ripudiare
repeat ripetere
republic repubblica
republican repubblicano
reputation reputazione *f.*
resort ricorrere *irr. v.* 253
respect rispettare
rest resto; riposo
restaurant ristorante *m.*
restore restaurare
result risultato
retreat ritirata
return ritornare
reveal rivelare
revolt ribellarsi
revolution rivoluzione *f.*
revolutionary rivoluzionario
rich ricco
right diritto; be —, aver ragione
ring *n.* anello; *v.* suonare
risk rischiare
Risorgimento Risorgimento
river fiume *m.*
roast arrosto
rocking chair sedia a dondolo
roll panino
Roman romano
Rome Roma
room stanza, sala; bath—, stanza
    da bagno; bed—, camera;
    dining —, sala da pranzo; wait-
    ing —, sala d'aspetto
rooster gallo
rose rosa
row *n.* fila; *v.* remare
ruby rubino
rug tappeto

rule regola; governo, (*in a bad
    sense*) dominio
ruler riga; uomo di governo

S

sacred sacro
sacrifice *n.* sacrifizio; *v.* sacrificare
sad triste
sail *n.* vela; *v.* partire
saint santo; *see* § 87
salad insalata
salvation salvezza
same stesso
Sardinia Sardegna
save salvare
savings department cassa di ri-
    sparmio
Savoy Savoia
say dire *irr. v.* 91
scaffold patibolo
school scuola
school janitor bidello
sculptor scultore *m.*
sea mare *m.*
season stagione *f*
seat posto
secret segreto
see vedere *irr. v.* 370
seem sembrare, parere *irr. v.* 190
self stesso
sell vendere
send mandare
sender mittente *m. or f.*
sentence frase *f.*
separate separato
September settembre *m.*
serve servire
set apparecchiare
settle stabilirsi
several diversi
she ella, essa

sheet lenzuolo (*pl.* le lenzuola);
— of paper foglio

shelf scaffale *m.*

shirt camicia; — waist camicetta

shoe scarpa

shore spiaggia

short corto, breve; — story
novella

show *n.* spettacolo; *v.* mostrare
(di)

Sicily Sicilia

sideboard credenza

siege assedio

sign firmare

signature firma

silk seta

sing cantare

sir signore *m.*

sister sorella

sister-in-law cognata

sit, sit down sedere *irr. v.* 307

skirt gonnella

sky cielo

slave schiavo

sleep dormire

sleeve manica

slow lento

small piccolo

smile sorridere *irr. v.* 323

snow *n.* neve *f.*; *v.* nevicare *imp.*

snowy nevoso

so così; — much tanto; — many
tanti

society società

sock calzino

soft morbido

soldier soldato

solution soluzione *f.*

solve risolvere *irr. v.* 273

some di + *def. art.*; alcuno, qualche, un po' di; *see* § 61

something qualche cosa

son figlio

son-in-law genero

soon presto, tra poco; as — as
appena, non appena; — after
poco dopo

sorrow dolore *m.*

soul animo

sound suonare

Southern meridionale

sovereign sovrano

Spain Spagna

Spaniard Spagnolo

speak parlare

special speciale

speech discorso

spend spendere *irr. v.* 333;
(*time*) passare

spirit spirito

splendid splendido

spoon cucchiaio

spread diffondere *irr. v.* 88

spring primavera

square piazza

stable stalla

stage palcoscenico

stamp francobollo

stand tavolino

start (*something*) cominciare; (*depart*) partire

state stato

stateroom cabina

statesman uomo di stato

station stazione *f.*

statue statua

stay stare *irr. v.* 338

steamer piroscafo

steward cameriere *m.*

stiff duro

stifle soffocare

still ancora

stock azione *f.*
stocking calza
stone pietra
store negozio
story novella, racconto
street via
strive sforzarsi (a)
strong forte
struggle *n.* lotta; *v.* lottare
student studente *m.*
studious studioso
study *n.* studio; *v.* studiare
stupid stupido
stupidity stupidità
succeed succedere *irr. v.* 343;
　riuscire (a) *irr. v.* 280
success successo
successor successore *m.*
such tale, come; — as quale
suffer soffrire *irr. v.* 314
suitcase valigia
suit of clothes abito
summer estate *f.*; next —, l'estate
　ventura
summit cima
supper cena
sure sicuro
surname cognome *m.*
swim nuotare
sword spada
Sylvia Silvia
sympathy simpatia
system sistema *m.*

T

table tavola; little —, tavolino
tablecloth tovaglia
tailor sarto
take prendere *irr. v.* 209; —
　breakfast fare colazione; —

place aver luogo; — part
　prender parte; — a walk pas-
　seggiare
talk parlare
tall alto
task compito
teach insegnare (a)
teacher maestro, –a
teaspoon cucchiaino
telephone *n.* telefono; *v.* telefo-
　nare
tell dire *irr. v.* 91
temperature temperatura
temporal temporale
term condizione *f*
terrible terribile
terrific terribile
territory territorio
terror terrore *m.*
than di, che; *see* § 119
thanks grazie
that *rel. pron.*; che, il quale;
　demonstr. codesto, quello; *conj.*
　che
theater teatro
their, theirs loro
them essi, esse, loro, li, le
themselves sè, se stessi, si
then (*afterward*) poi; (*at that
　time*) allora
thenceforth da allora in poi
there costà, costì, là, lì, ci, vi;
　— is c'è; — are ci sono
thesis tesi, *f.*
they essi, esse
thing cosa
think pensare (a)
thinker pensatore *m.*
this *adj.* questo; *pron.* questo, ciò
thou tu
threaten minacciare (di)

throne trono
through per
thunder *n.* tuono; *v.* tuonare *imp.*
thus così
Tiber Tevere *m.*
ticket biglietto
tile mattone *m.*
time tempo; (*turn*) volta; on —,
  a tempo; have a good —,
  divertirsi
time table orario
tired stanco
to, a, ad, per, di, in
today oggi
together insieme
tomorrow domani
tongue lingua
tonight stasera, stanotte
too: — much troppo; — many
  troppi
touch principio
Toulon Tolone *f.*
tourist viaggiatore *m.*
tragedy tragedia
train treno; express —, treno
  diretto; in a —, in treno
transact trattare
transfer trasferire
transfiguration trasfigurazione *f.*
translation traduzione *f.*
travel viaggiare
trip viaggio
triumph trionfo
troop truppa
true vero; come *or* become —,
  avverarsi
trunk baule *m.*
truth verità
Turin Torino
Tuscany Toscana
twice due volte

tyranny tirannia
tyrant tiranno

U

ultimatum (*Latin*) ultimatum *m.*
unchain scatenare
uncle zio
undeniable innegabile
under sotto
understand capire
unfortunately sfortunatamente
unite unificare, unire
united unito
unity unità
university università
unless a meno che . . . non
until *prep.* fino a; *conj.* finchè
upper *see* floor
us noi, ci
use usare
used to *see* § 45
useful utile
useless inutile
usher usciere *m.*
usually di solito

V

vain vano; in —, invano
valise valigia
vandalic vandalico
Vatican Vaticano
veal vitello
Venetia Veneto
Venetian veneto
vengeance vendetta
Venice Venezia
verb verbo
very molto
veteran veterano

vice vizio
Victor Vittorio
victory vittoria
violent violento
violin violino
virtue virtù *f.*
visit visitare
voice voce *f.*
voluntary volontario
volunteer volontario

W

wagon carro
wait, wait for aspettare
waiter cameriere *m.*
waiting room sala d'aspetto
walk *n.* cammino; *v.* camminare;
   take a —, passeggiare
wall muro, parete *f.*
want volere *irr. v.* 374
war guerra; World War Guerra
   Mondiale
wash lavare
watch *n.* orologio; *v.* sorvegliare
way cammino
we noi
weak debole
wear portare
weather tempo
wedding sposalizio
well bene
what che, che cosa, quale; (*that
   which*) quello che; (*that of
   which*) quello di cui
whatever checchè
wheat grano
when quando
where dove
whether se
which che, cui, quale, il quale

while mentre; in a little —, tra
   poco; a little — ago, da poco
   tempo
white bianco
who *inter.* chi; *rel.* che, il quale
whole tutto; the — summer
   tutta l'estate
whom *inter.* chi; *rel.* che, cui, il
   quale
whose il cui, la cui, etc.
why perchè
wife moglie *f.* (*pl.* le mogli)
wild selvatico
willing volenteroso; be —, volere
   irr. v. 374
willingly volentieri
win guadagnare
wind vento
window finestra; (*of an office*)
   sportello
winter inverno
wise saggio
wish desiderare (di)
with con
within entro
without *prep.* senza, (*before a
   pron.*) senza di; *conj.* senza che
wood legno; bosco
word parola
work *n.* lavoro; *v.* lavorare
world mondo; the — over in
   tutto il mondo; the World War
   la Guerra Mondiale
worse *aaj.* peggiore; *adv.* peggio
worst il peggiore
worth valore *m.*; be —, valere
   irr. v. 369
wretched misero
write scrivere *irr. v.* 305
writer scrittore *m.*
wrong torto; be —, aver torto

Y

year anno; **last —,** l'anno passato; **next —,** l'anno venturo
yellow giallo
yes sì
yesterday ieri
yet ancora
yoke giogo
you tu, voi, Ella, Lei, Loro, ti, vi, la, li, le

young giovane; **— lady** signorina
your, yours tuo, vostro, suo, loro
yourself te stesso, voi stesso, Lei stesso, Ella stessa, ti, vi, si
youth gioventù *f.*, giovinezza

Z

zero zero

INDEX

337